THE FINISH LINE

THE FINISH LINE

GOING THE DISTANCE IN THE MARATHONS OF LIFE

ROBERT A. STROMMEN

BEAVER'S
POND
PRESS

ISBN 13: 978-1-59298-979-9

Library of Congress Catalog Number: 2013909114

Printed in the United States of America

First Printing: 2013

17 16 15 14 13 5 4 3 2 1

Cover and interior design by James Monroe Design, LLC.

BEAVER'S POND PRESS

Beaver's Pond Press, Inc.
7108 Ohms Lane
Edina, MN 55439–2129
(952) 829-8818
www.BeaversPondPress.com

To order, visit www.BeaversPondBooks.com
or call (800) 901-3480. Reseller discounts available.

In Dedication to Those Who Work Toward Their Own Finish Lines

I am frequently asked about the significance of **purpose+3**, my branded identity for writing and speaking. **purpose+3** represents three elements of my life to which I dedicate this book: my children, my parents and my personal and professional relationships.

First and foremost, to my three children, Bjorn, Hans and Tjersti: From the day you were born my purpose as a parent was centered on my commitment to do my best as a father, to be actively engaged in your life and to guide your development in a manner that allowed you to be well grounded as you entered your adult lives. My wish for you has always been and is to:

- Know the value of hard work, friends, relationships, grace, forgiveness, pride and humility;
- Develop the foundation that will allow faith to be a part of your and your family's life;
- Find meaning in family and relationships;
- Live life to the fullest, with absolute intentionality;
- Recognize the importance and value that others play in your success and development and to acknowledge their help with a thank you;

- Know that hard work has its rewards and creates opportunities that at first are not recognized or realized;
- And to discover your passions and live your life with a meaningful purpose.

I dedicate this book to my love for each of you.

Secondly, I dedicate this book to my mother and father. My father was a rock in my development. My mother is a superb definition of MOM and was an incredible life partner to my dad. They were wonderful parents who always did what they felt best and had the right intentions in mind, something that I did not always recognize at the time.

It has been twelve years since my dad passed away. His life, compassion, grace, kindness, toughness and friendship remain with me. These attributes also describe my mother who is a vibrant eighty-nine years old. She has become my friend. Thank you, Mom, for being my closest critic and most ardent supporter. You have the empowering aspects of grace, forgiveness and love that have been the foundation of the Strommen family. I dedicate this book to our wonderful friendship and support for each other. Just prior to Dad's passing he said, "Take good care of your mother for me." I hope I have lived up to his expectations.

And, finally, I dedicate this book to the professional relationships that have guided and shaped my career, to my dear close friends (you know who you are) and the Strommen extended family. A special thanks to Karen for her assistance and support through the editorial process.

I once saw this post on Facebook: "There comes a point in your life when you realize who really matters, who never did and who always will!"

CONTENTS

INTRODUCTION

First things first: This is not a book about running, it's about what really matters—LIFE!

Life presents each of us with a series of marathons—long-distance challenges of one kind or another. Some we suit up and train for while others may carry us along, stumbling and gasping for air, feeling less prepared than we'd like. Marathons can take the form of careers, achieving business or financial success, personal growth and more. There are things in life we wish to accomplish, some of which, like marathons, have finish lines we're determined to cross. However, it's not so much the finish line we should be striving for but, rather, learning to appreciate what happens along the journey; how we treat ourselves and those around us during the journey; and the feeling once we get there—the sense of accomplishment (or the good burn!)—that is so rewarding and, really, the true prize.

I'm a daily patron of my local Caribou Coffee. In fact, not only do they know my name but when the baristas see me walk in the door, they often have my medium light roast sitting on the counter waiting. Caribou has become such a part of my routine that their slogan is one of my mantras, "Life is short. Stay awake for it!®"

This book represents one of those "Stay Awake" dimensions of my life. *Staying Awake* is about being engaged, being challenged, being thankful, being driven to strive for the best. For me, *Staying Awake* is about embracing those who support, nurture and challenge me to have a meaningful physical and spiritual life. It's about having the grace (and patience) to know we are all human. I have true friends and family who challenge my weaknesses and mistakes in making my life better and more impactful. *Staying Awake* allows me to make the most of my life and to give back to others. *Staying Awake* is looking for opportunities to say THANK YOU.

A friend once told me that one of the most disappointing feelings in life is the sense of regret and the "I wish I had done, or not done, x, y and z." This negative self-talk is something most of us would like to avoid. Let me expand on a personal level: I always wanted to get my law degree, not to practice law, but to support my financial services practice and enable me to better develop critical-thinking and problem-solving skills. Yet I did not pursue it. I let negative thinking about the (short-term) inconvenience of attending law school distract me from achieving a long-term goal and desire.

As you reflect back on your life, are you reminded of areas where you feel you failed, did not do well or just didn't do it at all? Are there areas that you wish you could do over? I know I have more than my share, in my personal and professional life, that haunt me. In fact, it has been some of those things in my recent past that have brought to the forefront an appreciation that:

- we only live once;
- we must embrace the power of true friends who challenge weaknesses and support strengths;
- we need people around us who have the ability to forgive, and exhibit grace;
- and we must appreciate the wonders of being engaged and having a well-defined purpose in life.

Essentially, we must *Stay Awake*!

> *To be able to look back upon one's life in satisfaction is to live twice.*
>
> —Kahlil Gibran

In part, this book reflects my desire to share my running experiences. More important, though, I want to share how I have applied—and continue to apply—what I am learning with each "marathon," be it a 26.2-mile run or that of achieving happiness, purpose and fulfillment in life and business. This book is about much more than running. It's about learning and growing. It is about life, sharing fulfilling relationships and moving toward something.

I started running—which ultimately provided the genesis of this book about personal and professional fulfillment—for personal reasons. I have never been a distance runner, but as a former high school and college soccer player and coach, I have always been active and fairly athletic. At the urging of my wonderful (and insistent) daughter, Tjersti, I began training for my first marathon at the age of fifty-six. We agreed we would start the race together, run together and support each other. When one needed to walk, the other would walk. We crossed the finish line hand-in-hand as we celebrated our accomplishment and our support, commitment and love as father-daughter. In 2011, we ran the Orlando/Disney Marathon. I would have never finished without the patience and support of my daughter. Success is not accomplished alone!

My first marathon experience greatly impacted my life. I've come to realize the significance of intentionality, purpose and fulfillment in my personal and professional life. Along the way I've learned a lot about running and life from fellow marathon runners. They've made an impact on me in a deep and meaningful way. I hope their stories will be inspiring to you as you run your own marathons in life.

I run for my reasons, not anyone else's. It is not about the time I clock but, rather, it's about the challenge, the sense of accomplishment, the setting of a goal, working methodically toward the goal, working through challenges during the training and then proving to myself that I have the willpower and fortitude to finish. The feeling at the finish line is indescribable and actually a very emotional sense of accomplishment. You realize you've just completed 26.2 miles. You've tested your fortitude, your mental and physical determination and won! I was proud of the personal accomplishment without regard to other runners' better finish times. The experience reinforced a feeling of self-satisfaction that no one could take away from me.

I have continued to run a couple marathons a year. I learn more about myself and find that each marathon has its own character, motivation, purpose and gratification. My aim isn't to win the race but to hone the skills that cross over into defining and living my purpose in life and business.

The 26.2-mile marathon is not much different than the marathons we run in our personal and professional lives. There are challenges, there are tests, there is a need for support and grace and encouragement, but above all, there needs to be purpose. As my dad often told me when things were tough, "Bob, this too will pass, and remember, anyone can be good when things are going well. The real test is the ability to make things good when they are going bad, to not give up, stay the course, stay focused and find a solution. Then you will know you are a winner in life and business!"

Sometimes life offers us turning points and opportunities to have a "do over." However, there's the saying that you only have one opportunity to make a first impression. You want to approach your tasks and goals the way you approach making a first impression. Depending on a do over is short-changing your personal abilities and sense of accomplishment. You'll find subsequent finish lines will be easier, more fulfilling and filled with a greater sense of accomplishment if each finish line is achieved with as little regret as possible.

Not to be too grim, but as we live our lives we all know we're eventually going to die and there's no "do over" at the end of *that* finish line. This is not a dress rehearsal for the real thing. We have before us the challenge that living a full and meaningful life cannot be left to chance, but must be filled with intentionality and purpose.

I've had the great privilege of doing this book in partnership with Grandma's Marathon (Duluth, Minnesota), a marathon I've run three times. I've interacted with lots of runners and dozens of them have shared their stories with me. In this book you'll learn through their experiences about the power of the human spirit and the individual drive for accomplishment and fulfillment.

"Running saved my life!!!"

Margaret H. tells a compelling story, just one you'll experience as you explore *The Finish Line.* Margaret believes running helped reverse a potentially fatal medical condition. Running brought her out of a life of hospital beds and medical specialists and opened the door to enjoying a vital, vibrant and vivacious personal and professional life. This liberated life has taken her to marathons in nineteen states and, most especially, nurtured a heartwarming connection to Grandma's Marathon in Duluth.

Margaret's and nearly thirty-five other runners' stories are sprinkled throughout *The Finish Line* to help you discover keys to personal growth through the power of running while examining the power of purpose, goal setting and planning, and the value and power of coaching and support. You'll read about Duluth's infamous Lemon Drop Hill and find metaphors for dealing with detours and adversity, defining a happy life and, finally, see how an annual community event in northern Minnesota helps bring out the best in people from around the country.

This book is a tribute to those who want to challenge themselves, to be moved by the stories of marathoners and use them as metaphors for the marathons of life, whether it's on the track of personal growth, professional success, relationships or, perhaps like Margaret, achieving better health. I want you to know you've fulfilled your purpose when life on this earth is over.

The Finish Line is presented as a series of essays that each stand on their own. Jump in anywhere you like. Reflect on the message and find those nuggets of gold that have meaning to you.

Thank you for joining me on this journey as we all aim for THE FINISH LINE.

CHAPTER 1

THE STARTING LINE: THE POWER OF PURPOSE

The purpose of life is a life of purpose.

—Robert Byrne

On July 11, 2001, I attended a funeral. The church was filled with over five hundred people who came to provide support to the family and pay tribute to the deceased. They didn't remember him for his business success or his magnificent career. They came to memorialize the man as a person, what he stood for, his grace and compassion, his ability to overcome obstacles and challenges, and the amazing and loving partnership of his spouse. They came together to celebrate what was really important, those things that last forever. The man, my father, understood the power of what was important. He realized life was short and made every day count. He understood mistakes are made but possessed an everlasting ability to forgive; a hallmark of the Strommen family.

That day impacted me to my core. To this day, I reflect, mourn, rejoice, give thanks and strive to exemplify the best characteristics that made him so special, not to be my dad, but to be a man who can honor his father in every way.

As a young man my father learned, in large part from being infected with tuberculosis, that we must lean on the strengths of others at varying degrees throughout life. He also discovered and believed that people have an incredible ability to exhibit grace, compassion and a desire to help. Learning this lesson as a young man became one of my father's defining characteristics and clearly outlined a purpose within his life: to share with others the appreciation that success and fulfillment is attained by complementing your own strengths with the abilities of those around you.

Purpose! It means something different for each of us, yet a well-defined and internalized personal purpose has the same effect on everyone—it provides motivation, satisfaction, feelings of accomplishment and sense of self. Caribou Coffee, a Minnesota-based regional line of coffee houses, has a straightforward approach to life with its slogan "Life is short. Stay awake for it!" What a simple yet meaningful phrase that encapsulates the essence of living a life of purpose, on purpose!

Webster's Dictionary defines "purpose" as:
That which a person sets before himself as an object to be reached or accomplished, the end or aim to which the view is directed in any plan, measure or exertion; view; aim; design; intention; plan.

One day, Jordan H. literally woke up and found a new purpose in his life. "I was eighty-five pounds overweight and taking medication for high blood pressure," he says. "I had recently quit a ten-year smoking habit. I had two little children and a beautiful wife and I wanted to make sure I'd be there for my family. I remember watching runners and thinking, 'Wow, they really look like they enjoy their runs.' I was trying to get in better shape and decided to start running. I woke up early on a Sunday morning and decided to run to the end of our road and back, about two miles. After that day I never looked back. It grew from there. I just wanted more. I have since run 5Ks, 10Ks and at least six half-marathons and nine full marathons. The longer the race is, the better I like it."

Jordan says he runs to inspire others to try something new. "After all these races and all the training miles I realized that God had blessed me with a gift I had to share. I have coached youth cross-country runners, coached a few adult walking and general health classes and, more recently, enjoyed the opportunity to lead a 'Run for God' class. I want to help others realize how this can change their life. Before I started running I was pretty depressed, but today I feel better about myself and I'm much more happy and healthy."

Jordan's story is a great example of how we can find purpose in our lives. What started out as a way to lose weight and get healthier ultimately provided a way for Jordan to inspire and help others. When he decided to take care of himself and make his own health a priority he discovered a whole new direction for his life.

Take Care of the Golf Balls First

Jordan's example reminds me of a story I've come across a few times. I don't know who the author is but I like the message about prioritizing what matters.

> A professor stood before his philosophy class at a table with a few items on it. When the class began, he picked up a very large empty mayonnaise jar and proceeded to fill it with golf balls. He then asked the students if the jar was full. They agreed that it was.
>
> The professor then picked up a box of pebbles and poured them into the jar. He gently shook the jar and the pebbles rolled into the open areas between the golf balls. He then asked the students if the jar was full. They agreed it was. The professor next picked up a box of sand and poured it into the jar. Of course, the sand filled up everything else. He asked once more if the jar was full. The students responded with a unanimous "yes."
>
> The professor then produced two beers from under the table and poured them into the jar, effectively filling the empty space between the sand. The students laughed.

"Now," said the professor as the laughter subsided, "I want you to recognize that this jar represents your life. The golf balls are the important things—your family, your children, your health, your friends and your favorite passions—and if everything else was lost and only they remained, your life would still be full. The pebbles are the other things that matter like your job, your house and your car. The sand is everything else—the small stuff.

"If you put the sand into the jar first," he continued, "there is no room for the pebbles or the golf balls. The same goes for life. If you spend all your time and energy on the small stuff you will never have room for the things that are important to you. Pay attention to the things that are critical to your happiness. Spend time with your children. Spend time with your parents. Visit with grandparents. Take your spouse out to dinner. Play another eighteen holes. There will always be time to clean the house and mow the lawn.

"Take care of the golf balls first—the things that really matter. Set your priorities. The rest is just sand."

One of the students raised her hand and asked about what the beer represented. The professor smiled and said, "I'm glad you asked. The beer just shows you that no matter how full your life may seem, there's always room for a couple of beers with a friend."

Finding Your Purpose

Katy K. runs for God's purpose. Katy is a missionary, a true reflection of her personal and professional life's purpose, yet it goes far deeper than that. Her faith not only drives her to run, but it makes her focus on her task, whether it be running to support her missionary work or praying during her runs. "Running gives me alone time with God, time to pray," she says.

Katy ran Grandma's Marathon, in part, as a fundraiser for a mission trip to South Africa where she spent a year with an organization called Ignite South Africa. The project trains people to educate others about disease, especially AIDS. Recently, Katy ran in the Chicago Marathon under the World Vision banner to raise funds to go to Rwanda where she's working as a family trauma therapist.

Katy clearly knows why she runs and her purpose and motivation, not just for running, but for her life.

Another committed runner, Kristie K., says her mother motivated her to start running marathons and it brought new purpose to her life. "My mom has had MS for many years. When I was a junior in college she told me there were so many things she wished she would have done when she was physically able.

I decided to challenge all of my smart couch-potato sorority sisters to commit to participating in three intramural sports. I thought about signing up for a 5K and Mom told me to 'do it while you still can!' I won it and was inspired to do something else. Three years later a friend convinced me to try something bigger and we trained for and ran our first marathon together. I came in second place for women, won a little prize money, made my dad cry, and could barely walk for two weeks. It was awesome!"

Since that first race, Kristie has qualified for Boston and has run thirty marathons since her mother first encouraged and inspired her to live life without regret and the "wish I had's!"

Kristie lived in Japan for a few years and ran the Osaka Marathon. "People alongside the road were yelling at me: 'White toe, white toe!' I thought they were insulting me. Later on, I found out they were shouting, 'Fight, fight, fight!'" Kristie did fight and finished yet another marathon.

"I've learned to set goals just a smidgen beyond achievable. You can surprise yourself and reach them. I've learned the power of positive thinking and mind over matter. My mom always said, 'Never wait until tomorrow to start something.' Take advantage of today. Thanks, Mom, for the inspiration so many years ago."

Kristie learned through her own experiences, as well as witnessing her mother's perseverance through health struggles, to live life to the fullest, to set challenges and work to achieve them. Kristie learned to be a marathoner, yet more importantly, she learned to be a more fulfilled person, something that has impacted all aspects of her life.

Life, Love and Death

Apple co-founder Steve Jobs—for many, the epitome of business success—shared his formula for a meaningful life as he gave the 2005 commencement address at Stanford University. He shared three stories about life, love and death.

Connecting the Dots

"You have to trust in something—your gut, destiny, life, karma, or whatever. The dots you encounter in life so often will eventually connect. Believing that the significance of your life and career journey will connect down the road will give you the confidence to follow your heart, even when it leads you off the well-worn path. That confidence will make all the difference."

We are not fortune tellers, we cannot connect the dots ahead of us; we can only do so by looking back on where we've come and making the most of our experiences, both good and bad.

Steve Jobs said some of the best things that happened in his life came as a result of being fired from his own company: He went on to found Pixar and fell in love with his future wife, two defining moments in his career and personal life. How's that for seeing the positive?

Have faith that what you are doing now, or experiencing now, will move you forward and will allow you to connect your dots in the future. Don't be afraid to follow your heart and your gut. You will be amazed by the unplanned opportunities that will present themselves when you do your best, follow your passions and keep an open mind.

Scott Keenan, founder and executive director of Grandma's Marathon, had just that experience. When asked what aspects in his life were most impactful on his career and success with Grandma's Marathon, Scott, without hesitation, gives credit to the Air National Guard. Scott enlisted at the age of seventeen. It was there, as a young man lacking in confidence and physical attributes, that he discovered the gift of running. Scott came out of the Air National Guard with confidence learned, discipline gained, organizational skills refined and a passion to run. His early years in the Guard helped him develop the incredible skills, confidence and passion that led to the establishment of Grandma's Marathon. Today it's one of the great marathons in the country and a jewel for Duluth, Minnesota. Connecting the dots helped Scott find and pursue his passion.

Love, do not settle!

Jobs said that knowing what was important to him and doing what he loved got him through some very dark times. "You've got to find what you love," he said. "And that is as true for your work as it is for your [relationships]. Your work is going to fill a large part of your life, and the only way to be truly satisfied is to do what you believe is great work. And the only way to do great work is to love what you do. If you haven't found it yet, keep looking. This philosophy applies to all relationships in your life. As with all matters of the heart, you'll know when you find it. And, like any great relationship, it just gets better and better as the years roll on. So keep looking until you find it. Don't settle."

What is your passion? What do you love? For some of us, we're lucky to do work we love. Some of us may be slogging through a job that simply pays the bills. Regardless of which category you fall into, are you offering up your best? Are you making the most of what's in front of you? For many, having an avocation—a way of giving back—fuels and inspires them and adds deep levels of contentment.

Death

Okay, probably not what a bunch of college graduates want to think about at commencement, but Jobs made some great points, which are all the more poignant as he would face the reality of his own death just a few years after making this address. Jobs said, "Remembering that you are going to die is the best way to avoid the trap that you have something to lose. Your time is limited, so don't waste it living someone else's life. Don't be trapped by dogma—which is living with the results of other people's thinking. Don't let the noise of others' opinions drown out your own inner voice. And, most importantly, have the courage to follow your heart and intuition; they somehow already know what you truly want to become. Everything else is secondary."

These may seem easy enough to nod your head in agreement to, but ask yourself, "How do I go about living so that my dots are connected, that I fall in love with my life, remember that life is short and maintain perspective?"

The Twenty-Five-Year Plan

I am of the notion that having a well-thought-out, articulated and written purpose (or set of purposes) for my life is a great starting point. So how, you might ask, does someone begin defining this purpose? Here is a great exercise to get you started:

Grab a pen and a yellow notepad and visualize yourself twenty-five years from now (if you are fifty, imagine yourself at seventy-five, if you are thirty-five, visualize yourself at age sixty). Don't be scared!

The exercise involves your reflections of what you see twenty-five years from now. Imagine you're sitting on the veranda, or on the porch, or in your favorite backyard lawn chair reflecting back on your life. What do you see? What are the things, activities, accomplishments and impacts that make you smile as you reflect? Who are the people that were important to you? What were the disappointments where you feel you missed the mark? As you think back on your life, how do you feel about what you see?

As you reflect, write down what you just visualized as you were sitting on the veranda twenty-five years from now. These reflections can serve as the framework for the life, career and relationships you want. This exercise, thinking ahead twenty-five years, and reflecting back from that point, will allow you to create direction and the start of a roadmap for your life, a roadmap that has at its foundation purpose and intentionality.

> *If you live each day as if it was your last, someday you'll most certainly be right.*
> —Steve Jobs

Going back to that Stanford commencement speech, Jobs told the gathered crowd that at the age of seventeen, he came across a quote: "If you live each day as if it was your last, someday you'll most certainly be right. It made an impression on me," said Jobs, "and since then, for the past thirty-three years, I have looked in the mirror every morning and asked myself: If today were the last day of my life, would I want to do what I am about to do today? And whenever the answer has been 'No' for too many days in a row, I know I need to change something."

Now What?

Every time I run a marathon, I have three emotional moments. First, when the gun goes off at the start of the race, I realize I am about to embark on an unnatural journey, a 26.2-mile journey to be exact. I have prepared for this. I feel the rush of fear, excitement, anxiety and anticipation all at once. Am I prepared mentally for the commitment of my purpose: to finish!

Second, at about the twenty-two-mile mark, after surviving Lemon Drop Hill in the Grandma's Marathon, I realize that I will finish. I get this feeling of happiness and satisfaction that it will be a successful journey.

Third, and finally, as I cross the finish line, there is a rush of emotions that comes with the reality of accomplishing "my goal." My dream has become reality. It's an incredible feeling. I've reached the finish line.

We all have finish lines we're aiming for. Once we cross them we must grapple with the question "Now what?"

What does finishing a marathon really mean? What does that finish line mean? In reality, very little in itself, yet the journey is what this was all about. The same holds true for our life, our career, our friendships, our faith and our family. It is the manner in which the journey plays out that places a fingerprint on what is important and helps us answer the question "Now what?"

Commitment to a Goal

Now here's a thought on mental, emotional and physical strength and endurance: Whatever your goal, whatever it is you are striving for, are you willing to put in the training miles to achieve it? How far can you push yourself (you'd be surprised!)? How far are you willing to push yourself to achieve your goal, to reach a particular finish line?

How you weather the challenge reveals a lot about yourself.

"I run for myself and my mind," says Brice A. "I run because I need to challenge myself and I know that it is as much a mental challenge as physical. Crossing the finish line is fantastic. I'm a goal-oriented person and it gives me something to strive toward. I need that challenge in my life."

A client and friend of mine, Jim H., once said, "The magic of the marathon, or mountain climbing, or whatever, is that nobody gets through it without hurting." So true of life, right? Regardless of conditioning, Jim went on to say, "At some point you are going to hit the wall. There are times when it's easier to give up. Your body is screaming 'Don't do this to me, quit!'" It's how you deal with the mental and physical pain that gets you through. It's a perfect metaphor for life: You can train and prepare for the event; however, you WILL want to quit—you WILL endure pain—but how you deal with it is what makes the difference.

How you weather the challenge reveals a lot about you. I have seen this in years of teaching and as an athlete, in my consulting career and as a business owner. There are different personalities and the real pros, the real successful people, are those who take responsibility, don't complain, learn from mistakes and move forward in a positive manner.

Remember my reference to Steve Jobs and connecting the dots as you look at where you've come? I believe you must first have a vision and purpose for the future that will guide you as you *live the dots.* The dots create the foundation for something that is not yet fully developed and discovered. The dots form the path that you discover and realize along the way. Yet with all this discussion of dots the foundation must be established for a well-defined *purpose*, a plan that is visualized, planned out and lived.

With all that said, remember that the path may take you on a side trip away from the dots already laid, a path not originally planned; this is not wrong, in fact, it just may be the path that was meant for you—your destiny—you just didn't realize it. Yet with focus, discipline, a sense of grace, appreciation for people and knowing that your success will not be accomplished alone (more on that later in this book), you will one day find as you reflect back that the dots did connect in an amazing, wonderful way.

Finding Purpose When It Seems Impossible

Margaret H. started running out of a desperate attempt to regain control from multiple medical issues that haunted her life. In 1995, Margaret was raced in and out of hospitals due to a series of respiratory infections.

After being told by her doctors that she had COPD and that her many chronic illnesses would always require hospitalized treatment, she refused to give in. With no training, or any idea how to begin, Margaret started running. "I didn't know what I was doing, really. I was just running," she says.

No matter how much it hurt, or how hard it was, Margaret believed anything was better than being in the hospital. That power of purpose (or reason for running) lifted her through several more diagnoses including a heart murmur, type II diabetes and a dependency on gamma globulin transplants. By channeling her energy into training and running, she has decreased the amount of medication she has to take and, most important, she has eliminated her visits to the hospital.

"I chose to run despite being told I probably shouldn't after having two vertebrae fused in my lower back. I run because I need to challenge myself," Margaret says. "I run because it is a very mental game for me." Interestingly, Margaret unexpectedly came full circle in running during a trip to Duluth for Grandma's Marathon. "I stumbled onto the very company—CSL Behring—that produces the gamma globulin I depend on to live." The serendipity of making this connection with CSL Behring re-energized employees, family members and even donors. "They were swept up in the explosive and exponential emotion of hearing how their product, along with running, had saved me from a lifetime of poor health. My running has since turned into an effort to raise money for leukemia and related causes."

When what we are is what we want to be, that's happiness.
—Malcolm Forbes

Margaret has found *purpose.* Margaret has connected her dots.

To come to one's end in life and feel there has been no purpose would seem such a waste. We live a finite time in the physical sense. I believe we are here for a reason, to make a difference in our own life and, perhaps, in the lives we touch directly and indirectly. Life shouldn't be about recognition, rewards or things, but rather the impact and manner in which we live.

My father taught me many important life lessons:

- We do not succeed alone.
- Do your absolute best and be proud of the effort.
- Win with grace and, more important, lose with grace.
- Understand we all make mistakes.
- Look forward and don't dwell on the past. Grudges can destroy the grudge holder's happiness and accomplish nothing.
- Forgiveness is the hallmark of the Christian faith.
- Don't forget the power of saying thank you.

Each day, purposely find ways to help others and be kind. Consider buying a cup of coffee for the car behind you at the drive-thru window, make an anonymous gift to someone in need, hold the door open for the person behind you, send a simple note to a friend or new acquaintance. It's the little kindnesses that are least expected that will be the most appreciated and impactful. You'd be surprised how rewarding it can be to incorporate this type of intentionality into your life.

The purpose for running doesn't need to be profound. Whether it is one person's desperate attempt to regain control of their chronic conditions, strip off the stress or deal with deep tragedy, for many running provides an escape from life's everyday frustrations. For some, the running itself addresses the problem. For others it's their preferred coping strategy. For all, the power of purpose (or the reason for the race) relies on running to satisfy, sculpt and shape their lives and the lives of those they step with.

Raise the Bar for Yourself:

Take a look back on your own life's journey. Where has your life brought you so far? Connect the dots. Do you see patterns? Where is your life taking you? Make a list of goals you'd like to accomplish. Identify one you can get started on now. Simply identify it for now. We'll work on laying out steps to achieving it in Chapter 3.

CHAPTER 2

DARE TO DREAM BIG

Only those who risk going too far can possibly find out how far one can go.

—T. S. Eliot

A scene from the new Disney movie *The Great and Powerful Oz*, the prequel to the classic *Wizard of Oz*, struck me as I was working on this book. The soon-to-be-anointed title character, a mischievous magician from Kansas, enchants curious audiences at a Kansas circus. He gains the wisdom to become a powerful ruler when he is inexplicably transported to the wondrous world of Oz. In the movie, illusionist Oscar Diggs (played by James Franco) says, "I do not want to be a good man. I want to be a great man." He gets caught up in a tornado, tumbling about, and soon finds himself in the Land of Oz. Now his perspective has changed as he says, almost in prayer, "I don't want to die. I haven't accomplished anything yet!"

Have you ever felt that way? Perhaps a far more relevant way to frame it is, have you given thought as to the meaning and purpose of your life? Are you prepared to challenge yourself to set goals that are meaningful to you? You are capable of more than you can imagine, so dream big!

In athletics, life and business, there are two words used to define a person's personality: egotistical or confident. Each comes with radically different connotations. The term egotistical equates to being overly impressed with one's self, possessing a deep and personal belief that success and knowledge revolves around oneself. Have you ever heard about someone who has enjoyed exceptional success as not being able to handle it? Or that it's "gone to their head"? They're often criticized for being too impressed with their own accomplishments without thought to those who helped them get where they are.

Invest in Confidence

Confidence, on the other hand, often belongs to those who are self-assured but also know the importance of hard work and commitment to a goal. They surround themselves with others they can learn from and who support them in their efforts. They know success isn't accomplished alone. Think about those athletes you admire who execute without hesitation. They hold a personal belief that success will prevail and, as a result, their performance is enhanced. This is not just an athletic phenomenon, it is found in life and business, too.

People who believe in themselves understand how to succeed. It's a process that doesn't come easily; however they are wholeheartedly invested in it. This belief results in the ability to present a positive and confident sense of self-knowledge and skill. This confidence level enhances ultimate performance and places the emphasis on a successful outcome, not on self.

So, how do you develop confidence in yourself and help nurture it in others?

- Strive for and accomplish attainable goals; the feeling of success is contagious.
- Look for positive reinforcement from those around you; the feeling of acceptance creates confidence and positive self-worth.
- As a leader, look for ways to recognize the success of those on your team.

Wilson Learning Corporation, one of the great sales training companies of the 1970s, '80s and '90s developed a sales training course, "Counselor Selling." The key principle in the course was "People do things for their reasons, not someone else's!" This principle is so concise, yet filled with such great value. If you don't believe, if you do not care, if you're not invested, if the outcome is of little personal value, then the response will be "NO WAY." Think about how this relates to life, future and success.

What would be your response to the following?

- A friend asks you to join her in training for a marathon. Would your response be, "No way, I can't run that far!"?

- When informed by your sales manager that this year's goals are going up 25 percent and the territory is being divided, would you think, "You've got to be kidding!"?

- Let's say you want to enter law school or med school or even the undergrad program of your choice but you learn you need to raise your GPA a full point. Would you think it impossible and give up on your dream?

Don't be too quick to say "No way!" to an opportunity dressed like an impossible challenge.

These and countless other scenarios may trigger the same reaction, but remember: you do not know the full depth and strength of yourself, your abilities or your faith until they have been arduously tested.

Believe in Yourself

Gina P. always saw herself as a casual but consistent runner. However, things changed when "a crazy ultra-marathon-running friend" came into the picture. "I was then given the challenge to try a half-marathon, which naturally became a challenge to run a full marathon!" says Gina.

The first time she crossed the finish line was quite an experience. "I was so incredibly high at that time! It's incredibly emotional. When I turn the corner and see the finish line, it's surreal . . . I feel like my feet aren't touching the ground, that someone's pushing me. I cry, I'm elated . . . it's beyond words. My family's there . . . it's such an awesome and moving experience crossing the finish line . . . such a sense of accomplishment."

Although Gina was once told she was not an athlete, she now sees herself as a runner and is learning more and more about herself with each race. "Other people's training and pace are not good for me. I've gotten over apologizing for not being like them. I believe in myself. I've proven that I can set a goal and achieve it. When you run a marathon, you need to do it for yourself. It's a personal sense of accomplishment. I proved to myself that I was capable of doing something big. The goal seemed unattainable, but I reached it! Runners who don't have a lot of confidence can look at me and think, 'I can do that someday, too!' I'm here to tell them they can! I'm slow but I run marathons!"

A friend of mine believes that the real purpose of running (for most of us) is not to win a race; it's to test the limits of the human heart. Doesn't this apply to challenges in all areas of our lives?

Don't avoid the hills in running, cycling and life. Strength is found when you tackle the seemingly impossible.

It has long been said that our goals need to be SMART (specific, measurable, attainable, relevant and timely) in order to have a reasonable chance of being successful. I wish to propose a broader set of meaningful dimensions to goal setting. I believe these can enhance the probability of success and, perhaps more important, provide greater satisfaction.

Goals need to be:

- **Filled with personal purpose** — Do the twenty-five-year-plan exercise (Chapter 1). It helps you develop a deep feeling for, and understanding of, what is important and will help you create a meaningful goal. Still struggling a bit? Do the visualization exercise (in Chapter 3). Take some time and cut out pictures from magazines that inspire you, make you feel good and make you dream. Do they reflect what's important to you in your life, career and relationships? Place them on a poster board and place it someplace just for you. These two exercises will help you visually sketch out the foundation for your goals.

- **Written down!** — Create a business and life plan. This is not a three-ring binder filled with dozens of pages of stuff; it needs to be concise, to the point and easy to review. A great resource to get you started is *The One Page Business Plan* by Jim Horan. This tool will help you define your vision (or goals) for your life or career and create steps for achieving it.

- **Measurable** — Any goal not measured is simply a dream. It is critical to track progress weekly, monthly and quarterly. Compare the results to the goal. If things are not on track, take time to assess (honestly) what has gone well and what is not working. Remember, do not be afraid to ask for outside help; get a coach who can challenge you, ask the tough questions and provide some feedback so you can discover what changes need to be made.

- **Realistic and attainable** — Being realistic is critical. I could dream big and set a goal of winning Grandma's Marathon and start training, but I would be setting myself up for failure. This goal is not realistic for me. Remember, goals are progressive building blocks. When I first came into the financial services business I had a goal of "activity" tasks that led to sales. This was controllable and realistic. I had a goal of reaching various production club levels. Each level required a higher degree of performance: Club 1, then Club 2 and finally the top production club. Interestingly, each goal was incrementally easier and attainable because of the planning and skills I developed as I progressed in my career.

- **Results need to be visualized** — As you strive for your goal, can you see yourself accomplishing what you desire? If the answer is no, stop and readjust, as a goal that cannot be visualized most likely will not be realized. Check out the visualization exercise in Chapter 3.

- **Flexible and adaptable to change** — We live in a changing environment—be prepared for change and adversity. Be prepared to adjust to the changes. Increase the goal if you discover you were too conservative, or do not be afraid to adapt to the goal that was set.

Allison M. believes runners are committed people and driven by goals. "We can become driven by our sport to an extent that often consumes us. Throw in marriage, a career and children, and getting out the door for a run becomes an escape from reality." Allison says no matter the length of the run, it provides one with time to clear their mind or to just get away from the rush of life.

Allison says that raising kids will always bring joy and frustration but "running brings me back to me."

After falling short of her goal of 4:30 in her first marathon, Allison chose Grandma's Marathon to attack her goal again. She took time from her busy life to incorporate a new approach to her running. She added a more grueling regimen that included faster runs and "fartlek runs," a training method that builds strength and endurance by varying speed and intensity. She did much of her running on her own and when asked if she thought that training hard, alone, helped her mentally in the tough parts of the race her response was, "Yes, because my mind is my own worst enemy."

Even on days where she came home from a tough day at work or a day full of driving her daughters to their activities, Allison found joy in pushing herself to achieve her goal. She was so focused and excited about the opportunity to prove to herself that she could reach her goal. On race day she applied the work that she had put in over the past months and found herself right on pace as she climbed the infamous Lemon Drop Hill around mile twenty-two of the Grandma's course. Lemon Drop Hill is considered by many to be the toughest part of the course.

As Allison pushed herself up the hill she saw her husband, parents and daughters waiting for her, giving her the encouragement that would push her past her goal of 4:30 to running 4:21:15. "They were at the perfect spot," says Allison. "I saw my father first and he told me that my husband and daughters were at the top. That gave me an extra boost to see them standing there with signs and cheering me on. It was great encouragement."

Many people would use a busy life to find reasons to miss a run or even as a way to deflect the fact that they missed their goal. Allison is not one of those people. She embraces her busy life and is motivated to accomplish her goals on and off the course.

Goal Orientation

A 2012 study by Stanford psychologist Paul O'Keefe, Adar Ben-Eliyahu of the University of Pittsburgh and Lisa Linnenbrink-Garcia of Duke University links one's ability to achieve goals to their mindset and environment. When we focus on learning or improvement, the team says, we are far more likely to be fully engaged. We want to grow and improve rather than show others how accomplished or smart we are. It's all about what motivates us—our goal orientation. The research goes on to describe two types of goal orientation—the mindset we apply to achievement-related activities: Mastery Orientation and Performance Orientation.

If we are *mastery oriented*, we place greater focus on learning and improving. If we are *performance oriented*, we place more focus on demonstrating our competence relative to others such as coworkers, friends or "The Joneses" down the street.

The study goes on to suggest that those who are mastery oriented often possess more positive qualities such as perseverance, seeking out challenges and a desire to learn. Whereas, people who are more concerned about outperforming others tend to have more anxiety and worry more. Which one describes you?

Debbie A.'s running career started as a casual three-mornings-a-week chance to spend time with a friend as a break from the pressures of being at home with young children. While at the time she didn't recognize the power of what she was starting, the enjoyment of exercise and talking while they ran soon became obvious. In other words, the situation went from trying something out as an "escape" to an actual desire to run. "In the beginning, it was all about companionship and burning calories . . . now I'm addicted!"

The feeling of accomplishment is addictive!

Now Debbie sees herself as a serious runner. She's run many half-marathons and recently completed her first full marathon. She's no longer a casual jogger. Debbie can clearly identify the moment when things changed for her. "It was the feeling of crossing that finish line," she says. "It was a rush like no other. I felt like Superwoman! The only other time I've felt that way is when I gave birth to my daughters. I am addicted to that feeling of accomplishment!"

Debbie self-identifies as a perfectionist and says running provides her with a source of continual opportunity to improve. Each new race brings an opportunity to compete with oneself for a faster time, a new personal record. She likes to set clear goals and work toward them. "I wanted to knock off one minute per mile and finish a half-marathon in less than two hours, and I did it!"

When it comes to training, there are many strategies.

Debbie uses a variety of them to keep the process of improving her running exciting. When asked which training strategy or method had disappointed her, the response was shocking. "There are no negatives. Everything I've tried has worked . . . running is pure joy!"

How has Debbie turned something most people would find grueling into such an overwhelmingly positive experience? The answer is clear as she shares what a happy, fulfilled and meaningful life looks like to her. "It's all about keeping a balanced life," she says. "I need a balance between friends, family, work, exercise, me time and faith."

I think Debbie's example is a great illustration of someone who has a clear mastery orientation. She has developed and tested strategies to help her accomplish her goals and is dedicated to improving herself through the process. In addition, Debbie's fully engaged with and enjoying the process of self-improvement.

According to the Stanford study, possessing a mastery-oriented approach is very beneficial for achieving a variety of goals.

We live in a society and culture where *performance orientation* is rewarded. Getting results, short term and immediate, is how success is assessed. Those results may take the form of good grades, job promotions or sales success, but there is an associated cost to overvaluing short-term performance. The cost of performance orientation is a diminished depth of knowledge, less creativity and innovation, less individual satisfaction, less long-term stability and fewer positive feelings related to the goal or task due to increased levels of anxiety and worry.

What a tough balance, living in a society that measures

results but also values satisfaction, stability and personal self-worth.

Don't get me wrong, results are critical in athletics, business, life and relationships. Yet creating a culture that nurtures long-term stability, maximum performance and maximum satisfaction pays dividends.

Strive for Your Best, Not Perfection

Recently I came across an article on running entitled "Mind over Miles" by Jerry Lynch, PhD, that appeared in the May 1996 *Runner's World* magazine. I'll do my best to paraphrase it. Basically, Olympic and other elite athletes use mental training to enhance their performance. Two fundamental principles stood out, not just for running, but for business, careers and life as well. First, stay relaxed. It is a proven fact that not being relaxed tightens muscles, clouds emotional perspective, minimizes creativity, drains energy and hinders performance outcome.

Second, strive for your best, not perfection. Striving to be perfect places a great deal of stress on oneself as we are not perfect, will not be perfect and cannot run the perfect race, whether it's a marathon, or in life or career. Instead, we can strive for *mastery*, doing our best, being realistic, being prepared for the unexpected and not worrying about perfection.

The outcome?

Being more relaxed equals better performance, less stress, more creativity and greater adaptability. You can translate this to a happier life and career. Mastery-oriented environments are great, but the real and meaningful question is whether mastery orientation and goals endure in less than ideal learning environments.

What does this study suggest for our personal, business and professional lives that are grounded on purpose, meaningfulness, satisfaction and happiness? And how do you balance the best components of mastery orientation with performance orientation?

The Best of Both Worlds: Mastery & Performance Orientation

As an avid golfer, I find that the elite golfer—think Arnold Palmer, Jack Nicklaus, Tiger Woods—possesses an amazing blend of performance and mastery orientation. Few sports place 100 percent of the responsibility for results on the performing athlete alone. Performance outcome, whether successful or not, points to the individual. So how do golfers reach the elite level that will get them on the PGA tour? It requires mastery of the skills to perform at a level that few of us will ever truly appreciate. Imagine the mental pressure of standing over a putt worth hundreds of thousands of dollars. The pros must have mastery of the swing and shaping of the shot: Do I want the ball to go straight, fade left, draw right, offset the wind, hit the green and roll, or hit the green and spin back to the pin? Mastery is required of the mind, the swing and the shot to effect elite performance.

I have a cousin who is an orbital eye cancer and facial surgeon. Do I want her to have a mastery (orientation) of her profession if I need her? Absolutely. Do I want her to perform at an exceptionally high level (performance orientation), with impeccable results? Absolutely. Do world-class surgeons embody both mastery and performance orientation? Yes!

What does this have to do with purpose, results and satisfaction in life and at work? It is about balance and determining how you go about defining and achieving happiness, satisfaction and success in your life.

I was sitting with the CEO of a major Fortune 500 company one afternoon. During the course of our casual social conversation, we talked about the performance of one of their NASCAR drivers who was off to a tough and less than productive year after coming off a great year. I quipped that it was a good thing the driver had built up some credits from his performance last year. The CEO's response was, "Maybe so, but we pay for current results, not past results!"

This is not just a business concept. I reflected on his response over the coming days and came to appreciate the reality of his comment about results. I agree that we cannot ride solely on past success and that while current results are critical, we need to maintain a sense of urgency to stay on task. I am of the belief, based on my own learning and experience, that there can and should be more to the sense of meaningfulness at work and in business, and in an individual's life, a meaningfulness that can pay long-lasting dividends. I have learned (from past mistakes) that being appreciated, having a feeling of belonging and knowing you bring value to an organization is not just for the sake of the organization, but also for the benefit and value of the team member and their family.

In *Drive: The Surprising Truth About What Motivates Us*, by Daniel H. Pink, we learn that the motivational paradigm of the last century, motivating ourselves with external rewards like money—the old carrot-and-stick approach—is the wrong way to motivate people for the challenges of today. According to Pink, "The secret to high performance and satisfaction—at work, at school, and at home—is the deeply human need to direct our own lives, to learn and create new things, and to do better for ourselves and our world." Knowing this, says Pink, gives us the knowledge to work smarter and live better.

According to Pink, in achieving meaningful, lasting and positive results you need to fully define your purpose with intentionality and thoughtfulness. You need to test your fortitude and understand the strength of the human spirit and your limits. Few people fully test themselves to their full ability. Why? In part because they have not defined what is important, what really matters. Until that is accomplished, you will continue to doubt yourself and eventually you'll look back on your life and say, "I wish I had done or tried X!"

Raise the Bar for Yourself:

Define an area in your life that you would like to strengthen. Set a goal. Now think about your personality. Are you more likely to assume a mastery or performance orientation to achieving this goal? Why? Think about some new ways of moving outside your comfort zone to achieve your goal.

CHAPTER 3

THE CHECKLIST: SUCCESS IS NOT AN ACCIDENT

If one advances confidently in the direction of one's dreams, and endeavors to live the life which one has imagined, one will meet with a success unexpected in common hours.

—Henry David Thoreau

I am thinking . . . 26.2 miles, am I ready? Will my body hold up? Am I physically and mentally strong enough to accomplish this challenge? Answering those questions is why I am here. Not for a time, not for a personal record, not for recognition, but for checking off a box in my life that yes, I can still do this, physically and mentally. I am pacing back and forth, listening to those around me talking of personal records, the weather and the run. I am nervous as I prepare for the singing of the national anthem and the sound of the starter's gun. I am scared and excited. The air force fighter jets scream down the start of the course as "The Star Spangled Banner" has begun. The race is about to start, the emotions are high as I am about to begin a journey that I have prepared for, perhaps more mentally than physically.

Rituals

There are two critical parts of gearing up for any important or significant activity or task: the physical/tangible preparation and the mental/emotional preparation; they usually go hand-in-hand. If you ask any great athlete about their preparation prior to game time you'll likely hear about rituals of one kind or another. For some, great care goes into what they eat the night before or morning of the event, what order they put their clothes on, the lucky socks they can't run without, the music they listen to while getting psyched up or the warm-up routine they run through. It's about the mental preparation—the details they "check off" that allow them to feel ready to go when the starter's pistol goes off.

"Marathoners have certain rituals that help us prepare for what's in front of us," says Crystal D. "I have to wear certain socks and I lay them out before every run; it's part of my preparation. A few years ago, I was lined up at the start of a 5K. I saw my then five-year-old son standing nearby ready to cheer me on. I noticed his socks were too big for him. He smiled and said they were mine. 'Why are you wearing my socks?' I asked.

'I want to run as fast as you, Mom!' he said, beaming." Apparently her son was creating his own rituals, too!

Crystal also understands and validates the unbelievable power of purpose to stay focused and motivated. "To celebrate my forty-fifth birthday, I signed up for a half-marathon. Two weeks prior to the race I was diagnosed with cancer. My doctor said I needed surgery immediately." Crystal got a second opinion and asked the doctor if the cancer would spread within two weeks if she held off on treatment. "You do what you have to do to work on your mind," he said. "We'll work on your body. Go run!" Crystal focused on the goal in front of her and poured her positive energy into it.

After finishing the half-marathon Crystal had a mastectomy. "My son was five and we chose to do chemo for four months," she says. "During that time, I ran. Running was the marker of being alive. There were times I couldn't walk, but I would tell my son I was going for a run." She'd put on her running shoes, walk to the end of the block, sit down for forty minutes, then walk back home. "'That was a workout!' I'd say. I wanted to show my son that everything was normal. My son needed to know that sometimes we just have to keep going and running was what I needed at that time. I explained to my son my treatments were like the crest of a hill; it's hard going up but once at the top, it only gets easier. Four months after the last chemo, I ran another half-marathon. Today I plan half-marathons around my surgeries."

Crystal finds purpose in running, using it as a means of healing and recovery for herself.

It's in the Details

I have my own set of rituals in my business. As an example, before a major presentation, I methodically review all my materials, detail by detail, checking everything off my "to do" list. I also visualize the upcoming meeting. I rehearse and review the presentation and anticipate possible questions that might arise. I nail down the flow of the meeting. Running through all these details is a ritual that helps me feel fresh and prepared.

I remember my very first post-college interview at a major school district. I had never done this before and walked in totally unprepared. Sure, I was dressed well, clean shaven and ready for a nice free-flowing discussion, but I had no clue as to what to expect. After a couple minutes of pleasantries, I was asked, "Bob, why do you want to teach and coach in our school district?" Without hesitation, and with all due candor, I responded, "Good question, I haven't thought about that." Right then I knew I wouldn't be getting a job offer. I walked out thinking, *What do you mean you haven't thought about that?* What a horrible reaction. Clearly I wasn't prepared. It's not that I didn't have a great answer. I had a poor reaction that I did not recover from. My poor performance was due to poor mental preparation. I hadn't yet developed a ritual, a way of formally preparing for this process. Sometimes overlooking the details can really get us in trouble.

Moving forward I vowed to be better prepared, to anticipate not only a wide range of questions but also how I would respond. The result? I had great interviews with subsequent teaching opportunities at different school districts that resulted in two teaching and coaching opportunities a few months later. I learned that taking the time to develop and practice rituals—the details that go into preparing for meetings, presentations, marathons or a myriad of other tasks—will help provide a sense of control and will go far in achieving positive results.

Focus on What You Can Control

Neely Spence is a twenty-two-year-old first-year professional distance runner who finished fifth at the 2013 U.S. Cross Country Championships, which qualified her to run in the World Cross Country Championships in Poland. Following the event, where she took thirteenth place, the best time for a non-African runner, she spoke about the importance of focusing on the basics and on what she can control.

"If there is one thing running has taught me," says Neely, "it's that being adaptable is one of the most critical components of success. With all the uncontrollable factors out there, I have to control everything I can and then not put energy into worrying about what is beyond my control. I consider myself to be a strong downhill runner; with four loops I had four opportunities to roll that downhill and that is where all my moves were made. The first lap, I nearly ran myself into the lead! That really surprised me, but I just stayed relaxed by focusing on my breathing and my rhythm."

The Role of the Checklist

Have a plan, work the plan! In preparation for the run we all do the same thing all successful people and businesses do—we review and reflect on our preparation and our plan. We have a checklist.

Having a checklist in place is essential to ensuring we don't overlook something. Pilots use them prior to takeoff (aren't you glad!) to check switches, wheel locks, flaps and more. NASCAR race teams use them as they prepare their car to leave the shop for the track. All major components, from the suspension to the wiring, brakes and fuel system, must be checked off. Flying down the track at two hundred miles an hour is a poor time to discover you overlooked something. Surgeons use them in the operating suite to ensure patient safety and lessen the chance of a clamp or sponge being left behind.

No matter what kind of adventure or goal you're working toward, having a checklist is a key element in your preparation. What should be on the checklist and why is it important?

Stay on Task

Don't let yourself think too far ahead. Focus on today and what needs to happen now. Although many of us pride ourselves on our ability to multi-task, in reality, there's no such thing. The brain can only successfully work on one thing at a time. Remind yourself daily of the purpose or motivation for your adventure, career move or personal goal. You can stay on task by focusing on your daily or weekly goals. You're the boss here. You get to determine how aggressive you will be in achieving your goals. Staying on task will firm up your resolve and make it far easier to keep moving down that checklist.

Here are some suggestions for helping you Stay on Task:

1. Define your goals. Write down your goals and why they are important to you. Put them somewhere you can see them. Whenever you get distracted, read your

goals and remind yourself of what you are trying to do and why.

2. Break it down. Create an actionable plan to help you identify how you can get from where you are now to where you want to go. Breaking goals into chunks or tasks provides motivation to get going and a sense of accomplishment when you can check them off one by one.

3. Prioritize. Some tasks are more important than others, or may be more time sensitive. Work on the urgent ones first to avoid feeling overwhelmed.

4. Track your progress. We all have good intentions for improving our lives, but sustaining our commitment is another thing. When you can track your progress, step by step, checking things off your list, you'll be able to see what you've done and will feel motivated to continue.

5. Reflect and reward. A great way to stay motivated is to periodically look back on what you've accomplished so far. Don't diminish the value of how far you've come. Find a way to reward yourself (without undoing your good work!) and celebrate.

6. Enlist the help of others. There's nothing like the support and gentle nudges from family and friends to keep you motivated. Share your goals with those closest to you. Let them be your cheerleaders and

counselors. They'll help you stay focused on what's important as you work toward your goals.

Years ago I was privileged to chair a national advisory board for a major financial services firm. I was given a great piece of advice from the chairman and CEO of the firm. "Bob," he said, "pick two or three key initiatives you wish to accomplish in your term, get buy-in and work the plan. Doing so, your tenure will be a success." What great advice: Trying to do too much in too short a time period often leads to less.

Be Intentional

Do things with good reason, have purpose, be thoughtful. Intention is a partner of planning. We can take baby steps each day, sometimes minute by minute, to accomplish our goals and become who we are meant to be. Only you can choose to engage with and live a purposeful existence. Living with intention will enable you to discover and celebrate your purpose and what's important to you. Not sure how to live with intention? Start with these simple questions:

- Am I being intentional about when I get up, and when I go to bed?
- Am I being intentional about what I put into my body?
- Am I being intentional about exercising?
- Am I being intentional about my work?
- Am I being intentional about my passions?

- Am I being intentional about being a spouse, parent or friend?
- Am I being intentional in my faith?
- Am I being intentional about my life?

Now, think about a way you wish to add greater fulfillment to your life or accomplish a specific goal. Create a list of ways you can be intentional in making it a reality. Remember, baby steps are good!

Harvey Mackay is a great businessman here in Minnesota as well as a nationally recognized author. He also writes a weekly column for the *Minneapolis Star-Tribune*. In a recent column, "What Is Your Next Marathon?" Mr. Mackay relays a message from Bill Wenmark, a fitness coach and marathoner: "You should run your first marathon for the right reasons because you will never be the same person afterwards. You must want to do it, for your reasons!" Interestingly, Wenmark has run over one hundred marathons with intention and purpose.

Webster's Dictionary defines "intentionality" as:
to be deliberate, done on purpose,
not by accident. It's a philosophy involving thought
such as beliefs and desires.

Running a marathon, succeeding in business, having a successful career or a broad network of close friends is accomplished through intentionality. Having a great mental attitude and being positive in thought takes intentionality. To live with grace, forgiveness, appreciation and happiness takes intentionality. As the definition states, intentionality is not by accident.

Be Committed

Every now and again I think it's important to do a self-check. Am I committed (to my purpose, my goal, my adventure) and do I walk the walk and walk the talk? Think about that for a moment. Few people can match the commitment, absolute power of purpose, intentionality and willingness to walk the talk of Bob Weiland and his running of the 1987 New York Marathon. Approximately twenty-three thousand runners started the race that year. Twenty thousand finished. The last person to cross the finish line was Bob Weiland, who ran the marathon on his hands, finishing in four days and two hours. Weiland is a Vietnam vet who, as a medic, lost his legs to a land mine while trying to rescue a buddy. Bob is an incredible example of being committed to a goal and having a well-defined and personal purpose, no doubt!

Prepare, Prepare, Prepare

If you want to get certain results you have to put the right conditions in place; there are no short cuts. Preparation is a critical component of achieving success in all your endeavors. As Abraham Lincoln once said, "If I had six hours to chop down a tree, I would spend the first four hours sharpening the axe." Preparation is the difference between a successful outcome and a failed outcome.

When I was a kid, my parents practiced consistency with my sister and me. Before an athletic event, concert or some other activity, we were told, "Do your best; that is all we can ask. If you do that, we will be proud and support you to the end." Afterward they would say, "You did a nice job, we are proud of you, you did your best."

Don't cheat yourself by failing to live up to your potential. Nothing, no matter how naturally gifted you are, can be accomplished to its limits without doing one's best in preparation.

Adam S.'s approach to running is "go big or go home." He trains by himself, focusing on his own abilities. Finding time to train is a challenge, scheduling around work and family life. As he was preparing for his first marathon, Grandma's in 2012, which he heard was a good beginner's marathon, he says some of the best advice he got was to start out slowly and pace yourself. "I learned not to treat it like a college exam, cramming everything in at the last minute to pass. Take training seriously and take your time. Training is the hard part," he says. "The marathon itself is the victory lap." Adam's family is a huge support system for him. On training runs they meet him halfway with water. His daughters cheer him on and his son blows a horn.

Running has provided Adam with lots of blessings. "I live each day to the fullest. I feel privileged to be healthy enough to run. Thinking about people out there who are physically unable to walk or run has pushed me through times when I was tired or sore or didn't want to do it. I don't take anything for granted."

Visualize the Goal

Dreams serve as our motivators in life and serve as the starting point for visualizing the outcomes we desire. Whether you desire improved health, a thriving business, a fulfilling relationship or a wonderful new home, there's a saying, "If you can imagine it, you can achieve it." As you think about the goal you are pursuing, close your eyes and imagine everything you will be seeing, feeling, smelling, hearing and tasting as you achieve your goal. The more sensory details you include, the more you will plant the vision in your psyche. Give it a try and with practice you will find this a fun and valuable exercise to keep you motivated for achieving your short- and long-term goals.

Phil G. believes a "personal sense of inner power" helps propel him forward in visualizing and accomplishing his goals. "When you're a runner, you can commit to a lot of things," he says. For Phil, the energy he absorbs from spectators along the marathon route helps him stay focused on his goal to reach the finish line. "I get jazzed from the electricity in the crowd," he says. He remembers a race where it was pouring rain. "I turned the corner on mile seven and heard my wife yell, 'Go Phil!' It was her enthusiasm that really uplifted me and kept my goal in sight," he says.

If you can imagine it, you can achieve it. If you can dream it, you can become it.
—William Arthur Ward

A few years ago, Ann J. was running during a very hot season. "During one marathon," she says, "there were heat warnings the whole time." At one point, around mile seventeen or eighteen she knew she wasn't meeting her time goals. "My husband and I have a tradition of going to Hell's Kitchen the next morning for breakfast. I knew I couldn't eat there in good conscience if I didn't finish the race. That's the lure that kept me going; that and seeing my husband at the finish line!"

In the Zone

Okay, I'm back at Grandma's Marathon. As I stand at the starting line, getting ready for that starter's pistol to go off, I begin to visualize my goal and the steps that will get me there. I visualize stopping periodically throughout the race for some quick encouragement (fuel!) from those supporting my journey. I see myself working my way through the "wall"—Lemon Drop Hill. Next I'm running by the old ore boat, docked at Canal Park. I know the finish line is not far off and I'm feeling the emotions of knowing I have won; not the race, but my purpose.

The starter's pistol has gone off. I'm back in the moment. We're running! The nervousness is gone. I'm feeling pumped. The adrenaline is doing its thing. I'm ready for this. This is what I've trained for. I'm in the zone. What a magical place to be. I seem to be gliding. The miles are clicking by and I feel so relaxed, so in touch with myself. I am smiling inside, I am excited as to how easy and fun it seems right now. Should I pick up the pace? Right now it feels as if I could do this for the balance of the race. I feel so free and comfortable and in control. My confidence is at a peak. I'm thinking this marathon will be a piece of cake.

But wait—I am reminded that I'm fifty-nine years old; I may need to adjust my thinking here, adjust my pace.

The winners of the race are now in their last mile and I have just crossed the thirteen-mile mark. Stay the course, stick with the plan; reconnect with your purpose. I'm not going to win—that was never part of the plan; it's not my purpose. Visualize the balance of the journey, reconnect with your plan and prepare. The infamous Lemon Drop Hill lies just ahead at mile twenty-two. Reality will be returning by then if not much sooner.

Play with Scissors

When I was young in my career, my father's company hired a consultant from Chicago to come in and do sales training for us. One day he asked us, a group of successful sales professionals, to get a stack of magazines from the corner of the room and grab a scissors, paste and a large piece of tag board. For the next hour we went through the magazines, cut out things that were important to us and then pasted them on the tag board. For a while there I felt like a second-grader, only with grown-up scissors.

Later that morning we went around the room and talked about what we'd put on our tag board. Some had boats, cars or large houses. Some had dream vacation destinations or prestigious golf courses. Some had pictures of churches or images representing social causes and family. We all had found pictures of things that were important to us, reflecting the personal reasons why we do what we do with our lives. While we were reminded of what motivates us, for many of us, it was perhaps the first time we actually connected these images to our thoughts, dreams and desires.

We were encouraged to put our personal visualization tag board someplace prominent in our offices. This would be a tool to help us stay on task. Those tag boards would serve as a personal reminder that when things are not going as planned we need to pick ourselves up and fight through the period of adversity.

To this day, that visualization board exercise is with me, not in a physical way, but mapped in my head. As I run and struggle in my training or in a race, I remind myself of the purpose and the reasons why I'm doing what I'm doing. I visualize the "finish line" and the feelings of success and accomplishment I'll feel when I get there. I fight through Lemon Drop Hill at mile twenty-two knowing that it is a necessary part of the journey if I want to experience satisfaction, success and a sense of accomplishment. Struggles make the journey that much more rewarding.

Raise the Bar for Yourself:

Imagine a time when you felt "In the Zone." Visualize the situation. What were you feeling? Trace the steps that got you to that place of fulfillment and accomplishment. What did you do to stay on task? How did you prepare? Remembering the sensation of being in the zone and what it took to get there can guide you in working toward your next goal.

CHAPTER 4

LEMON DROP HILL: DEALING WITH ADVERSITY

What lies behind us and what lies before us are small matters compared to what lies within us.

—Ralph Waldo Emerson

For those who have run a marathon, you are familiar with the term "hitting the wall." We slam into it somewhere around mile twenty or twenty-two, when we've used up the vast majority of stored energy. For Grandma's Marathon runners, "the wall" is also known as Lemon Drop Hill.

Lemon Drop Hill is a transition point in the race. You're leaving the gorgeous tree-lined streets sprinkled with magnificent homes nestled on the edge of Lake Superior and entering the commercial side of Duluth. You can see "the hill" clearly. The crest is on the horizon. On the surface this does not seem to be an overly daunting task; it's a climb that appears to be rather short. The problem, however, is that you have already run more than twenty miles. Your stored energy is gone. You're likely running on fumes. Your mental strength is being challenged. Fatigue is knocking rather loudly at your front door.

Here comes The Wall . . . will you slam into it, letting it stop you in your tracks, or fight through it? This is one of the last big tests in the race. Suck it up. Slow down and talk to your inner voice. *I've trained for this . . . what a great feeling . . . I will make it.*

Your body continues to scream "DON'T DO THIS TO ME—QUIT!" It's how you deal with the mental and physical pain that gets you through. It's a perfect metaphor for life.
—Jim H.

In running, you need to be prepared for this natural event to occur. It is physiological in nature as you can store only so much energy. Yet preparation, both physically—and equally as important—mentally, for this event will provide you the fortitude to push through.

Dick Beardsley, a Grandma's Marathon record holder, likens "the wall" to "feeling like an elephant has jumped out of a tree onto my shoulders and is making me carry it the rest of the way." Hitting the wall is when self-doubt casts a deep shadow over your mind, your confidence, your goal and your very soul.

According to Bob K., another Grandma's runner, "The real purpose of running is not to win the race—it's to test the limit of the human heart." The physical training is critical and most runners have their regimen for the physical part of enduring a marathon, yet fueling both the body and mind throughout the marathon is important. Runners refuel with their energy of choice to keep the body moving at its optimal levels. They also need to sustain the mental and emotional confidence that they can reach the finish line.

Hitting the Wall

Think of this as a metaphor for the fuel you need both physically and mentally as you work to achieve your own goals in life. Hitting the Wall is not just a marathon phenomenon—it happens in various areas of our personal and professional lives, too.

"It is easy to find success when things are going well; the real test is how you respond when things are not going as planned!" My dad said this to me when I joined his financial services firm. Things were going well—actually better than I could have ever imagined. I was relaxed, confident and on a roll; I was "in the zone." My dad said, "Remember, Bob, the real test of professional and long-term success in business is how you handle things when it's not going as well. How you react, how you pull yourself out of less productive cycles will be the real test of your skill and professionalism. Prepare yourself, as that day will come!"

He was so right. Like the market, there is no such thing as a straight line of perpetual upward success. There are detours, downturns and turning points that force you to assess, recalibrate, retool, accept responsibility and find a solution in a positive, constructive and productive manner.

I have observed and discovered different types of

personalities in life and business. There is the "blame someone else" personality. The person who, when something goes wrong, immediately finds someone else to blame: "The professor was hard to understand." "My supervisor doesn't know anything." "The coach is an idiot." Any of these sound familiar? It's easy to find excuses to insulate ourselves from accepting the fact that accountability and responsibility and, ultimately, our success or failure rests on our shoulders. Placing blame on others to gloss over our own personal weaknesses is the death knell in athletics, business, careers, finances and relationships.

On the other side of the coin is the positive, "I accept responsibility" personality, the person who looks at the issue and honestly assesses how they contributed to the problem. This personality determines how they can improve, perhaps consulting with others for advice, communicates their mistakes and works to collaboratively find ways to move on from the failure and take it as growth and learning experience. It is this personality that remains well positioned to grow within a corporate environment, business, life and relationships. Being able to accept responsibility underscores one's sense of confidence and reinforces the foundation of purpose and meaningfulness in their personal and professional lives.

MaryEllen Tribby is the founder and CEO of Working Moms Only.com, an online newsletter dedicated to empowering working moms. Ms. Tribby has a lengthy background in publishing and has interviewed many successful entrepreneurs during her career. Based on her work, she created a chart outlining the characteristics and behaviors she has identified in successful versus unsuccessful people. With her permission, I've included the chart on the following page.

THE SUCCESS INDICATOR
By MaryEllen Tribby
SUCCESSFUL PEOPLE
Have a sense of gratitude
Compliment
Forgive others
Give other people credit for their victories
Accept responsibility for their failures
Keep a journal
Read everyday
Talk about ideas
Want others to succeed
Share information and data
Keep a "to-be" list
Exude joy
Set goals and develop life plans
Embrace change
Continuously learn
Keep a "to-do/project" list
Operate from a transformational perspective
UNSUCCESSFUL PEOPLE
Criticize
Have a sense of entitlement
Hold a grudge
Take all the credit for their victories
Blame others for their failures
Watch TV everyday
Say they keep a journal but really don't
Think they know it all
Fear change
Fly by their seat of their pants
Operate from a transactional perspective
Talk about people
Secretly hope others fail
Hoard information and data
Don't know what they want to be
Exude anger
Never set goals
Copyright © 2012 MetEdge, LLC

Persevering through adversity is an essential and meaningful part of achieving our goals. Victory is all the sweeter when you can look back on all the bumps and bruises you've survived. There is no failure for those who continue to push forward, learning as they go.

The harder the conflict, the more glorious the triumph.
—Thomas Paine

Calvin Coolidge said, "Nothing in the world can take the place of persistence. Talent will not; nothing is more common than unsuccessful men with talent. Genius will not; unrewarded genius is almost a proverb. Education will not; the world is full of educated derelicts. Persistence and determination alone are omnipotent. The slogan 'Press On!' has solved and always will solve the problems of the human race."

Purpose + Goals + Motivation =
Success, Satisfaction and Happiness

Goals are the "what," motivation is the "inner drive and commitment" and purpose is the "why." Without purpose, goals won't take shape. Motivation alone will not carry you through the Lemon Drop Hills in life and on the home stretch to the finish line.

Beauty Emerges from Adversity

Are you familiar with The Butterfly Story? It's been modified over the years, but basically the story goes that a man was sitting and watching a monarch butterfly struggle to emerge from its cocoon. He sat and watched the butterfly for several hours as it struggled to squeeze its body through a tiny hole it had created at the end of the cocoon. Then it stopped, as if it couldn't go any further.

So the man decided to help the butterfly. He took a pair of scissors and snipped off the remaining bits of cocoon. The butterfly emerged easily but it had a swollen body and shriveled wings. The man continued to watch it, expecting the wings would enlarge and expand enough to support the body, but nothing happened. Instead, the butterfly spent the rest of its life crawling around. It was never able to fly.

Although the man had good intentions, what he didn't understand was that the restricting cocoon and the struggle required by the butterfly to get through the opening was nature's way of forcing the fluid from the body into the wings to prepare the butterfly for flight.

Struggle serves a purpose in our lives. Going through life without obstacles would actually be detrimental to our personal and professional growth. Struggle and adversity serves to strengthen us and enable us to fly.

The struggle is equally critical to crossing the finish lines in business and life. We all get in the zone and feel that things are so easy, everything seems to fall in place, and we are relaxed and have this amazing sense of confidence. Yet life, like the stock market, is not a straight line upward. It has a frustrating way of reminding us that we need to stay the course, stay on task, have patience and not get overly greedy. We also find that when the cycle takes a downward move, it's our purpose, well-defined goals and process that will allow us to work through the falls and missteps that may come.

Get Yourself a BHAG

Recently I heard Chris Killingstad, CEO of Tennant Company in Minneapolis, speak about corporate culture. His view is both wonderfully startling and refreshing. Mr. Killingstad says that when considering the essential elements for business success in the twenty-first century, it is imperative to create a compelling vision, encourage crazy ideas, reward failure and instill in your team a confidence to dream big and not be afraid to take risks. That combination, he says, sets the stage for amazing potential, rewarding results and excited employees and staff.

What struck me was the masterful way that instilling creativity, dreaming big and removing some of the barriers that can destroy creativity and collaboration can get everyone involved in being part of achieving a compelling vision and experiencing an exciting journey.

Mr. Killingstad reminded me that dreaming big and having a BHAG (Big Hairy Audacious Goal) sets the stage for unusual results.

I love the idea of BHAGs. Just saying "B-HAG" is fun. When was the last time you came up with a BHAG for yourself? Before going any further, why not take five minutes to conceptualize something you've always wanted to do. Go ahead, think about it.

Take Five.
Imagine elevator music here. . .
Okay, come on back.

I'd like to share an example of how my goal setting and definition of success has been impacted by perspectives learned from running. In sales and consulting, success is most often defined by end results. I used to focus on being at the top of the game. I worked to be in the top 10 percent of the group and to achieve as much success in my career as possible.

Today, my BHAG is to create a balance between achieving client success and satisfaction, and having ample time for personal interests and travel, building adult relationships with my children and having a meaningful and purposeful personal relationship.

How do I hope to accomplish this BHAG or at least give it a good shot? I'm going to take a lesson from myself in Chapter 3 on "Checklists" where I've included a list of baby steps you can take for helping you "Stay on Task" as you work toward a goal. I'll save you the time of going back by adding the list here adapted for developing a BHAG.

Staying on Task:

Define your BHAG.

Write down your BIG HAIRY AUDACIOUS GOAL (BHAG) and why it's important to you. Put it somewhere you can see it. Whenever you get distracted, read your BHAG and remind yourself of what you are trying to do and why.

Break it down.

Create an *actionable* plan to help you identify how you can get from where you are now to where you want to go. Breaking a BHAG into chunks or tasks provides motivation to get going and a sense of accomplishment when you can check them off one by one.

Prioritize.

Some tasks are more important than others, or may be more time sensitive. Work on the urgent ones first to avoid feeling overwhelmed.

Track your progress.

We all have good intentions for improving our lives, but sustaining our commitment is another thing. When you can track your progress, step by step, checking things off your list, you'll be able to see what you've done and will feel motivated to continue.

Reflect and reward.

A great way to stay motivated is to periodically look back on what you've accomplished so far. Don't diminish the value of how far you've come. Find a way to reward yourself (without undoing your good work!) and celebrate.

Enlist the help of others.

There's nothing like the support and gentle nudges from family and friends in keeping you motivated. Share your BHAG with those closest to you. Let them be your cheerleaders and counselors. They'll help you stay focused on what's important as you work toward achieving your BHAG.

Dreams (and BHAGs!) are the foundation of purpose. Dreams are the visualization board of your mind. Dreams are the emotional dimension of motivation. If you cannot dream it, you will never be able to accomplish it.

Personally, the journey toward various finish lines in life has not been without bumps and stumbles in the road. I think of past failures as a kid and have come to the conclusion that those failures and how I dealt with them, how I prepared for what became a failure, and the ongoing encouragement by my parents and those around me allowed me the freedom to fail and learn from the experience.

> *When your reach for the stars, you may not get one, but you will not come up with a handful of mud either.*
> —Leo Burnett

Chris Killingstad from the Tennant Company reinforced that to me and reminded me to have BHAGs, to reach for the stars, not to be afraid of failure but to learn from it, and not to look for blame in others. To be a "blamer" is a sure ticket to failure and unfulfilled success due to the label that is branded on your cultural pedigree.

Never Give Up . . . Even if You're Hallucinating

Dan R. started running when he was ten years old. He was pretty serious about running but not winning. "I believed that just doing the best I could was good enough," he says. Now at the age of fifty-seven, with an incredible two-hundred-plus marathons under his belt, he still strives to do the best he can. "Running a marathon has turned into something like Groundhog Day over and over again," he says. During the run things come back to him: "I'll think, Oh, I always forgot about this or that," as he relives a memory, physical feeling or experience. When he first began he struggled. "I was the worst, but never giving up turns into mastery. I was actually hallucinating in my first marathon," he says.

Running with his brothers is a bonding experience for Dan; they still enjoy running and spending time together. During one race Dan says, "My older brother passed me. I was shocked and I spent the whole race trying to catch him. I beat him by thirty seconds. The family still talks about it."

During Dan's first Grandma's Marathon in 1987 he broke his personal record by nearly sixteen minutes. However, after his awesome personal victory, he wasn't feeling well and ended up nearly passing out, needing medical treatment. After a couple hours, the medics released him and he began to search for his friends. The worst part of the story, Dan says, is that he couldn't find anyone he knew. "All I had with me was my running outfit and a solar blanket." Dan finished a tough marathon that day by hitchhiking home, ultimately getting a couple rides from friendly drivers who recognized him as a disoriented marathon runner.

Dan believes that never giving up allows a person to achieve and master almost anything.

Raise the Bar for Yourself:

Now your assignment is to create a Staying on Task list for your new BHAG. Start by creating an actionable plan and break it down into digestible bits you can tackle one by one.

CHAPTER 5

I DID IT! (BUT NOT ALONE)

When he took time to help the man up the mountain, lo, he scaled it himself.

—Tibetan proverb

I have fond memories as a child and young athlete playing summer baseball and golfing. There was so much I took for granted during those days. My father, a former baseball player with the St. Louis Cardinals, was my baseball coach for as long as I could remember, maybe always. We had practices that were filled with drills and game situations. As I reflect on those practices now, I have come to realize that my dad was teaching and coaching team play. He focused on the importance of communication and the mental skills that contribute to success more than relying on raw ability. We won games because we were a good team, not because we had great players. In fact, we didn't. We had good players who played great together as a team. Our success was based on a team effort.

As I grew older, I loved to play golf. However, I was often frustrated that my best friend, Steve P., kept beating me on the short par-three course across the street each and every time we played. I had never taken lessons . . . but what's so tough about golf? I thought that you play and you get better. I was wrong. It wasn't that simple. Instead, I learned from my mistakes and poor mechanics and the more I played, the more I refined my technique. The old saying "practice makes perfect" was absolutely on target. I discovered that at least my mistakes were consistent and repeatable as I added up my score in disgust, once again losing to my buddy.

Later I played more golf with my dad, socially and at events. We were always committed to doing our best and winning. Winning did not happen at first as those repeatable, learned and refined mistakes that I made as a young man on the par-three course remained entrenched with me.

At the suggestion of my dad, I took a series of lessons from a professional. As with baseball, I learned there was more to the game than being a good athlete. There were mental, emotional and mechanical skills that needed to be learned and practiced. I found that my game started to improve. My scores were lower and I discovered moments of greatness, followed by longer moments of mediocrity. I learned that instruction and practice created value. I learned that purpose and strategy applied to golf as well as life.

I discovered that controlling my emotions, accepting that mistakes will be made and not dwelling on mistakes greatly helps. Figuring out what happened, learning from it and using it as a growth experience would keep me "on par" as I approached the next shot. Today, I find that golf has had an exceptionally positive impact on my life and how I approach challenges.

> *Arrange whatever pieces come your way.*
> —Virginia Woolf

Golf reinforced the belief that I could not improve alone. I had help along the way from the professional instructor and from my dad, who reminded me to have patience, to forget about the last bad shot and not try to overcompensate on the next shot. I learned to stay the course with my purpose and get the game back on track by keeping my emotions in check, concentrating on the mechanics and moving toward the next opportunity. Couldn't the same be true for our approach to life, careers and relationships?

Since we're on the sports track here, I can share with you that I so desperately wanted to be a good basketball player in high school. Admittedly, I had some physical limitations in my early years in high school. I was short, weak and slow. But I didn't let that stop me. I was a smart player. However, it didn't take long to realize being smart with limited physical skills did not paint a rosy prospect for my future dreams.

Between my junior and senior years in high school I decided to take things into my own hands. I worked hard, ran, lifted weights, played ball daily and refined my shot. I became strong, tough, quick and fast. The result? I became a rather good soccer player (another passion) and never got off the bench in basketball.

Was all my work a failure? Absolutely not. It taught me a great deal about being the best reserve and the best practice opponent for the starters. I had a purpose! I believed that without tough competition in practice, the starters would not be well prepared and the team would not succeed. I was part of a team, and I contributed to our success as much as the starters; I just never got on the court to demonstrate what I had gained in the summer of hard work. My conclusion: We succeed—as in life and work—not as individual players, but as part of a team. I learned that connecting the dots (like Steve Jobs said) can result in a more fulfilling outcome and path than expected—as soccer, not basketball, became a sport that I excelled at in college and led to my career as a coach.

Interestingly, in college, I was blessed to play soccer for four years, all because of my passion to be a great basketball player. Soccer was a rather new sport where I grew up and we were a rag-tag group of individuals who wanted to play some soccer while getting a great education. We had a superb coach, Rolf Erickson, a former Norwegian national soccer player, who was a tactician and master of strategy. He also was a gentleman. Rolf was always well dressed and classy. His signature hounds-tooth fedora easily identified him as the iconic Augsburg College

soccer coach. Rolf taught us the mental and physical attributes and skills to play as a team.

My fellow players were not caught up with individual accomplishments, but rather this intense desire to win as a team. We clearly were not the most talented individually, but over the next four years we became a great team. We won games and we excelled as a team. The individual skills and abilities of those players shined and many were recognized on a conference and regional level. At the foundation of our success was our commitment to a common purpose: to be the best team.

Running and Marathons (of all kinds!)

Five years ago, Adam B. found himself weighing nearly three hundred pounds. A friend suggested they start to hold each other accountable, so they started running together. "I thought about running a marathon but it seemed like a very tall task," Adam says. He made the marathon his goal and began training. "It was cold during the race but there were tons of people out there cheering; they really embraced their roles as motivators!" One memory about that marathon made a lasting impact on him: "At the end of the race there was a man running hurt. People helped him and he just wouldn't give up until he finished. Everyone out there has the mentality, 'Don't give up. We can do this.' It motivates you to push to the end and it's a celebration when you finish."

Cassie F. moved to Duluth, Minnesota, in 2011. "At Grandma's, everyone is involved, it's the thing to do. People run, cheer or volunteer. The entire city supports it, including the University of Minnesota–Duluth students. Everyone has a role."

I love the book *Running Marathons for Dummies*, which offers a simple, straightforward approach geared to the lay runner. The book provides a foundational process along with a roadmap for helping make the marathon journey a successful and less painful experience (note I did not say pain free!).

There is no question that for a runner to participate in a marathon and finish takes personal training, motivation, purpose, drive, mental stamina and fortitude. With all that said, most everyone has a support network around them and resources that keep them on track and on pace with achieving the goal. Some runners join a running club to prepare for the run. Most have a personal and well-defined purpose and reasons for running. The next time you're at a marathon (as a runner or supporter), look at the back of the T-shirts of those around you. They bear colorful, passionate and personal tributes to their purpose and cause. For many of us, it's those loyal supporters (families and others) who are sprinkled along the racecourse, cheering us on or offering a cup of water, that fuel us.

Personally, I could not do it without the 26.2 miles of support, encouragement and expressions of excitement and awe for the runners. As Craig T. says, "I run each of the last six miles in tribute and dedication to six people close to me, one for each mile." Without meaningful people in our lives, motivation and meaningfulness is so difficult to hold onto.

A Little Help from My Friends

As Ringo Starr sang on the 1967 Beatles's *Sgt. Pepper's Lonely Hearts Club Band* album, we all need a little help from our friends. Nothing significant is really accomplished without the help and support of others. All great leaders, businesspeople, athletes and other celebrated achievers have a great and talented team working with them.

I remember the early days of my career in the family financial services business. My dad had assembled a remarkable group of team players to support the exceptionally entrepreneurial sales dimension of the firm. Pam H., Dan A., Wayne S., Frank F. and Karen G. made everyone look and perform better. The firm did not succeed because of the founder, but because of those he gathered around him who believed in the mission, purpose and direction of the company. It was a remarkable example of team effort that enabled so many individuals to succeed at incredible levels.

> *The way a team plays as a whole determines its success. You may have the greatest bunch of individual stars in the world, but if they don't play together, the club won't be worth a dime.*
>
> —Babe Ruth

Many of us are part of some type of team. It could be at work, in a volunteer capacity, in our faith community or at school. To be successful, all teams need to develop a team attitude dedicated to a common goal. Here are a few things that need to happen to support a group's efforts:

1. Leaders must put away their ego and provide their teams with the tools (including a role or job description) they need to succeed. They must consistently praise their team's efforts and accomplishments. A leader's success is directly related to the success of those around her.

2. Teams need a clear, articulated and agreed-upon purpose and goals that are:
   - Collaboratively established;
   - Well communicated;
   - Consistently measured;
   - And crafted to allow for individual ownership in the successes and failures.
3. Leaders need to demonstrate that they care about the team. Individuals need to be thanked, positively acknowledged and encouraged with expectations and support to improve. *Leaders must establish a relationship with the person and focus less on the job.*

As individuals, we often forget one remarkable aspect of life: the power of others in our overall success and growth, individually and organizationally. I have learned that very fact both personally and professionally, not just from success, but also from failures. Without unselfish support, potential is missed and success for the organization and individual fails to materialize.

What kind of support am I referring to?

Support at home

The individual careers and roles of spouses need to be defined and supported. We are each driven by our own unique passions. Whether both parents/spouses are career focused or one stays at home, there needs to be unwavering support for each family member. Everyone has a role and each role is important, whether it's earning money, being primary care giver (CEO of

LEADING the STARBUCKS WAY

5 Principles for Connecting with Your Customers, Your Products, and Your People

Joseph A. Michelli

Mc Graw Hill Education

NEW YORK CHICAGO SAN FRANCISCO
ATHENS LONDON MADRID
MEXICO CITY MILAN NEW DELHI
SINGAPORE SYDNEY TORONTO

1 2 3 4 5 6 7 8 9 0 DOC/DOC 1 9 8 7 6 5 4 3

ISBN 978-0-07-180125-6
MHID 0-07-180125-1

e-ISBN 978-0-07-180126-3
e-MHID 0-07-180126-X

Design by Lee Fukui and Mauna Eichner

Library of Congress Cataloging-in-Publication Data

Michelli, Joseph A.
Leading the Starbucks way : 5 principles for connecting with your customers, your products, and your people / by Joseph Michelli.
pages cm
ISBN-13: 978-0-07-180125-6 (alk. paper)
ISBN-10: 0-07-180125-1 (alk. paper)
1. Starbucks Coffee Company—Management. 2. Customer relations. 3. Product management. 4. Corporate culture. 5. Success in business. I. Title.
HD9199.U54S7357 2014
658.4'092—dc23 2013015527

This book was prepared with the assistance of The Starbucks Coffee Company. The titles of the Starbucks partners and other Starbucks facts were accurate at the time the book went to print.

The author is not employed by or affiliated with Starbucks.

All internet addresses provided in the book were accurate at the time the book went to print.

This book is printed on acid-free paper.

This book is dedicated to the memory of my wife,
Nora Leigh Michelli (September 7, 1961, to February 11, 2013)—
the woman with whom I shared more than half my life.
You've been released from your six-year battle with breast cancer,
and I know you heard, "Well done, good and faithful servant."
Nora, it is your time to enjoy the Master's happiness!

Contents

Foreword

Many business leaders today face a dynamic set of challenges. How does one choose employees who have the talents and interpersonal qualities necessary to deliver memorable customer experiences? How can leaders bring on board, train, and acculturate team members so that they develop a passion for product excellence and the skills required to become consummate service professionals? How can technology be leveraged to strengthen, *not* diminish, personal service delivery?

If you are fortunate enough to be a manager or leader in a company with a global footprint like The Ritz-Carlton Hotel Company or Starbucks, you face the added challenges of constantly refining your products and services to connect with changing and culturally diverse customer groups—all the while maintaining operational excellence and the loyalty of your existing customer base.

Each of Dr. Joseph Michelli's books offers a learning laboratory that's rich with examples from leaders as they address the aforementioned challenges and opportunities. They provide information, insights, and analysis on how leaders seek to create a high-performance organization that operates through the lens of humanity. This book demonstrates both the setbacks and the breakthroughs that the Starbucks leadership has encountered as it has attempted to position its products and people to deliver consistent, engaging, and loyalty-enhancing experiences.

I first met Dr. Michelli approximately six years ago. At that time, he brought his background as a customer experience professional, business consultant, and author to The Ritz-Carlton Hotel Company and chronicled our never-ending commitment to foster the engagement of our "Ladies and Gentlemen" and the guests whom we are fortunate to serve at our hotels and resorts in 27 countries presently.

As president of The Ritz-Carlton Hotel Company, I believe that a company's culture is critical to its success. At The Ritz-Carlton, we strive to anticipate and exceed guests' expectations in a warm, relaxed, and refined setting. We are constantly looking for ways to infer and go beyond the wants, needs, and desires of our Ladies and Gentlemen and of our guests. All of the Ladies and Gentlemen of The Ritz-Carlton (myself included) invest in and communicate about our cultural foundation on a daily basis.

American author M. Scott Peck suggested that we should "share our similarities, and celebrate our differences." While The Ritz-Carlton and Starbucks are different organizations in many respects, *Leading the Starbucks Way* is a powerful and useful reminder that every one of us (no matter what our function or our industry) can contribute in some way to improved product quality, enhanced service delivery, emotionally engaging experiences, and enriched community involvement.

I wish you a fond farewell and joyful reading.

Herve Humler
President and Chief Operations Officer
The Ritz-Carlton Hotel Company, L.L.C.

Acknowledgments

Physician, philosopher, and theologian Albert Schweitzer once wrote, "At times our own light goes out and is rekindled by a spark from another person. Each of us has cause to think with deep gratitude of those who have lighted the flame within us." In the next few paragraphs, I am challenged to express the depths of my gratitude to so many people who have blessed my life with a willingness to kindle the flame that made this book possible.

Leading the Starbucks Way would not exist were it not for the support of Howard Schultz and the leadership team at Starbucks. While a list of Starbucks partners who contributed to it can be found in the Bibliography, special recognition must be provided to Gina Woods, director, Executive Communications, and Heidi Peiper, program manager, Corporate Communications. Both Gina and Heidi were involved in all strategic and tactical aspects needed to take *Leading the Starbucks Way* from idea to reality. Thanks for your patience, enthusiasm, insights, and diligence.

Lynn Stenftenagel has worked on five books with me, starting with *The Starbucks Experience*. Through years of book writing, unimaginable business success, and our share of headwinds, I can resoundingly say that there is no one I admire and respect more than Lynn. While we continue to grow and refine our business relationship, there is no denying the transformational impact that Lynn has had on my career and my life. When it comes to our work, Lynn is the true "keeper of the flame."

During that same five-book run, I have been fortunate to work with Donya Dickerson and Lloyd Rich. Lloyd, my publishing attorney, is the epitome of professionalism. He is an exceptional subject-matter expert with an amazing ability to create win/win solutions. Donya, an executive editor at McGraw-Hill, has the enviable ability to spark people to perform at unexpected levels. Donya sets clear performance expectations and dives in to help realize those objectives; but it is her unfailing encouragement, even temperament, and resourcefulness that push people past what they think they are capable of doing.

While this book is dedicated to Nora Michelli, I must provide some context if the remainder of these acknowledgments is to make sense. Nora and I met in 1987, married in 1989, and parted in the final stage of this book's completion. In fact, my earthly time with Nora ended in 2013 as our children and I sat at her bedside while she took her final breath.

Over the course of our journey, Nora and I brought into the world two children: Andrew and Fiona. We laughed, fought, delighted, angered, prayed, and battled cancer—together. I am happy to say that Nora knew everything about me and forgivingly loved me anyway, and for that I am eternally grateful.

During her extended cancer fight, and upon her death, many people have relit my life flame. Andrew and Fiona, you are my most significant inspirations. I know your lives have been painfully altered with the loss of your mom, but I pledge to be the best parent possible to carry forward the part of her that was delighted by and believed in your greatness and your ability to change the world. Andrew, may your nursing career allow you to transfer your loving spirit into acts of healing. Fiona, congratulations on Loyola and your journey into a life of leveraging business leadership to do significant good in the world.

Jim Collins talks about the people you would place on the board of directors of your life. The following have earned that place for me by their sage counsel, amazing depths of compassion, leadership vision, and resolute friendship, particularly during the challenges of late. Thank you, Rob Graf, Bob and Judy Yarmuth, Tommy and Diane Nance, Jeff Woodell, Barry and Lori Torman, Matt Lurz, Paul Prouty, Leanne Hadley, and Michael Pollard.

Thanks as well to those who have taught me so much about serving others through their example. Not the least of these include Kim Blankenburg, Carolyn Churchill, and so many others at Janus Capital Group, as well as Christie Schatz and staff members at Sonny's Franchise Company. Similarly, I offer gratitude and praise for Saint Peter's Healthcare System in New Brunswick, New Jersey, Jackie Houston, and the special nurses of Suncoast Hospice.

As always, I conclude with a word of gratitude to you the reader. *Nothing plays a greater role in sparking me to write than an appreciation for the willingness of someone like you to take the time to read, learn, and grow.* Philosopher Eric Hoffer said, "In times of change learners inherit the earth; while the learned find themselves beautifully equipped to deal with a world that no longer exists." I extend a heartfelt thank you for allowing me to learn and to share with you. May *Leading the Starbucks Way* play a small role in helping us all move forward in this grand adventure!

CHAPTER 1

The Starbucks Connection

A couple in Switzerland make their first visit to a Starbucks® store and are welcomed enthusiastically. When asked what they'd like to have prepared for them, they both respond that they aren't there to make a purchase. They just want to see "what all the Starbucks fascination is about." They become regulars at that store.

A partner (as employees are called at Starbucks) shares how he was "moved" while attending the funeral of a regular customer. During the eulogy, the son of the deceased expressly mentioned the significance of those daily interactions between his father and that Starbucks partner.

A man sits alone at lunch in his favorite Starbucks store and tells a green apron–clad Starbucks barista (coffee preparer) that the store is his midday refuge, noting, "At Starbucks, you are nice to me, you remember me, and you seem genuinely grateful that I am here."

These actual stories exemplify a company whose leaders establish a compelling vision and manifest behaviors that culminate not only in product sales but in powerful, loyalty-rich human connections. You are probably looking into the pages of this book to essentially understand how "all this Starbucks fascination comes about." How do leaders at Starbucks strategically and tactically steward the company's products and people to build customer engagement, loyalty, advocacy, and even brand love? How do these leaders model and inspire excellence in product delivery, the creation of moments of authentic service, an enterprise-wide appreciation for the importance of shareholder value, and a contagious demonstration of social conscience? You are probably also interested in what Starbucks partners are doing to expand relationships beyond the café environment, how they leverage technology to enhance customer experiences, and the ways in which they customize offerings to address local desires across the globe. Ultimately, lessons from Starbucks leaders, managers, and frontline partners will teach you to build connections with those you serve to effectively enrich your business and personal life.

STARBUCKS: A LEADERSHIP BENCHMARK

Starbucks is consistently recognized as one of the world's most effectively led and beloved brands. For example, *Entrepreneur* magazine ranks the company among the 10 "most trusted" businesses, and *Fortune* magazine places it among the "most admired" global brands. Before delivering an important jobs speech, U.S. president Barack Obama placed a call to the president, chairman, and chief executive officer of Starbucks, Howard Schultz, because of Howard's leadership on job creation. *Fortune* magazine has named Howard Schultz as businessperson of the year, and other magazines have suggested that he is among the top tier of global leaders when it comes to his impact on business ethics. Leadership across all levels of the company has produced more than 54 million Facebook fans, and millions more follow the company on Twitter and Pinterest.

Most important, Starbucks leaders are responsible for substantial global economic and social impact as well as considerable workforce stewardship. Starbucks leaders guide more than 200,000 people who serve the more than 60 million weekly customers frequenting more than 18,000 stores in more than 60 countries worldwide.

My previous book about Starbucks, *The Starbucks Experience: 5 Principles for Turning Ordinary into Extraordinary*, looked at how Starbucks leaders positioned the company for meteoric growth through much of the 1990s and early 2000s. Following the publication of that book, Starbucks leaders faced challenges resulting from their frenzied speed of expansion, decisions they made to drive year-over-year sales numbers, the effects of a sliding global economy, and less frequent visits from loyal customers to Starbucks U.S. stores. In 2008, Howard Schultz, who had been serving as the chief global strategist for Starbucks, returned to the helm as the company's chief executive officer. At the fiscal 2008 second-quarter earnings conference call, when Howard was explaining a 21 percent earnings decline over the prior year period, he noted, "While our financial results are clearly being impacted by reduced frequency to our U.S. stores, we believe that as we continue to execute on the initiatives generated by our Transformation Agenda, we will reinvigorate the Starbucks Experience for our customers, and in doing so, deliver increased value to our shareholders."

Howard's "Transformation Agenda" is detailed in his 2011 book titled *Onward: How Starbucks Fought for Its Life without Losing Its Soul.* At its core, Starbucks leadership crafted a transition plan that established a forward-looking vision that enhanced the company's established mission. While the Starbucks mission was "to inspire and nurture the human spirit—one person, one cup and one neighborhood at a time," the transformation vision set an energizing and rallying objective, "to become an enduring, great company with one of the most recognized and respected brands in the world, known for inspiring and nurturing the human spirit."

Tactically, Starbucks leaders identified "seven bold moves" to focus on existing strengths and identify innovations and process improvement objectives that should position the company for long-term viability. Those bold moves were stated as follows:

1. Be the undisputed coffee authority.
2. Engage and inspire our partners.
3. Ignite the emotional attachment with our customers.
4. Expand our global presence—while making each store the heart of the local neighborhood.
5. Be the leader in ethical sourcing and environmental impact.
6. Create innovative growth platforms worthy of our coffee.
7. Deliver a sustainable economic model.

Adherence to these seven bold moves has resulted in desired financial outcomes, as evidenced by 13 consecutive quarters of global comparable store sales growth greater than 5%. While Starbucks was making its turnaround, global economic factors were triggering peak business failure rates, as Dun & Bradstreet reported: "The number of formal bankruptcy filings in the 12 months ending June 2010 . . . increased by 10% . . . and the year over year increase between 08 and 09 was 50%." Unlike the leaders of the proliferation of businesses that failed in 2008, 2009, and 2010, Starbucks leadership positioned the company for enduring profitability and brand respect.

This book, *Leading the Starbucks Way*, outlines the foundational principles that have guided Starbucks leaders during sustained periods of meteoric growth, economic downturn, recovery, and transformation. Like the tactical course defined in the Transformation Agenda, *Leading the Starbucks Way* looks at key strategies and tools that leaders are deploying to achieve sustainable success, particularly in the areas of product creation, category growth, international expansion, and technological and social media innovation. These guiding principles and strategies are presented in language consistent with the Starbucks culture, even though that language may be somewhat unusual for most leadership discussions. The foundation for Starbucks leadership is reflected in terms like *connection*, *humanity*, *humility*, *passion*, and, yes, even *love*.

WHAT'S LOVE GOT TO DO WITH IT—LEADING A HIGH-PERFORMANCE ORGANIZATION

When you're sitting across from Howard Schultz, it doesn't take long for him to get to the heart of leadership excellence. From Howard's perspective, much of leadership comes down to three traits: "Take love, humanity, and humility and then place it against a performance-driven organization; these are in conflict to the naked eye. But I believe that performance is significantly enhanced by this kind of leadership. I am so convinced of it because we have become more performance driven than at any other time in our history and the values of the company are at a high level. If we can infuse love, humanity, and humility on a global basis and build it into a performance-driven organization, we are unbeatable."

While Howard's views about positive emotional connections and high performance standards are somewhat unusual among CEOs of large corporations, that perspective is consistent with a groundswell of opinions and findings from leadership experts and researchers. Leadership author James Autry, for example, notes, "Good management is largely a matter of love. Or if you're uncomfortable with that word, call it caring, because proper management involves caring for people, not manipulating them." Professor Leonard Berry of Texas A&M summarizes decades of consumer research by noting, "Great brands always make an emotional connection with the intended audience. They reach beyond the purely rational and purely economic level to spark feelings of closeness, affection, and trust. Consumers live in an emotional world; their emotions influence their decisions. Great brands transcend specific product features and benefits and penetrate people's emotions."

Consumers are not the only ones who "live in an emotional world." Employees do so as well. Starbucks demonstrates, and research confirms, high levels of partner (employee) engagement, retention, and productivity when supervisors positively penetrate the emotions of those they lead.

At Starbucks, leadership champions the human connection in all aspects of business. Additionally, leaders build their business strategies based on opportunities that emerge from connections with partners, customers, communities, and shareholders. Ultimately, they manage through a lens of humanity and high performance expectations.

STANDARDS, OPPORTUNITY, AND CONNECTION: FORGING A HOLISTIC LEADERSHIP APPROACH

This book shares essential principles used by Starbucks leaders as they forge emotional connections that drive innovation, grow new business product lines, and foster employee and customer loyalty. These principles are especially relevant in a service world that has been revolutionized by mobile technology, social media, and increasing consumer choice. Each principle is outcome-focused and is easily applied, no matter where your business is in its developmental journey. The principles in *Leading the Starbucks Way* are the result of more than two years of research spanning all regions that Starbucks serves. Access was granted to leaders and partners at all levels of the company. More than

500 hours of interviews and research produced the following five leadership principles:

1. Savor and elevate.
2. Love to be loved.
3. Reach for common ground.
4. Mobilize the connection.
5. Cherish and challenge your legacy.

Executing on these principles produces powerful bonds with employees, customers, suppliers, and even noncustomers. In turn, these operational and emotional bonds will help any leader achieve sustainable profits, increase brand equity, and fuel online and offline stories of loyalty and love.

One such story involves Diana Kelly, a Starbucks district manager who ran across a circumstance that she had seldom encountered in her suburban location of Fredericksburg, Virginia—a homeless man in her store. Rather than treating that man, Dominic, as an unwanted intrusion in her business operation, Diana bought him a hot chocolate and asked him about his life. To her surprise, she found that he lived in a makeshift homeless encampment in a nearby woods. Diana and several other Starbucks store managers and baristas decided to go to the woods to "connect with" and serve Dominic and dozens of people like him.

Based on those experiences, Diana and her team shared stories from the homeless camp with customers and leveraged their customer connections by placing collection bins in each of the 14 stores in Diana's district. The bins became a repository for items like toothbrushes, toiletries, and clothing for distribution at the homeless camp. A local businessman (and Starbucks customer) donated the necessary funds and found a local attorney to help this grassroots community effort become an actual nonprofit organization called Project Dominic.

Why did Diana take an interest in Dominic? What good could possibly come out of such an act, particularly as it relates to Starbucks sustainable profits, brand equity, and love? While I suspect that her initial intentions were based on nothing more than a genuine concern for Dominic irrespective of his ability to produce a visible impact on a Starbucks cash register, Starbucks benefited from Diana's willingness to offer Dominic a few moments of human connection.

Specifically, Starbucks partners in Fredericksburg have had the benefit of making a tangible difference in their community and engaging regular customers. Those partners and customers have been enriched through the chance to work together for good. Finally, without Diana and her team ever meaning for this to be a benefit, people close to and far away from Virginia are reading about and being inspired to engage in actions like those that began so humbly in Fredericksburg. Writing in *The Washington Post*, columnist Petula Dvorak noted, "The City Council called for hearings and solutions. Some residents demanded that all the homeless be rounded up and jailed. The leaders at Micah Ministries, a Christian outreach program that provides social services, asked for calm and understanding. . . . [Diana and Project Dominic] bring hundreds of supply bags into the woods and, with each delivery, try to talk the folks into going to one of the city's outreach centers for counseling, medical care and shelter. They are helping more than 200 people." Call it what you want—kindness, compassion, or love. I call it the Starbucks connection and leading the Starbucks way!

My hope is that this book helps you, as a leader in your organization, build and grow your business through a genuine relational strategy, guided by the leadership excellence of individuals like Howard Schultz and his team at Starbucks. In so doing, you will not only drive success and profitability but develop a significant and purposeful business anchored in engaging and compassionate leadership practices.

PRINCIPLE 1

SAVOR AND ELEVATE

Before we start our deep exploration of Starbucks, I challenge you to think about your own business. Something drew you to sell your goods or services. Hopefully, that original attraction came from positive connections you formed with your product or industry, and those original favorable feelings have grown over time and spread to those you lead and serve.

"Savor and Elevate" is a business principle that emphasizes the importance of maximizing enthusiasm for the products, services, and experiences your company provides. It reflects the importance of helping your people autonomously master product knowledge, develop strong emotional connections to your products, and innovate timely solutions and experiences that build on the strengths of your product array.

Like each of the principles in this book, "Savor and Elevate" is explored in two chapters. Chapter 2, "If You Don't Have Passion for Your Product, Why Should Your Customer?," focuses on how Starbucks leaders communicate and demonstrate their personal passion for their product. It explores ways in which passion is fueled through formal training, company rituals, immersive experiences, and corporate strategy.

Chapter 3, "From Replicable and Consistent to Magical and Unique," sets product passion and consistent service execution as the foundation for fostering craveable customer experiences. By defining an authentic and attainable set of desired experiences, and by engaging in active and continuous dialogue, Starbucks leaders have inspired and empowered employees to deliver products and services in the context of genuine human connections that result in uplifting customer moments. Chapter 3 explores the ways in which Starbucks leadership communicates with partners and empowers them to create extraordinary experiences. When good is not good enough, it's time to lead your people to "Savor and Elevate."

CHAPTER 2

If You Don't Have Passion for Your Product, Why Should Your Customer?

Only passions, great passions, can elevate the soul to great things.

DENIS DIDEROT, *French philosopher*

Many books and articles suggest that with the right techniques, anyone can sell anything. The authors of these works seem to imply that you can be successful at selling any product, even if you do not particularly like what you sell. Certainly, some entrepreneurs achieve success without having a positive emotional connection with their goods or services. Steve Chou, the founder of Bumblebee Linens, reports that his online store went from zero earnings to more than $100,000 profit in a single year, despite the fact that he was "not terribly passionate about wedding linens. Decorative pieces of fabric don't really make me excited and to be honest, I'm not in love with what we sell. . . . When my wife and I first started our business, it was all about the numbers and whether the business could make enough money so my wife could quit her job."

Even Tony Hsieh, the CEO of Zappos, a company I wrote about in my book *The Zappos Experience: 5 Principles to Inspire, Engage, and WOW*, notes that he is "not passionate about shoes at all." Despite running a company that has an inventory of more than 50,000 varieties of shoes, Tony has reported he owns three pair. Instead, Tony acknowledges that he is "passionate about customer service and company culture," which may be why Zappos has reached a level of success that most other stores that just sell shoes have not.

While passion for the product may not be necessary for sales success, it certainly differentiates sales leaders from most of their competitors. Additionally, employee passion for the product fuels the emotional engagement of customers and facilitates sustainability. Sales consultant Troy Harrison defines the link between employee passion and customer engagement by suggesting, "Passion is the indefinable something that creates and builds interest and excitement on the part of the customer." From Troy's perspective, customer excitement emerges when your people have "a need to make buyers feel the same excitement" that they do. To achieve that level of customer enthusiasm, Troy suggests you have to first sell yourself "on your products or services. If you were in the position of a target customer, would you buy? . . . All else is meaningless."

Starbucks chief executive officer Howard Schultz explains the transference of passion slightly differently: "You can walk into any store and you can feel whether the proprietor or the merchant or the person behind the counter has a good feeling about his product. If you walk into a department store today, you are probably talking to a guy who is untrained; he was selling vacuum cleaners yesterday, and now he is in the apparel section. It just does not work."

Howard consistently transfers his excitement for Starbucks offerings and anchors that enthusiasm to the product that is at the center of the company—coffee. He reports that his enchantment with coffee was heightened in 1982 when he joined Starbucks. As he described in his book *Onward*, he gained an enriched awareness of the "magic" of coffee and the coffee ritual a year later when he visited Milan, Italy, and experienced coffee artisans who "seemed to be doing a delicate dance as [they] ground coffee beans, steamed milk, pulled shots of espresso, made cappuccinos, and chatted with customers standing side by side at the coffee bar." Reflecting on his Italian experiences, Howard concluded that espresso, coffee, and cappuccino creation was not a "job" but a "passion."

To achieve the company's mission "to inspire and nurture the human spirit—one person, one cup and one neighborhood at a time," leaders at Starbucks crafted a set of principles to be lived daily, the first of which involves passion for:

> Our Coffee. It has always been, and will always be, about quality. We're passionate about ethically sourcing the finest coffee beans, roasting them with great care, and improving the lives of people who grow them. We care deeply about all of this; our work is never done.

In support of this principle, Starbucks leaders have developed a variety of mechanisms to help everyone who comes to work for the company (not just those in customer-facing roles) understand and hopefully gain a deep connection with the rich history of coffee; the journey of coffee from farm to Starbucks cup; the economic, social, and environmental aspects of the coffee industry; and also a sophisticated respect for the special nuances of coffee flavor profiles. In short, Starbucks leaders have produced diverse tools to help Starbucks partners develop or deepen a genuine product passion.

The remainder of this chapter will look at the wide-ranging product passion-enhancing tools that Starbucks deploys internally and examine how those tools build excitement for customers. In the process, you will be challenged to consider how training, corporate rituals, immersive employee experiences, and aligned strategies for product excellence can incite passion in your people and your customers.

SETTING THE STAGE THROUGH KNOWLEDGE

When you think of someone who works at Starbucks, you are likely to envision a barista. In fact, many of us have a personal connection with the brand through frequent contact with this group of service providers. As in many large organizations, however, the barista is only one essential part of a complex array of professionals who function across corporate, international, regional, and store-level functions.

While many employees seek careers at Starbucks because of their interest in coffee or as a result of experiences that they have had as customers, a large number of applicants seek employment despite *not* having had a taste for the primary product the company sells. Virgil Jones, director, Partner Services, at Starbucks, shares his introduction to Starbucks by noting, "I used to walk by Seattle's Capitol Hill Starbucks store when I was in college, and I knew nothing about coffee or about Starbucks. One day I decided to go inside, and I was confused by a number of items on the board. When the store manager asked if I was a new customer, I said yes, and he responded, 'I'm going to make you a mocha,' and he handed it to me. He then said, 'This one is on me, but I want you to come back, and the next time I'll introduce you to some of our brewed coffees.' I walked away that day being impressed. So I did some research on the company, and my junior year in college decided I wanted to work for Starbucks. When I was graduating, I applied for probably 15 to 20 positions at Starbucks and got hired as temporary full-time help for the holiday season in the warehouse." Like so many other Starbucks partners, Virgil continued to evolve, and professionally grow from that temporary warehouse job into his career as director of the Partner Services team.

While a passion for coffee is not required in order to be hired at Starbucks, new partners across the company do receive a strong introduction to the significance, specialness, and importance of coffee. At the store level, for example, Starbucks onboards baristas by a "first impressions" meeting with the store manager. That visit typically begins with the new barista experiencing a coffee tasting of the store manager's favorite coffee and continues with activities and conversation that emphasize the centrality of coffee and the desired Starbucks Experience.

Over the days and weeks that follow, new baristas learn a great deal about coffee-growing regions, trade practices in coffee purchasing, processing methods for removing the coffee bean from the coffee cherry, coffee roast profiles, the skills necessary to pull a high-quality espresso shot, the fundamentals of coffee brewing, steps in coffee tasting, foundational taste characteristics of coffee, and all aspects of preparing Starbucks wide range of beverages and other offerings. This training combines a formal curriculum with individual development discussions and job practice sessions with the new hire's store manager and an experienced barista who functions as a learning coach.

This coffee education reflects a 70/20/10 growth and development approach. Based on research on how people integrate and utilize new information, new baristas at Starbucks receive approximately 70 percent of their initial coffee education through on-the-job experience and hands-on practice. Another 20 percent of their training is the result of feedback and mentorship from their peers, their learning coach, and store management, and 10 percent is derived from an online modularized curriculum. (See the sidebar for the specific learning blocks presented in Starbucks barista certification training.)

To be certified as a barista, a new partner must complete the following curriculum:

Learning Block 1: First Impressions and Customer Experience, Starbucks Experience, Coffee Brewing and Tasting, Espresso Bar Basics, and Food Warming

Learning Block 2: Beverage Essentials, Cold Beverages, Coffee Growing and Processing, and Point of Sale

Learning Block 3: Beverage Preparation, Customer Service Essentials, and Coffee Roasting and Packaging

At intervals during the certification training and development process, new partners must pass a knowledge test and demonstrate to their store manager skill competency in tasks such as preparing a cappuccino. While rich knowledge and skills-based education alone do not guarantee that certified baristas will have a passion for the products that they prepare and serve, education and personal growth do increase a barista's awareness of and appreciation for coffee. Ryan, a Starbucks barista from Denver, Colorado, notes, "After I started working at Starbucks, I changed my drink preference to brewed coffee. I learned so much about different blends and regions. I now love Asian coffee; Sumatra is my go-to drink. I never really knew how much taste could change from coffee to coffee."

At Starbucks, leaders also help new hires begin to understand the importance of coffee-growing communities and the economic challenges they face. Early training experiences identify coffee as a socially powerful product (in fact, it is one of the world's most heavily traded agricultural commodities, and it bolsters the economies of many equatorial countries). New Starbucks partners are given insights into the importance of fair trade and price transparency throughout the supply chain of coffee sourcing.

In addition to offering a social context for the substantial social, economic, and political impact of their product, leaders encourage baristas (both new and veteran) to view themselves as artisans of a handcrafted product. In essence, a person can become passionate not only about the coffee itself, but also about the artistry involved in its creation. Howard Schultz notes in *Onward*, "Pouring espresso is an art, one that requires the barista to care about the quality of the beverage. If the barista only goes through the motions, if he or she does not care and produces an inferior espresso that is too weak or too bitter, then Starbucks has lost the essence of what we set out to do 40 years ago: inspire the human spirit. I realize this is a lofty mission for a cup of coffee, but this is what merchants do. We take the ordinary . . . and give it new life, believing that what we create has the potential to touch others' lives because it touched ours."

REFLECTION ON CONNECTION

1. Are you driving product knowledge and certifying service excellence from the onset of employment?
2. What is your team's overall level of product passion? How does it compare to the product passion levels at the best service providers you have encountered?
3. What first impressions do you create for new hires so that they can be intrigued by the products that you provide? What are the nuances or uniquely important aspects of your offerings?

Can you imagine how different our lives would be if most business owners worked to infuse product passion into their entire workforce? What if those owners also believed it was their job to improve or elevate the products that they touch? How would your next visit to your dry cleaner, post office, electronics store, or supermarket be different? Better yet, imagine how your customers might feel if all your people were passionate about your products and felt responsible for elevating them with each touch.

While the opportunity for developing a passion for coffee and the artistry of its preparation is built into the formative learning experiences of Starbucks new hires, the company's leadership understands that this passion is reinforced, sustained, and deepened through corporate rituals, immersive learning opportunities, and core business strategy. But before we look at the Starbucks approach, let's define corporate rituals and explore their relevance to developing a culture of product passion.

CORPORATE RITUALS

For some people, the word *ritual* tends to conjure up images of religious or personal behavior; however, S. Chris Edmonds, a senior consultant with the Ken Blanchard Companies and coauthor of *Leading at a Higher Level*, defines corporate rituals "as events which communicate and reinforce desired performance and values." Chris believes, "Few senior leaders leverage corporate rituals as an intentional strategy to define and reinforce a company's desired culture."

Edmonds provides a structure for looking at rituals and criteria to assess their effectiveness. Specifically, he breaks leadership rituals down into those oriented toward celebration and those directed toward communications. In assessing the effectiveness of either approach to ritual, Chris suggests that intentional efforts should be made to "ensure that all corporate rituals create a common bond, inspire commitment and innovation, and build the 'finely woven cloth' of an effective culture." Let's look at how Starbucks leadership builds a culture of product passion through celebration and communication rituals, and also define ways in which you can do the same.

CELEBRATION RITUALS

When I described the first impressions meeting between a newly hired Starbucks barista and a store manager, you were given a preview of one of the key celebration rituals at Starbucks—the coffee-tasting ritual. When a store manager celebrates the first day with a new hire by preparing a coffee tasting, that manager is producing an event that both communicates the desired behavior of learning the unique flavor profiles of coffee and demonstrates values that support coffee passion.

The coffee-tasting ritual is also a prominent feature at major cultural events for Starbucks. For example at the October 2012 Leadership Conference, Dub Hay, then senior vice president, Global Coffee Authority, who was nearing retirement after 10 years at Starbucks (with whom I have done coffee tastings in Costa Rica), led the assembled store managers and other leaders in a tasting of the newly released Starbucks® Thanksgiving Blend. Addressing the crowd, Dub noted, "I can't tell you all how humbling it is to be on this stage . . . knowing all the work and care and love that went into this coffee that now sits in your hand. This is probably one of the largest coffee tastings I've done in my history at Starbucks. I can't think of a better combination than to be tasting Starbucks Thanksgiving Blend with 10,000 store managers, the 200 Houston partners who delivered their coffee to you, and, as you see ringing the stage, the senior leadership team and managing directors from around the world." Dub then led a massive tasting. Just think about the logistics of having 10,000 Starbucks partners taste a cup of coffee simultaneously. Some might say that such an undertaking is a pointless exercise; however, Starbucks leadership sees it as a ritual that reinforces the essence of the brand.

Starbucks district manager Tisha Kimoto explains how she integrates coffee tasting into her leadership ritual, noting, "With the district manager role, we are not in the office, we are always in the field; I get to meet with the store managers. We start the meetings with coffee tastings. What do we not know about the coffee? What more can we learn? And for us it really is, how can we be passionate about the product that we sell?" Howard Schultz, Dub Hay, leaders and district managers with store managers, store managers with new hires and their teams . . . the coffee-tasting ritual is alive and well at Starbucks.

This ritualization of coffee tasting is further supported by guidelines set for employees throughout the company. For example, new hires are encouraged to complete a "Coffee Passport" within their first 90 days of employment. A Coffee Passport (see next page) serves as a road map and journal to guide partners through tasting all of the coffees that Starbucks offers. A barista from New York notes, "When I was first learning about coffee three years ago at a Starbucks in Connecticut, I tasted Caffè Verona®. The partner who was doing that tasting poured some mocha sauce into a cup. We smelled the mocha and we smelled the Verona, and it was a newfound experience full of joy. I realized there were different depths of flavor to coffee that I never knew existed. I thought coffee was just something to keep you awake when you were tired. So that was the beginning of my love affair with coffee. Part of Starbucks training is completing the Coffee Passport. . . . You have to taste and describe every coffee that we offer. I finished my passport within the first two weeks of my time at Starbucks. In the process, I discovered some of my favorite coffees and my least favorite coffees, and I couldn't stop telling people about the vast array of flavors that existed between coffees. It was a brand-new world. It was exciting, and my

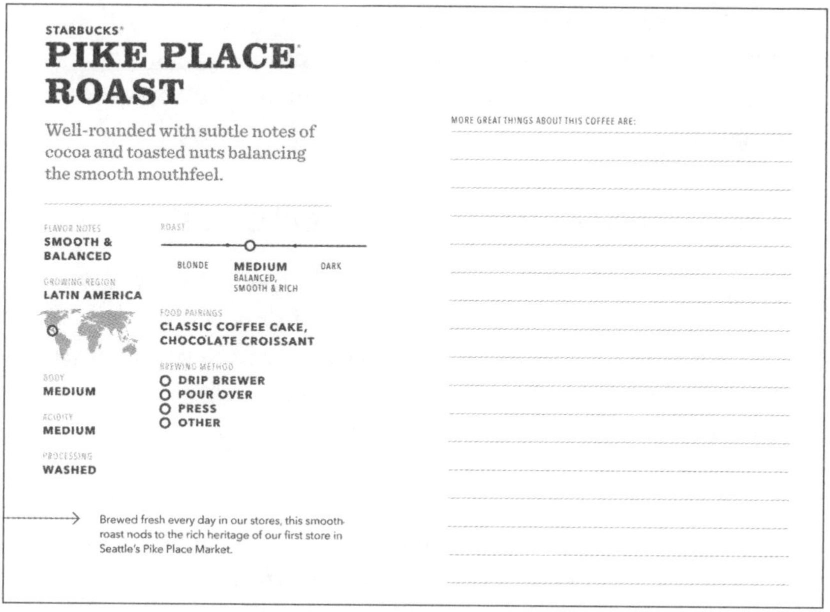

STARBUCKS®

PIKE PLACE® ROAST

Well-rounded with subtle notes of cocoa and toasted nuts balancing the smooth mouthfeel.

FLAVOR NOTES
SMOOTH & BALANCED

GROWING REGION
LATIN AMERICA

BODY
MEDIUM

ACIDITY
MEDIUM

PROCESSING
WASHED

ROAST
BLONDE **MEDIUM** DARK
BALANCED, SMOOTH & RICH

FOOD PAIRINGS
CLASSIC COFFEE CAKE, CHOCOLATE CROISSANT

BREWING METHOD
O DRIP BREWER
O POUR OVER
O PRESS
O OTHER

Brewed fresh every day in our stores, this smooth roast nods to the rich heritage of our first store in Seattle's Pike Place Market.

MORE GREAT THINGS ABOUT THIS COFFEE ARE:

A page from the Starbucks Coffee Passport.

manager seemed to understand my excitement. She nurtured my passion for coffee, and I never stopped."

Similarly, Samantha Yarwood, director of marketing, Switzerland and Austria, shares how she has seen new baristas not only get excited about the coffees they taste but also lead others through tastings: "I met a new barista who had been with the company for only two weeks when she conducted a coffee tasting of her own. I wish I had a picture that I could share of the amazing presentation she arranged. It was incredible. She presented chocolates, cookies, cakes, and fruit that reflected and paired well with the coffees she was tasting with us. She was so engaged and engaging. I later found out that she stayed up the night before to prepare all the food items she had presented. That coffee tasting left me saying, 'Wow.'"

Coffee-tasting rituals and the Coffee Passport tool serve to create a patterned exploration of the richness and complexity of coffee mastery that opens up many Starbucks partners to a genuine fascination with and passion for the product. All the while, these rituals ingrain coffee's centrality in the way things are done throughout the company.

COMMUNICATION RITUALS

Starbucks leaders have also ritualized corporate storytelling. Rather than providing messages that just describe the "what" and "how" of their products, leaders listen for and share stories that help connect partners to coffee farmers and the journey that coffee takes before it is served at Starbucks. While I was talking to Howard Schultz about the rituals of communication at Starbucks, he noted, "One of the strengths of Starbucks is storytelling and being able to infuse an authentic, genuine story about the journey of a coffee—where it comes from or how we do things. . . . Those stories are enriched by the passion and feeling we have about what we do. You cannot fake that. The customer is too smart, and our people are too smart. If our people do not believe in what you might loosely describe as the love story behind the coffee or the truth behind it, it is over before it starts."

While the methods of story delivery at Starbucks are varied (one-on-one, group, or video), the themes of communication regularly highlight the coffee journey, the coffee-farming experience, and the impact of ethical sourcing on the lives of suppliers. Clarice Turner, senior vice president, U.S. Business, shares, "As we educate our partners on our coffee, we talk about how the sale of coffee beverages changes the lives of farmers around the world, and we have a lot of specific examples that we use to demonstrate the importance of fair pricing and transparency." Through storytelling, Starbucks leaders humanize and connect Starbucks partners to the very real impact of farmer support and ethical sourcing efforts like C.A.F.E. (Coffee and Farmer Equity) Practices. C.A.F.E. Practices were created in partnership with Conservation International (a nonprofit environmental organization committed to benefiting humanity through biodiversity and protection of nature) to define guidelines to help grow coffee in a way that sustains farmers and the planet. By deploying measurable objectives, including Starbucks quality standards; transparency of verified payments across the coffee supply chain; third-party-verified measures of safe, humane, and fair working conditions; and environmental leadership, Starbucks is able to work with coffee farmers to increase sustainability.

Kelly Goodejohn, Starbucks director, Ethical Sourcing, exemplifies the effectiveness of leadership storytelling by sharing, "I was in Costa Rica recently visiting small-holder farms who were participating in C.A.F.E. Practices. Given that many of these farmers only work a couple of acres of land, everything they earned is essential for their families to thrive." Kelly notes that, as always, she was greatly affected by the uplifting stories shared by farmers concerning the impact of the premiums Starbucks pays in accord with the farmer's level of engagement with C.A.F.E. Practices. Many talked about how those premiums made the difference in their children getting a quality education and in some cases going on to universities.

Noting that her visit followed a rainy period in the steep hills and mountains of the Tarrazú region, Kelly reported being particularly troubled by a farmer who said that he had been participating in C.A.F.E. Practices in a limited way. Kelly shares, "The farmer pointed to a hill where an enormous landslide had sheared off coffee trees. He then told me he hadn't been paying enough attention to erosion control measures, and as such he had lost a third of his trees in one rainy time of the year. He wasn't going to be able to harvest coffee there for about three to five years, and a third of his income was lost. The look on his face expressed regret and sorrow for the impact of his choices. That touched me deeply. He then asked if Starbucks could help him manage his farm more effectively, and our agronomists are working to give him the technical tools so that in the future, he'll be able to mitigate some of the severe impacts of weather change. It is these experiences that result not only in passion for the coffee but a deep compassion for the people and families who work with us all along the journey."

Stories of coffee farming, the journey of the bean, and ethical sourcing (like the one provided by Kelly) clearly engage Starbucks partners. Katie McMahon, national account executive, Branded Solutions, shares, "One of the images that resonates with me is the image of the coffee farmer. You look at their hands and they are covered in dirt. For me, that's at the core of who we are as a company, and I think about them every day when I work with other partners and customers." Barista Ruth Anderson notes, "Our coffees travel so far before they reach us. I often hear about the first 10 feet of the coffee's journey and about the lives of coffee farmers. I care that our product is ethically sourced and that the people at the beginning and throughout the coffee journey are cared for. As a barista, I need to be at my personal best to deliver that coffee for the last 10 feet of that coffee's journey as I craft drinks for our customers. I see my job not just as a coffee preparer. I see my job as having impact on the world through coffee."

Aristotle once said, "We are what we repeatedly do. Excellence is not an act but a habit." While the celebration and communication rituals in your business will certainly differ from those of Starbucks, isn't it worthwhile to examine the habits, rituals, and messages that you deploy? Are they facilitating emotional connections, a sense of community, and product passion excellence? By effectively building authentic rituals into your business, you will also define unique aspects of your culture and reinforce your business's broader purpose, particularly when the rituals are supported by enriched experiential learning and a congruent business strategy.

REFLECTION ON CONNECTION

1. How have you used celebration rituals to increase the connection between your staff members and your products?
2. What, if any, parallels to the Coffee Passport program at Starbucks do you have? What might you create?
3. Overall, how effectively have you used corporate rituals to intentionally "create a common bond, inspire commitment and innovation, and build the 'finely woven cloth'" of a culture of product passion?

IMMERSIVE EXPERIENCES

It is one thing to have leaders telling stories that will help link staff members to product passion and quite another to place staff members directly in positions where they can garner stories of their own. When it comes to conversations about coffee farming and the impact of ethical sourcing, Starbucks leaders have taken a number of different approaches, including having coffee farmers tour Starbucks stores and a rather unusual program called the Origin Experience. If you would like to get a glimpse of an Origin Experience trip, please visit: http://tinyurl.com/mrrk5wr or direct your QR reader here:

Valerie O'Neil, Starbucks senior vice president, Partner Resources and Brand Leadership, shares the idea behind the Origin Experience trips: "My team and I spearheaded the pilot program where we took 35 to 40 partners from U.S. and Americas to Costa Rica. We took Asia-Pacific partners to Indonesia, and then Europe and Middle Eastern partners to Tanzania. They spent a weeklong immersion seeing how coffee is grown, produced, processed, and then shipped out to our roasting plants. What that helped to do was not only infuse passion for the product, but it also helped our partners understand what happens in the lives of the farmers and processors and all that we do to support those communities as well. It's not only about what we buy and give to the farmers; but it's also about the schools and the support programs in those coffee-farming areas. Participants are also planting seedlings and picking coffee cherries themselves."

As you might imagine, selection for these regularly scheduled Origin Experience opportunities is highly competitive, and most of the participants come from customer-facing store-level functions. Criteria for participation include overall job performance, demonstrated coffee knowledge, and communication skills. Valerie notes, "The participants have to be able to and want to share the stories from the experience. As much as we would love to send 200,000 partners to these regions, it would not be respectful to the communities or practical for us. We are relying on the partners who go to give their own authentic accounts to other partners throughout the organization."

In a culture of ritualized storytelling, enriched and immersive experiences provide unique opportunities for reinforcing important messages. In the case of coffee knowledge, Starbucks has also created an intensive training curriculum that produces impassioned subject-matter experts referred to as Coffee Masters and Coffee Ambassadors. Before we get to these masters and ambassadors, let's look at the motivational importance of creating opportunities for "mastery."

CREATING STATUS FOR PRODUCT EXPERTISE

Considerable research on human motivation suggests that mastery is a key driver of human performance and that extrinsic reward programs can undermine the intrinsic joy of personal growth and development. Daniel Pink, author of the book *Drive: The Surprising Truth About What Motivates Us*, notes, "Rewards can perform a weird sort of behavioral alchemy: They can transform an interesting task into a drudge. They can turn play into work. And by diminishing intrinsic motivation, they send performance, creativity and upstanding behavior toppling like dominoes." With this context in mind, leaders at Starbucks encourage the pursuit of coffee expertise through a mastery- and social recognition–based approach, not through a monetary or reward solution. The first level of this two-tiered coffee knowledge program is aptly referred to as Coffee Master, with a more advanced level being referred to as Coffee Ambassador.

Carrie Dills, a former Starbucks barista, shares her journey to Coffee Master by noting, "The manager who hired me was a Coffee Master, and when he talked about the product, there was just this love and passion, and he infused it into me. I don't even work for Starbucks anymore and should have no incentive to talk about coffee, but I get googly-eyed sharing about the way a bean is harvested, the farmers that harvested it, or how Starbucks takes care of those people." Carrie notes that she has encountered people who are skeptical of the authenticity of her product passion. "People would say, 'You're just spewing company rhetoric,' and I would push back that I feel it, I believe it, and I've gone out of my way to see it for myself and interview farmers." While she was a barista, Carrie reports, she went on a personal vacation in Costa Rica, and "I visited a farm where they harvest Starbucks beans. I told the farmers that I was employed at Starbucks, and they were in awe. I sought out that experience because of involvement with the Coffee Master program and the level of interest it generated in me."

Opportunities for Coffee Master status are not limited to U.S.-based Starbucks operations or exclusively to those who brew and serve coffee in Starbucks stores. Wang Bin Wolf, a Starbucks partner and supervisor at the Jianwai SOHO branch of Starbucks in Beijing, China, shares that he was not motivated by his prior employment in a printing factory and often felt exhausted and drained after his workday. Wolf reports that his prior negative work experience was in stark contrast to the friendliness and knowledgeability of the baristas he personally had encountered at Starbucks, and that because of this, he made a conscious decision that he would work at Starbucks. Upon his employment, he became involved in the Coffee Master program.

As a result of his participation in the Coffee Master training, Wolf appreciates that "coffee-making is a form of art. . . . To someone who had never had coffee before Starbucks, it simply tasted bitter to me. During the process, I had to keep on tasting, and learning from others to gain more experience. Gradually, I discovered the complexity of flavors. . . . Once a stranger, coffee has now become my very good friend. . . . Through my learning and effort, I continued to improve. Eventually I was able to wear the black apron and carry the title of Coffee Master. Personally, I am very proud and happy."

Like many partners who do not serve in a customer-facing coffee preparer role, Jenny Cui, business analysis manager, who works in the Starbucks Support Center in Seattle, Washington, shares her journey to Coffee Master: "I grew up with tea, and coffee was not really my thing. When I joined Starbucks, I was swept into information and experiences about coffee-growing regions, different taste profiles, and how to make beverages. It was a totally different world for me, but I enjoyed it. And now, I'm proud that I am certified as a Coffee Master." Based on her early learning experiences after her arrival at Starbucks, Jenny reports that she decided to sign up and learn more about coffee and how the human connection is forged through coffee: "Through my work to achieve the Coffee Master designation and based on the general culture here, I'm regularly part of groups who taste different blends and talk about coffee. I also attend regular coffee-roasting events to better understand how our coffees are crafted." When asked why, as a finance professional, she would invest so much time in the pursuit of coffee knowledge, Jenny stated, "It's just a great feeling to learn about the product that drives our business and to develop a deeper appreciation for the complex characteristics of coffee and the way it comes to market."

While the Coffee Master designation represents a sufficient growth challenge for many Starbucks partners, the leaders at Starbucks have created an additional level of coffee expertise referred to as a Coffee Ambassador. Andrea Bader, Coffee Ambassador for Starbucks in Switzerland, wears a special brown apron and offers insights on how she achieved her title: "Ten Coffee Masters and our store managers participated in an event judged by the district leadership team for our region in Switzerland. Each of the Coffee Masters had to present two Starbucks coffees and craft perfect food pairings. After being selected to represent my district, I joined the other district representatives in the Coffee Ambassador challenge for Switzerland. This time all store managers from Switzerland and the entire leadership team evaluated our coffee presentations and our food pairings. I am delighted to have been chosen as the Swiss Coffee Ambassador." When asked if she was being financially rewarded (extrinsically motivated) for achieving this level of expertise, Andrea responded, "I did this to have a greater impact on coffee knowledge in my company. In fact, recently I had this crazy idea to do coffee tastings over Skype and Facebook. Literally, 1,000 people from around the world joined me in the experience. People were asked to prepare a specific blend of coffee, and we used the Skype call to discuss the flavor experiences of the participants."

Leaders at Starbucks have crafted ways to immerse staff members in enriched learning experiences that create opportunities for product passion. Moreover, they have found ways to spark mastery of product knowledge by relying on an intrinsic sense of accomplishment that comes from advanced learning and the ability to teach others. What immersive opportunities and volunteer training recognition resources should you consider to enhance product passion among your people?

STRATEGY CONSISTENT WITH PRODUCT PASSION

Jim Collins, author of the bestselling business book *Good to Great: Why Some Companies Make the Leap and Others Don't*, asserts that visionary companies are led by individuals who are constantly assessing their company's strategy and ensuring that it is in "alignment to preserve an organization's core values, to reinforce its purpose, and to stimulate continued progress towards its aspirations. When you have superb alignment, a visitor could drop into your organization from another planet and infer the vision without having to read it on paper."

For all their effort to value coffee quality, passion, and knowledge, there was a time in Starbucks history when the strategic decisions of the leaders failed to support product passion. In fact, Starbucks leaders became so focused on driving positive sales numbers (reflected in year-over-year same-store comparables, or "comps") that coffee excellence was compromised. Howard Schultz readily acknowledges that comps "were a dangerous enemy in the battle to transform the company. We'd had almost 200 straight months of positive comps, unheard-of momentum in retail. And as we grew at a faster and faster clip during 2006 and 2007, maintaining that positive comp growth history drove poor business decisions that veered us away from our core." Howard goes on demonstrate what he calls the "comp effect" by describing a store visit where he encountered a large pile of stuffed animals for sale: "'What is this?' I asked the manager in frustration, pointing to a pile of wide-eyed cuddly toys that had absolutely nothing to do with coffee." In response, the manager pointed out that the stuffed animals were good for his store's comps, building incremental sales and high profit margins. This led Howard to conclude that the comp effect had produced a "mentality that had become pervasive. And dangerous."

In his book *Onward*, Howard detailed a series of strategic moves that were made at the senior leadership level in an effort to retain the "soul" of Starbucks. A number of these efforts clearly demonstrated the leadership's passion for coffee and a declaration that Starbucks was "reclaiming its coffee authority." Some of these coffee-specific strategies included closing all U.S. Starbucks stores for an afternoon to retrain baristas on how to make the perfect espresso shot and espresso-based beverages, the creation and launch of the Pike Place® Roast (a transformative balanced coffee roast that brought the aroma of grinding fresh beans back into Starbucks stores), and the acquisition and thoughtful deployment of the Clover® brewing system (an advanced brewing method that creates a personalized high-quality coffee by drawing water down through finely ground coffee, thus retaining the coffee's most flavorful oils).

Since the company's turnaround, leaders have maintained their alignment with the centrality of coffee. This is evidenced by coffee product innovations such as Starbucks® Blonde Roast. For years, Starbucks leaders had been aware that a large number of coffee consumers (approximately 40 percent) rejected dark roast coffee or preferred lighter roasts. Evaluations of coffee-roasting taste profiles consistently had shown that lighter roasts were grassy with a sour green flavor, resulting in significantly lower quality ratings than those for the darker roasts of Starbucks.

Brad Anderson, one of the key coffee roasters responsible for Blonde, shares how the lighter roast emerged after 80 attempts.

"We wanted a mild sweetness and the taste of cereal to be flavor notes for Blonde. We didn't know how to get there with our existing roast styles. So we started from scratch and tweaked things over and over again. For me, it was a technical and personal challenge, and we spent a lot of time developing that coffee. Every time the product came back to us, we asked how we could make it better. I am extremely proud of our final product and the teams of people who stayed so dedicated to its creation."

Partners at the store level appreciate it when product-based strategies and values align. More important, partners experience the positive impact of that alignment on the lives of their customers. Barista Elisha shares, "I like dark coffee, but I think that making Blonde available to customers is wonderful, because many aren't dark drinkers. Blonde is in keeping with our commitment to product excellence, and it hits a market of new customers. Bringing in those new customers allows us to talk

REFLECTION ON CONNECTION

1. How do you help your staff fully experience your products or services? What are your parallels to a Starbucks Origin Experience?
2. Are you incorporating mastery and social recognition into your training programs? If so, how?
3. How aligned are your strategies and your stated values concerning product excellence? In the words of author Jim Collins, if "a visitor could drop into your organization from another planet," would that visitor be able to know your vision for product excellence "without having to read it on paper"?

to them about coffee and lets them in on an experience others have enjoyed for years." When you combine innovative products that add new customer segments with a loyal customer base, you have a recipe for business success and sustainability.

CONNECTING CUSTOMERS TO PASSION

With Starbucks leadership investing a great amount of energy in creating an environment where partners are passionate about coffee, it is important to determine the return on that investment. Do product-impassioned Starbucks partners actually incite product passion on the part of customers?

In this chapter, you've seen how fueling a customer's coffee passion can contribute to an interest in becoming a Starbucks partner. While most customers won't be moved to the point of seeking employment with Starbucks, many will strengthen their relationship with Starbucks and expand the frequency, depth, and breadth of their purchases. For example, barista Paul Quinn shares how a customer's purchase patterns changed as he shared his coffee passion with her: "I am in the process of becoming a Coffee Master, and I have found that the process has reinvigorated my whole-bean passion, and has in turn enhanced my ability to sell. Everyone has regulars, and with the knowledge gained . . . from my Coffee Master Journal, I've turned one of my Friday night regulars into somewhat of a coffee buddy." Paul reports that he and this regular had talked about a variety of Starbucks roasts and appropriate food pairings. As a result, Paul prepared a small coffee press of Guatemala Casi Cielo® and sampled it with a slice of lemon loaf. Paul adds that the customer's "face lit up as she began to understand exactly what I meant as I explained how the citrus enhances the taste of the coffee. . . . Now, I see her almost every Friday between 10:30 and 11 p.m., and we have a chat about what's brewing . . . or snacks and pastries that go well with certain coffees." For example, Paul notes that he recommended Gold Coast Blend® with a Snickers bar. As a result of their relationship, Paul notes, "She almost always picks up a pound of coffee. . . . There is a genuine connection with the customer, which is fantastic, and the Coffee Master program is only helping me become more knowledgeable and a better barista."

Increased visit frequency, wider product penetration, greater customer engagement, consistent product sell-through, and employee pride and professional development are enviable by-products of igniting the passion of your team members. Will you give your customers a reason to be passionate about your products? What specifically will you do to champion product passion in your business? We know, thanks to mounting research evidence, that "knowledgeable employees" is one of the top items on the wish list for customers today. Imagine what knowledgeable and passionate employees can do, not only for your customers, but for the morale and enthusiasm associated with your business. Starbucks isn't imagining!

CONNECTING POINTS

- When frontline staff members are passionate about your products, they build interest and excitement on the part of your customers.
- Passionate staff members not only sell products, but have a magnetically positive impact when it comes to turning customers into future employees and brand fans.
- Research suggests that effective staff growth and development often follows a 70/20/10 approach, with 70 percent of education coming from on-the-job experience and hands-on practice, 20 percent from

mentoring and coaching, and 10 percent from a formal curriculum.

- Corporate rituals are powerful ways to create a common bond, inspire commitment and innovation, and build an integrated and effective culture.
- Authentic corporate rituals also define unique aspects of your culture and reinforce your business's broader purpose, particularly when those rituals are supported by enriched experiential learning and a congruent business strategy.
- Rather than providing messages that solely describe the "what" and "how" of your products, listen for and share stories that will help connect your people to the nuances of your products and/or special aspects of the customer journey.
- As Aristotle said, "We are what we repeatedly do. Excellence is not an act but a habit."
- Rewards can transform an interesting task into drudgery and diminish intrinsic motivation. Rather than relying on rewards, consider the power of autonomy, mastery, and purpose.
- Evaluate every strategy to ensure that it aligns with your core values, reinforces your purpose, and stimulates continued progress toward your aspirations.
- When you combine innovative products that add new customer segments with a loyal customer base, you have a recipe for business success and sustainability.

CHAPTER 3

From Replicable and Consistent to Magical and Unique

Men are rich only as they give. He who gives great service gets great rewards.

ELBERT HUBBARD

While passion for coffee has been and continues to be essential to Starbucks, leaders like Howard Schultz emphasize that human experiences are at the heart of the brand. For example, Howard notes, "Starbucks is at its best when we are creating enduring relationships and personal connections." Building on that theme in 2008, while strategizing how to mount a resurgence for Starbucks, Howard communicated to partners that the "Transformation Agenda includes . . . re-igniting our emotional attachment with our customers by restoring the connection our customers have with you, our coffee, our brand, and our stores. Unlike many other places that sell coffee, Starbucks built the equity of our brand through the Starbucks Experience. It comes to life every day in the relationship our people have with our customers. By focusing again on the Starbucks Experience, we will create a renewed level of meaningful differentiation and separation in the market between us and others who are attempting to sell coffee." People can copy your products and your services, but seldom can another business effectively or consistently execute a differentiated experiential offering—this is equally as true for a visit to an Apple Store as it is for a visit to Starbucks.

So, how does a company like Starbucks take a product that can easily be commoditized and offer it in a way that produces differentiation anchored to enduring relationships and personal connections? This chapter unpacks multifaceted aspects of Starbucks customer experience excellence, including how Starbucks leaders:

- Define and communicate the desired and unique Starbucks Experience.
- Select individuals with the requisite talent to deliver that experience consistently.
- Train partners on the key pillars necessary to engage customers routinely.

More important, this chapter allows you to see the strategic and tactical customer experience–based efforts deployed by Starbucks, so that you can consider how those approaches fit with the challenges and opportunities that you face.

WHAT EXPERIENCE DO YOU WANT CUSTOMERS TO HAVE?

American personal development pioneer Earl Nightingale observed, "Success is the progressive realization of a worthy goal or ideal." As was the case with product passion, the worthy customer experience ideals at Starbucks are expressed in the company's mission statement (to inspire and nurture the human spirit—one person, one cup and one neighborhood at a time) and are supported by the principles of how this mission is lived every day, including:

Our Customers
When we are fully engaged, we connect with, laugh with, and uplift the lives of our customers—even if just for a few moments. Sure, it starts with the promise of a perfectly made beverage, but our work goes far beyond that. It's really about human connection.

Our Stores
When our customers feel this sense of belonging, our stores become a haven, a break from the worries outside, a place where you can meet with friends. It's about enjoyment at the speed of life—sometimes slow and savored, sometimes faster. Always full of humanity.

That's brief and clear—leaders like those at Starbucks put customers, products, and experiences at the purposeful center of their businesses.

LOOKING FOR EXPERIENCE CREATORS

By using words like *inspire*, *nurture*, and *uplift*, Starbucks leadership defines the Starbucks Experience as being much more than the accurate and efficient service of high-quality beverages. Partners should aspire to deliver moments, products, and environments that elevate and transform those who are served. Human connection is the magic at the core of the Starbucks brand. In order to make the magic happen, Starbucks looks for prospective partners who are authentically and consistently interested in others. That interest can cut through the chaos and unpredictability in the lives of customers, thus producing reliable and positive experiences at your business. Consumer data, consistently reflected in studies such as the American Express Global Customer Service Barometer, validate the perspective that customer service is chaotic, unpredictable, and in decline. But how does an organization select individuals who have an interest in "authentically and consistently" serving others?

Charles Douglas III, a paralegal at Starbucks, believes that the key element in selection is observing and interviewing for enthusiasm and service talent. In fact, he believes he was selected for his first job at Starbucks (as a barista) based largely on those factors. According to Charles, "I was looking for a place that closely aligned with my personal values and a place I would be proud to say that I worked." Charles reviewed the company's guiding principles and felt they were credibly reflected in the experiences he had as a customer. Charles then reports that he put on a dress shirt and green tie and "with a smile on my face, ran up to a store manager as she was opening her store at 4 in the morning. I noticed that she was scared, but I did my best to say, 'I am here because I really want this job, and I bet you I want it more than anybody else.'" Charles goes on to note, "Starbucks store managers are really good at hiring based on enthusiasm, your sense of purpose for serving others, and a willingness to learn. We really look for those people who are willing to live by what the company holds most important, and we will train them from there." Résumés, past work history, and even favorable recommendations notwithstanding, there is something to be said for observing and interacting with prospects to determine whether they are eager, teachable, and authentically interested in others.

GUIDING EXPERIENCE DELIVERY

Many businesses orient new hires by teaching them the tasks to be performed on the job but fail to educate them on service excellence skills and/or the experience that they want those employees to consistently deliver. At Starbucks, however, initial training dives quickly into courses like "Customer Service Basics" and the "Starbucks Experience."

During these training sessions, new hires are provided guidance on what "customer experience" means at Starbucks, and they are placed in positions where they can observe the service experience from the customer's perspective. For example, newly hired baristas are exposed to a process tool called the "Store Walk Thru," where they move through the café environment observing and recording salient aspects that a customer is likely to encounter as she journeys from her arrival through her departure. Starbucks leadership sets the expectation that after initial training, the new hire will be a part of these customer-perspective walks, which occur once per shift at each store. Like all tools of this nature, store managers must constantly reinforce the importance and value of taking the customer's perspective and ensure that this process does not become a perfunctory and routine task.

In addition to this customer empathy tool (Store Walk Thru), initial customer service and desired experience training help new hires reflect on their personal history of consumer experiences (inside or outside of Starbucks) to identify what makes an experience memorable, uplifting, inspiring, or elevated for them. The training hones in on the concept of "branded" experiences and how customers need to be assured that all encounters that they have with a brand will deliver consistent products, processes, and engaging experience elements. Execution on the branded/consistency dimension is reflected in comments from customers like Jenny, who notes, "When I travel, I try to spot a Starbucks. It feels like you are connecting with a little bit of home wherever you are in the world. . . . It carries a set of expectations for products, feelings, and the way you are treated." Even if a business operates from a single location, the issue is the same: Will I have a comparable experience the next time I visit? Will the expectations set today be matched or exceeded tomorrow? Or will I have a random, unreliable collection of encounters that erode the concept of the brand?

To deliver consistent experiences at Starbucks, the leadership offers a defined service vision that describes what needs to be achieved during service experiences. Additionally, it provides four customer service behaviors that help partners understand how the customer service vision is to be accomplished. The Starbucks customer vision statement reads: "We create inspired moments in each customer's day." To accomplish this objective, partners are encouraged to focus on the following customer service behaviors:

- Anticipate
- Connect
- Personalize
- Own

In essence, the leadership offers partners the desired service experience outcome ("inspired moments") and the key actions needed to deliver it. For example, if a barista reads the customer's need state, the barista can anticipate, connect, personalize, and own that customer's experience to create an inspired moment for him. To be more specific, if a customer looks rushed, the barista can anticipate and take responsibility for delivering an accurate and expedited beverage with a brief but personal moment of connection (something as simple as a genuine smile). By contrast, if a customer is a regular who enjoys conversation, the partner can make a connection by remembering his drink or calling him by name and taking responsibility for personalizing the drink or conversation in a way that produces meaningful, if not inspired, moments in his day.

Customers often share the joy they experience when baristas execute the Starbucks service vision. Alli Higgins, a 10-year Starbucks customer, notes, "Baristas remember my drink and my name. It's amazing, since it usually takes only one or two times and they already know my name. That stands out in a world where you don't see much of that care or thoughtfulness. Baristas also remember when I take a trip and ask me about it. Because of the way I am treated at Starbucks, I'll occasionally bake cookies for them. Now they'll jokingly say, 'Hey, Alli, where's our cookies?' That's the kind of thing I want to do because I consider them part of my family." By providing the desired destination and ways to arrive there, you help your teams develop exceptionally strong bonds with customers (in Alli's words, "I consider them part of my family") that powerfully differentiate your company from the competition.

REFLECTION ON CONNECTION

1. If asked, what percentage of your employees could articulate your customer experience vision or the way you want customers to feel as a result of the experiences they have with your brand? What would you hope to hear?
2. Do you provide tools like the "Store Walk Thru" to help your staff empathize with customers and adopt their perspective?
3. Have you outlined key behaviors such as anticipate, connect, personalize, and own which will help your team members understand how to deliver your desired experience?

CREATING THE ENVIRONMENT—KEEPING IT CLEAN AND LEAN

So you sell excellent products, you've ignited product passion throughout your organization, and your staff authentically and consistently delivers your branded experience. You have mastered the customer experience challenge, right? Not exactly. To be on the same trajectory as world-class service providers like those I write about (Starbucks, Zappos, or The Ritz-Carlton), you need to possess at least three additional competencies: (1) the ability to maximize customer engagement through environmental design, (2) integration of key sensory factors, and (3) a capacity to listen and adapt your offerings to meet the changing wants, needs, and desires of your customers.

In the late 1990s, business theorists and economists like B. Joseph Pine and James H. Gilmore started to suggest that we were entering an age in which "memorable experiences" served as key drivers for economic growth. Rather than simply focusing on the benefits and attributes of products or the financial advantages of efficient service delivery, these pioneers initiated discussion about the benefits accrued from scripting sensory-rich experiences upon the "stage" of a business. Borrowing themes from the world of live theater, they offered guidance on how to remove negative and align positive cues in order to build experiences that not only engage customers but "transform" them. While theatrical metaphors for customer experience design can be problematic when they refer to "staging" and "scripting" (which imply inauthenticity or robotic transactions), these references allude to the importance of sensory elements and to the attention that is needed to build the right environment or platform on which service experiences are cast.

In a variation of Shakespeare's immortal line delivered by Jacques in *As You Like It*—"All the world's a stage. And all the men and women merely players"—all business settings are a stage from which all experiences emerge. At Starbucks, the design of the stage (the store environment) and the sensory elements placed on that stage are carefully considered to heighten the customer experience.

Starbucks leaders understand that the design of extraordinary experiences involves a willingness to see the environment from the customers' perspective and to attend to the need states of core customer segments. While many leaders look for ways to improve experiences by adding elements to the environment, the best outcomes often come from the removal of negative cues that detract from a memorable experience. Howard Schultz, for example, removed breakfast food items from Starbucks stores until he could be assured that any negative smells of food preparation (charred bread or burnt cheese) did not intrude upon a key sensory element in the coffee shop—the smell of coffee. This battle involved the leadership's willingness to forgo revenue from breakfast food sales until preparation technologies could be developed to abate unwanted food aromas. Similarly, decisions by Starbucks leadership to reduce non-coffee-related merchandise (like the stuffed animals referred to in the previous chapter), even if that merchandise contributed to positive margins, reflect a commitment to the elimination of cues that compromise an ideal experience. In the end, great customer experiences depend on both the addition and the removal of emotional stimuli and environmental design elements.

Lest you think that "stage" design considerations relate only to brick-and-mortar storefronts, every contact point between your customer and your business serves as an opportunity to engage customers through thoughtful presentation. For example, Mike Peck, creative director, Packaging, Starbucks Global Creative Studio, who led the team responsible for the redesign of the Starbucks iconic logo, saw opportunities to enhance the customer experience and modernize the brand through the newly updated mark.

The original 1971 Starbucks logo had the words "Starbucks Coffee and Tea" encircling the siren (the mythical character at the center of the logo that is often confused with a mermaid). The revised logos of 1987 and 1992 dropped the word *tea*, but still had the siren bound by the words *Starbucks* and *Coffee*.

Starbucks logo introduced in 1992.

According to Mike, "Although not a core reason for the update to the icon, the words on the logo actually created confusion in the customer experience. For example, we had Starbucks ice cream flavors like vanilla, chocolate, and strawberry, none of which have coffee in them." With the existing logo, people who glanced at those particular ice cream containers might assume coffee was an ingredient. Mike shares, "Putting a big stamp on the container that says 'coffee free' is a rather inelegant solution. You want your design to be as clean and pure as possible. Consumers, when they looked at it, just saw coffee and strawberries, not an optimal taste combination. We have other beverages domestically and internationally that are not coffee-based, yet they would have the word *coffee* affixed to them by virtue of the logo. Ultimately our redesign opened up the siren, let her be the hero, broke down some barriers, and even streamlined the customer experience." Looking across all your contact points with your company, from its logo to its product return policies, where can you clean up your clutter and confusion?

Starbucks logo introduced in 2011.

Since eliminating clutter and increasing clarity improve customer experiences, Starbucks has entered a "Lean" transformation process, focusing on a shift from traditional efforts toward enhancing value to an approach based on a discipline modified from pure manufacturing settings to minimize waste and increase customer value.

During this transformation period, Starbucks leaders have had individuals at all levels of the organization comprehensively look at processes to identify issues and streamline their efficiency. Troy Alstead, chief financial officer and chief administrative officer, states, "As good as we were about spontaneity at forging human connections, we weren't as good at removing waste and creating processes that maximized efficiency and customer value while making it easier for partners to serve our customers. Over the recent past we have made great strides in these areas of discipline. So the idea now is to remove the things that really aren't critical to customer value. We shouldn't be putting our partners in positions of having to be creative with processes. Let's leverage their best practices that maximize efficiency for the partner and for the customer. Our partners should be encouraged to bring every bit of their creativity to how they interact with our customers, but quality and execution ultimately should be designed and measured by the benefit it brings to partners, customers, and our business." Inherent in Starbucks approach to reduce inefficiencies is the understanding that to be truly effective, those reductions should produce routines that free up people or resources to make stronger interpersonal connections.

Unlike many other businesses that deploy Lean strategies, Starbucks takes a frontline empowerment approach to achieve its objectives. John Shook, a former executive at Toyota (the company from which much of Lean manufacturing practice emerged) and a past advisor to Starbucks, compares the strategy taken to increase efficiency at Starbucks with the methodologies used by McDonald's: "McDonald's very business model seeks a highly cookie-cutter approach. Therefore, McDonald's may be successful in implementing traditional Industrial Engineering (Taylorism and all that—not lean) in a very traditional, top-down, programmatic way."

By contrast, John suggests, "Starbucks decided long ago—and reconfirms this every day—that a cookie-cutter store approach is not the pathway to success for their product, which is a higher-end, higher-priced coffee that emphasizes the customer's experience. . . . Each Starbucks store is different. The footprint is different, the customer experience is different. I believe Starbucks wants the customer experience from store to store to be consistent but unique. McDonald's wants the customer experience to be exactly the same, totally common from store to store."

Given that the drink and syrup combinations at Starbucks allow for more than 80,000 different beverages to be ordered by any given customer, John suggests that at Starbucks, "The goal is to make as many things as possible routine so that the barista can spend just a few more seconds talking with the customer. . . . No workarounds due to the line backing up, no shortcuts to get caught up—handling each unique order as it should be handled, in stride, without burden, and to the customer's satisfaction." If you are looking to create consistent but unique experiences, Starbucks approach to Lean serves as a template. Develop expertise in Lean-type strategies and engage a dialogue with and informative observation of those who perform important operational tasks. Those conversations and observations will readily enable you to create effective routines and efficiencies. Ultimately, this effort should result in more time for your people to create personally engaging experiences.

ADDING, ERRING, AND PERSISTING

When it comes to the customer experience, quite often enhancements take the form of trial-and-error adjustments in an attempt to hit upon the right ingredients in the right quantities necessary to deliver an optimal customer experience. Frequently, key elements are sensory in nature, such as music. Author and journalist Nick Chiles notes, "For companies looking to make an emotional connection with consumers, music continues to be one of the most reliable devices in the marketer's toolbelt. . . . Take the case of Starbucks, which endeavored to turn its coffee shops into a fully experiential adult playground that tickled and stroked every one of the customers' senses while they were in the café, making them want to stick around all day. A big part of that was music—interesting, off-beat, quirky musical finds that thrilled customers with a feeling that they had made a new discovery."

Because customers became so connected with the music that Starbucks played in the stores and the discovery moments associated with that music, Starbucks began selling compilation and compact discs of featured artists.

What role do sensory elements play for your business? What do your customers hear at key touch points in their journey with you? Are there opportunities to incorporate sensory elements (auditory, olfactory, visual, or tactile) that will authentically enhance the customer's experience?

KEEPING IT CORE AND EVOLVING

As we've explored previously, extraordinary customer experiences rely on processes of simplification and a willingness to experiment with sensory enrichment. The path to excellence also requires an ability to merge design elements in a brand-congruent fashion. Arthur Rubinfeld, chief creative officer for Starbucks and president, Global Innovation and Evolution Fresh Retail, notes, "As an architect, I believe that everyone can have an impression and an opinion on how to create a coffeehouse experience. The key, however, is to support the brand's position seamlessly in the physical design. The most difficult part of retail store design is connecting the gestalt of the company, the mission of the company, the culture of the company to the physical solution. I've often said that in judging a store design, if you were to remove the logo discs and the signs from the fascia of the storefront tonight, would people shopping in that retail space tomorrow know that it was a Starbucks store?"

Throughout the 1990s Starbucks certainly seemed to be mixing the right ingredients to deliver coffeehouse experiences that contributed to the brand's meteoric growth. Because they serve the ever-changing needs of people, physical spaces can't remain static. In addition to sharing the importance of environmental factors in store design (which will be addressed extensively in Chapter 11), Arthur suggests that much has changed in creating Starbucks environments. "Our concepts in the 1990s were rooted in a thematic design, with a leading-edge color palette and extensive iconography. For example, we used a wonderful group of icons and swirls that gave us opportunities to present the siren and other nautical graphic design elements in fixture designs."

By contrast, today Arthur indicates that his design teams work to provide flexible design approaches that allow individual in-house designers to use local artists and materials to make them more locally relevant in their look and feel. He also suggests that customers are looking for authenticity, seating choices, and places where they can connect with their community. According to Arthur, "We promote interaction and community gathering by providing unique and specific elements. The community table is one of them. The community table also allows for group meetings and participatory conversations about whatever is on someone's mind. In addition, we're trying to provide as many alternative-seating areas because of the varied need states of our customers who come in the morning, at noon, and in the evening. Maybe they will sit on a comfortable chair, in a nice settee, or at a community table. We are also incorporating 42-inch-high tables which complement the 30- and 36-inch tables. If you are coming in to work on a laptop, a 42-inch-high table is ergonomically better for you, as you can stand. It's also an alternative kind of perch for people to experience the 'life' of the store that goes on versus sitting in a settee in the front or back section of a store."

Starbucks leadership is comfortable experimenting with design elements that the leaders believe will address the evolving need states of the company's customers. They consider emerging trends and observed customer behavior as they refine the stage on which their experiences are provided.

REFLECTION ON CONNECTION

1. Take a moment to put yourself in the place of your key customer group. As you walk through their experience, what elements of clutter or confusion stand out to you? What can be done to clean up these experience detractors? Repeat the exercise with other important customer groups.
2. If you were to do a "sensory audit" of your business, what would be your strengths, weaknesses, and opportunities? What sights, sounds, smells, and tactile elements do your customers experience at key contacts with your brand?
3. Have you used or are you using disciplined processes like Lean (or Six Sigma) to increase efficiencies, improve your customer experience, or even determine the root cause of service breakdowns? If so, how has the customer experience improved? If you aren't taking a disciplined approach, what would cause you to explore such processes?

Whether it is connecting the design of your physical space to your company's mission, vision, and values; streamlining efficiencies to improve the customer experience; or adding sensory elements, successful customer experience enhancements have one unifying component: the need to execute the details. As Arthur puts it, "One of my mantras is, 'The difference between mediocrity and excellence is attention to detail.' The attention to detail that we put into every aspect of our business is geared toward staying on the leading edge of design and providing the most powerful, unique experience possible in our stores."

Executing details to achieve leading-edge customer experiences works for Starbucks. How are you doing on perfecting the details of your desired customer experiences?

CO-CREATE THE EXPERIENCE WITH YOUR CUSTOMER

To provide the "leading-edge" experience that Arthur referred to, Starbucks leaders do more than observe, try, evaluate, and refine their offerings. Starbucks engages with customers to help the leaders prioritize experience improvement targets. In 2008, Starbucks was at the forefront of the online "co-creation with customers" movement. Cecile Hudon, online community manager at Starbucks, explains, "When we first launched the My Starbucks Idea website in March 2008, we felt we were losing some of the connection we had with our customers. So Howard Schultz spearheaded our effort to let customers know that we were listening. We did that by creating one of the earliest and most successful online idea sites at MyStarbucksIdea.com."

Members of My Starbucks Idea can share, vote on, and discuss product, experience, and involvement ideas. As ideas are shared, site-goers vote on those ideas and also interact with Starbucks partners who can evaluate them and affect change. According to Cecile, "The secret to the success of the site is our customers

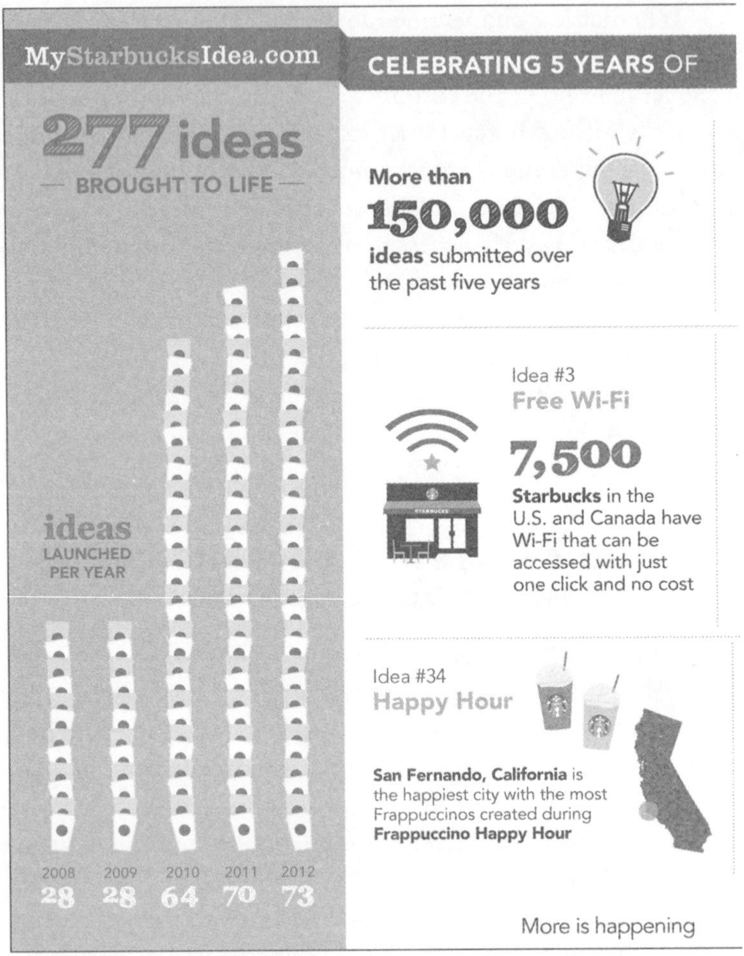

Infographic prepared by Starbucks for the five-year anniversary of My Starbucks Idea.

get to talk to subject-matter experts who function as moderators. So as customers offer food items or suggest gluten-free products, for example, a partner from the Starbucks food team looks through those suggestions. If we had tried to support this site with a single person from, say, the marketing department, they may not recognize a good and relevant idea, because they

are not as close to the work being done in each department and the process would be slower to move ideas forward. Today we have about 40 moderators that are on the site from all over the company listening to the ideas that are relevant to their work. Customers interacting with Starbucks partners in areas that they care about helps the customer feel a part of the company. Their opinion matters."

As items gain popularity through the votes of members in the community, moderators engage in dialogue about those ideas. Cecile notes, "We encourage the moderators to comment and look for responses to the most popular ideas each week, and also look for diamond in the rough ideas—innovative ideas that have low point scores because they may be too new of a concept for people to recognize as a good idea."

Beyond commenting on ideas, moderators move the best options through a series of possible categories: "under review," "reviewed," "coming soon," and "launched." As ideas go under review, functional teams look at whether an idea is innovative, whether it is a differentiator for Starbucks, how quickly the idea can go to market, how much impact it will have on the customer experience, and whether it is a good business driver. Examples of ideas launched from My Starbucks Idea were identified in the infographic on the preceding pages.

More than 150,000 ideas have been submitted on the site, and 265 ideas launched, as of this writing. My Starbucks Idea has helped shape the Starbucks loyalty program, inspired the Starbucks Card eGift program, encouraged the company to sell reusable cup sleeves, and prioritized its recycling efforts. Years after the launch, the community is vital and active, with some users visiting more than 200 times a month. As customers continue to share their ideas with Starbucks partners, leadership continues to listen and respond. Partners participate on the consumer site, and a separate site has been created for them to offer ideas that affect their work lives and the experience of their store's customers.

While Starbucks has developed a variety of other tools for engaging customer input, My Starbucks Idea demonstrates how customers and partners can be engaged in an advisory counsel function to suggest, prioritize, and invest in the evolution of experience offerings. How effectively are you mobilizing your engaged customers to help them help you address their wants and needs?

PERMISSION TO BUILD ON AN EXPERIENCE PLATFORM

If you deliver high-quality products in experiential environments, served up by knowledgeable and passionate staff members, customers not only will support your growth through that product line but are also likely to explore other offerings you innovate in the context of those core competencies. For Starbucks leadership, this has meant a growth plan that includes café environments serving other high-quality beverages—enter the Evolution Fresh™ and Tazo® tea stores.

In late 2011, Starbucks announced that it had acquired Evolution Fresh, Inc., "as part of its commitment to evolve and enhance the Customer Experience with innovative and wholesome products." The move signaled that Starbucks would takes its beverage expertise into the $3.4 billion superpremium cold-pressed juice market and broadly into the $50 billion health and wellness sector.

Upon announcing the acquisition, Howard Schultz noted, "Our intent is to build a national health and wellness brand leveraging our scale, resources and premium product expertise. Bringing Evolution Fresh into the Starbucks family marks an important step forward in this pursuit." Prior to the acquisition, Evolution Fresh sold premium juice products through health supermarkets such as Whole Foods. Evolution Fresh, which was created by the founder of Naked Juice, uses patented technology to pasteurize most of its juices without exposing them to nutrient-depleting heat.

By acquiring Evolution Fresh's existing bottled juice products, Starbucks leadership expanded its presence in the consumer products goods space (which will be discussed in detail in Chapter 9, "Personal Relationships Translate: Sharing the Love from People to Products") and also created a new experiential platform, Evolution Fresh retail stores. These stores focus on the same principles of customer experience crafted in a traditional Starbucks café environment, but adapt that experience in keeping with the health and wellness products that they sell.

Starbucks rolled out its first Evolution Fresh stores in the Seattle area. The centerpiece of these stores is the "tap wall," which dispenses seasonal cold handcrafted juices like Field of Greens (a low-calorie blend of ginger, greens, organic apple, and cucumber) and natural smoothies. The stores also offer globally inspired, personalized food experiences with hot and cold selections, including breakfast items, lunch and dinner wraps, soups, sandwiches, and bowls (such as an under-300-calorie offering made up principally of quinoa, organic kale, and butternut squash). Of course, Evolution Fresh stores also sell Starbucks coffee and Tazo teas.

Kevin Petrisko, director of business operations, Evolution Fresh, describes the experience he wants customers to have in Evolution Fresh stores by noting, "Our vision is, a customer walks out and says, 'Wow, that was a fantastic experience. I learned something new, I had an amazing human connection with the juice partner who guided me through this experience, ultimately the food or the drink taste like the fruit and vegetable it came from, and I have to return. I have to tell my friends how high the quality is of the food I'm eating and the beverage I'm drinking. I've learned something, and I understand how this is going to help me think differently about what I put into my body.'"

Other than the mention of Starbucks coffee on the menu board, there is no signage linking Evolution Fresh to Starbucks, yet online customer reviews frequently make the connection. This is exemplified by one review that reads, "Evolution Fresh is Starbucks newest addition to health food. Although spendy, it's totally worth the experience. The partners behind the counter are knowledgeable and happy." While Evolution Fresh is its own independent-branded store experience, the human connection anchors the retail stores to the essence of Starbucks.

Unlike Evolution Fresh, which represents a fairly recent foray into an adjacent beverage category, the Tazo tea stores are a newly evolved retail concept that links back to the origins of Starbucks. When it was founded in 1971, Starbucks was known as the Starbucks Coffee and Tea Company. As the company grew, the leaders positioned Starbucks with coffee at its core, but in 1999 they purchased a premium tea brand. A *New York Times* article from 1999 described that acquisition by noting, "Tazo, the Oregon company that once aspired to be the Starbucks of teas, has been bought out by the Starbucks Corporation. . . . The Seattle-based Starbucks hopes that with Tazo it can attract new customers."

Effectively, Starbucks built Tazo from an $8.1 million purchase price in 1999 into a brand with more than $1.4 billion in sales, and recently positioned a retail concept to further grow the brand in a Tazo tea store setting. The first Tazo store opened in Seattle in November 2012 and provides a retail experience where customers can purchase more than 80 varieties of loose-leaf teas or enjoy a freshly brewed cup of tea—hot, iced, or prepared as a latte. In fact, customers

Tazo tea retail store, Seattle, Washington, USA.

work with Tazo partners to create their own unique tea flavors and can buy those personal blends by the ounce or by the cup.

According to Charles Cain, vice president, Tazo Merchandise and Operations, "In our Tazo tea retail store, we want to create an experiential offering and a place where customers can get a rich sense of our extraordinary teas. Additionally, we want to take a leadership role in exposing people to premium tea. When we hit our stride, we anticipate that 25 percent of our sales will be from prepared tea beverages and the remainder will be from the purchase of loose-leaf teas and related supplies for customers to prepare their beverages at home."

Like the Evolution Fresh concept, the Tazo tea store is not branded with the iconic Starbucks logo. While having less emphasis on prepared beverages and more on take-home purchases, a Tazo tea retail store is marked by the same product passion and attention to experience detail highlighted throughout this chapter.

Annie Young-Scrivner, executive vice president and president, Starbucks Canada, expresses the aspiration of the leadership as it relates to the market relevance of decisions like the creation of the Tazo tea retail stores: "The tea category is exploding right now; it's literally at the point where coffee was a number of years ago. The majority of tea is in filter bags, not full leaf, and we hope to elevate tea-drinking experiences across the global landscape. This is a particularly relevant opportunity given our commitment to beverage delivery in tea-drinking counties like China and India. Hopefully, our collective efforts around Tazo tea will represent a big win that is very complementary to what we are doing with coffee." Stacy Speicher, director of category brand management, Tea, adds, "As we move into stores designed around products other than coffee, we guide our decisions by the most important common denominator—the customer. At the heart of everything we do are our customer insights and data. We need to understand who is buying tea, where they are, even how to reach them through social media or advertising. We need to understand our consumers backwards and forwards in order to do what we do best—connect with them."

While the true success of Evolution Fresh or the Tazo tea retail concept won't be fully known for years to come, it is clear that Starbucks success in product execution, customer connection, and experience design have allowed it to explore adjacent categories. Starbucks leadership appears to explore new business opportunities by asking questions like:

- How can we translate our core competencies into future opportunities for our existing and prospective customers?
- What external factors or consumer trends can guide us as we leverage our strengths?
- How will this possibility serve our mission and elevate the experience of our customers and all stakeholders?
- How will this opportunity enhance a connection of trust and love for those we serve?

In my view, these types of questions are relevant to every business leader. The final question, "How will this opportunity enhance a connection of trust and love?", is addressed directly in the chapters that immediately follow under the principle titled "Love to Be Loved."

CONNECTING POINTS

- Human experiences are at the heart of your brand.
- People can copy your products and your services, but seldom can they build the powerful connections with customers that emerge from the well-designed experiences that you deliver.

- Observe and interact with your prospective employees to determine whether they are eager, teachable, and authentically interested in others.
- Define your service vision in such a way that it describes what needs to be achieved during service experiences.
- Well-designed experiences involve a willingness to see the environment from the customers' perspective and attend to the needs of core customer segments.
- Great customer experiences depend on both the addition and the removal of emotional stimuli and environmental design elements.
- When it comes to the customer experience, quite often enhancements take the form of trial-and-error adjustments in an attempt to hit upon the right ingredients in the right quantities necessary to deliver an optimal customer experience.
- Whether it is connecting the design of your physical space to your company's mission, vision, and values; streamlining efficiencies to improve the customer experience; or adding sensory elements, successful customer experience enhancements have one unifying component, the need to execute the details.
- Co-create your experience with your customers.
- If you deliver high-quality products in experiential environments served by knowledgeable and passionate staff members, customers will support your growth through that product line and are also more likely to explore other offerings you innovate in the context of those core competencies.

PRINCIPLE 2

LOVE TO BE LOVED

I don't need to tell you that these are challenging times for leaders. We all seek to engage staff members, create innovative products, satisfy customers, and drive brand loyalty despite operating in an environment of consumer anxiety. To make things more complicated, we have to differentiate ourselves from the competition in as cost-effective a manner as possible and react to the increasing service demands of customers, who expect immediate responses through their desired communication channels or on their preferred social media platforms. The silver lining in what appears to be a dark cloud is the fact that every leader is faced with these exact same opportunities and market conditions. Leaders at companies like Starbucks have found ways to maintain strong emotional bonds with their customers and achieve their business objectives despite a landscape of heightened consumer empowerment and corporate cynicism. At the center of these sustained emotional bonds is a leadership principle that I refer to as "Love to Be Loved."

"Love to Be Loved" is presented in Chapter 4, "It's a Matter of Trust and Love," and Chapter 5, "It Must Thrive Inside to Be Experienced Outside." Chapter 4 explores the hierarchical nature of customer engagement and how Starbucks leaders model integrity to secure stakeholders' trust. In addition, the chapter explores the role that leaders play in charting a course toward brand passion.

Chapter 5 takes a broad look at the many and varied efforts that Starbucks leaders deploy to maximize the company's connection with partners. Given the diversity and international nature of the Starbucks workforce, the chapter offers insights into effective communication methods that maintain personalization and intimacy.

In these two chapters, you will see how employee and customer satisfaction will keep your company's lights on today. More significantly, you will come to appreciate that in order to be a viable force well into the future, you will most likely need to "love to be loved."

CHAPTER 4

It's a Matter of Trust and Love

Trust is . . . the beginning place, the foundation upon which more can be built. Where trust is, love can flourish.

BARBARA SMITH

On January 5, 1914, Henry Ford more than doubled the minimum wage for many of his employees by introducing a $5 a day minimum pay scale for employees of the Ford Motor Company. On that same day, Ford began offering profit sharing to his employees and reduced shifts from nine hours to eight. Ford's treasurer at the time, James Couzens, explained these bold leadership moves by saying, "It is our belief that social justice begins at home. We want those who have helped us to produce this great institution and are helping to maintain it to share our prosperity."

On January 5, 2012, 98 years later, embittered individuals who identified with the Occupy Wall Street movement were in the 111th day of a protest that began in Zuccotti Park in New York City's Wall Street financial district. These protestors were expressing what they perceived as economic unfairness and inequality resulting from corporate greed. The group's mantra, "We are the 99 percent," reflected cynicism and distrust for business, financial, and governmental systems that they viewed as sacrificing the interest of the country's 99 percent in favor of the wealthiest 1 percent. Where had we come in a century?

Dov Seidman, founder, chairman, and CEO of LRN, a company that helps businesses develop and maintain effective corporate governance, suggests, "This crisis of trust in our basic institutions is so troubling precisely because the lack of trust is in so many cases well deserved. Broken promises, obfuscation, spin, concealment, all have created a suspicion—often unfortunately true—that there is something to hide."

Given these global trust issues, LRN commissioned research among U.S. citizens and executives to assess their attitudes concerning the trustworthiness of corporate America. According to Dov, "The results were dismal. Over two-thirds (71%) of the Americans polled said that none, very few, or only some corporations operated in a fair and honest manner. Nowhere is the crisis of trust more acute and widespread than in corporate America, although the recent scandals overseas point to a global problem that defies national borders. In light of the power, influence, and impact of corporations, any hope of stabilizing . . . and restoring trust will not only need to involve business; it must, I believe, be led by business and business leaders."

Starbucks chief executive officer, Howard Schultz, also champions the importance of business leaders stepping up to address social problems like unemployment, destructive government partisanship (more on these two topics in Chapter 11), and distrust of businesses by employees and consumers. Howard suggests, "Most people come to work for a company having had previous work experiences. In many cases, their experience has been bad. As such, they enter with cynicism, and the burden of proof is on leaders to demonstrate that this is a different place."

Howard views the rise of distrust among employees and consumers as a "seismic change" that produces opportunities for those who behave in socially conscious ways. Howard shares,

"There is a longing by the consumer, a longing to do business with companies they trust, respect, and admire. Those companies, whether it is Whole Foods, Costco, or Timberland, that have done the right thing for a long time are winning and winning for a reason. We all have competitors, and there is disparity in the marketplace of social responsibility. Consumers are smart and will reject companies that are not making deposits in the reservoir of trust or who are not authentic about the way they appear to go about it." Alli Higgins, a regular Starbucks customer from Denver, Colorado, acknowledges that authentic social responsibility matters to her: "If I am going to frequent a company, I want to feel good about how it treats its employees, its suppliers, and the earth. I think we all have to do our part with this by looking into the companies we support. I am all for businesses making healthy profits, as long as they still do the right thing. So that's why I go to Starbucks."

This chapter is about, in Howard's terms, making authentic "deposits in the reservoir of trust." It also explores how those deposits produce returns in the form of engagement loyalty and beloved brand status. Let's start with a conceptual framework for accessing brand passion by first focusing on competence and trust.

NO POINT IN SEEKING LOVABILITY IF YOU AREN'T LIKABLE OR TRUSTWORTHY

Most of us have had some exposure to the work of Abraham Maslow. Reflecting back on your high school or college coursework, you may recall that Maslow's 1943 paper "A Theory of Human Motivation" identified a hierarchy of five human needs (physiological, safety, belongingness and love, esteem, and self-actualization). Later in Maslow's lifetime, he went on to expand his theory to eight definable need levels (adding cognitive, aesthetic, and transcendence needs). While the number of need levels may be subject to debate, Maslow is credited with appreciating that basic survival requirements take precedence over more evolved social and transformational needs. In his hierarchy, Maslow identifies biological and safety needs as having primacy over the need for love. In essence, Maslow suggests that humans have to answer the question, "Am I safe?" before they will seek to answer the question, "Am I loved?" Maslow's hierarchical view has enjoyed a renaissance among business theorists addressing the motives of customers and employees. Maslow is also relevant to our exploration, as we examine the hierarchical nature of consumers' need states when it comes to business trust, belongingness, and love.

Theorists and researchers at the Gallup Corporation, for example, have defined a hierarchy of customer perceptions that escalate from low levels to full customer engagement. In the Gallup model, the first hurdle a company must face is the question, "Are you competent?" If you provide a satisfactory experience and customers report that they are likely to purchase from you again, you have established foundational competence and achieved an entry level of engagement by the consumer. Your customers are content with your offering, and for reasons of habit or convenience are likely to purchase from you again. Your product or service delivery did *not* disappoint your customers, and therefore they feel no need to actively look elsewhere for similar products. Unfortunately, your customers also have no strong reason to stay loyal to you, and they are vulnerable to being lured away by competitors.

Being viewed as competent is a necessary but insufficient threshold for business success. In large measure, competence and satisfaction (which is used to determine perceived competence) are intellectually based perceptions that offer no protection from the effective marketing strategies of competitors or from the entrance of new businesses into your marketplace. In essence, your customers are a coupon away from exploring elsewhere.

If you are to ensure a more secure relationship with your customers, they must be able to answer the question, "Can I predict that this company will demonstrate fairness and consistency in the way it delivers products and experiences?" In essence, customers must conclude that the company operates with honesty and integrity. Based on what they have experienced firsthand or gleaned from friends, online reviews, and the media, they are determining whether a company will honor its implied and stated promises. Are senior leaders acting in accordance with their values? When problems arise, are those problems resolved in a reasonable and appropriate way? Do representatives of the company behave in a manner that is consistent with what they promise or what the marketing materials suggest?

If customers view your company as being competent and having integrity, you have created the environment for consumer trust. That trust can set the stage for yet deeper levels of customer engagement, such as brand passion or beloved brand status.

In the Gallup hierarchy, for example, being perceived as having integrity establishes the opportunity for customers to experience a heightened level of emotional engagement—"pride." In order to derive pride from a business relationship, customers must be able to offer a resounding yes to questions like, "Was I smart to have made the choice to buy here?" "Do I want to be known as a customer of this company and tell my friends and family about my positive experiences?" Customer pride comes when your business is viewed as a positive force in your customers' lives or in the lives of others they care about, as well as when you behave in ways that leave them pleased to associate with you. In some cases, pride comes from status that is derived through a connection to your brand.

The pinnacle of Gallup's customer engagement hierarchy is *passion*. To determine the presence of consumer passion, Gallup's customer engagement measurement tool (CE-11) asks questions that get at whether a company is "perfect for someone like" the customer or whether the customer can "imagine a world without" that business. (A detailed exploration of the 11 questions that Gallup used in the CE-11 can be found in my book *The New Gold Standard: 5 Leadership Principles for Creating a Legendary Customer Experience Courtesy of The Ritz-Carlton Hotel Company.*)

For our purposes here, the Gallup model serves to explain that trust is a gateway emotion on a journey to greater levels of engagement. As a consumer, I can be satisfied with the product you provide today, but I need to know that the product will be delivered consistently tomorrow or at other locations that carry your brand name. I also need to know that in the rare instances where something goes wrong, you will make it right and make me whole. Finally, if possible, I would like to feel esteem from my association with your brand and an even deeper sense that you play an intimate and personal role in things that bring pleasure to my life. In this context of hierarchical thresholds of customer engagement, let's look at how Starbucks leadership first establishes trust through integrity. More important, let's connect Starbucks actions to the way you wish to affect your customers' perceptions concerning your competence, your integrity, pride, and passion.

WATCH YOUR FEET

From my vantage point, brand integrity is the result of leaders authentically striving to align expectations and actions. Valerie O'Neil, senior vice president, Partner Resources and Brand Leadership at Starbucks, supports this view by noting, "When I joined the company, I was struck by the authenticity of our senior leaders and how they create alignment around the importance of doing the right thing for partners, customers, shareholders, and the sustainability of our planet. By acting in accord with a moral compass to 'do what is right,' leaders set the stage for the execution and integrity of partners who also want to do what is right. That has become wired into the DNA of our brand. It drives operational excellence, it affects how we fulfill promises, it guides the respect we offer customers, and it reinforces our commitment to be good stewards for our shareholders and neighborhoods."

Striving to do "the right thing" is at the core of leadership excellence, and, in today's interconnected world, it involves both the public and private behavior of leaders. Dov Seidman notes, "Virtue has been, is, and always will be its own reward. The best companies have always understood this and have refused to pursue the easy path to short-term gains at the sacrifice of long-term value and reputation. But there has been a sea change. Circumstances have combined to tangibly reward adherence to virtue. It has become practical to be principled. Why? Because the rules have changed to lay bare corporate behavior forever. The profound impact of technology has enabled greater transparency in evaluating business, institutions, and organizations. The corporate veil has been pierced."

Even before the Internet, scholars like Albert Einstein suggested that success should be measured not only through short-term profitability but also by morally considering the betterment of others. Einstein opined, "The most important human endeavor is striving for morality in our actions. Our inner balance and even our very existence depend on it. Only morality in our actions can give beauty and dignity to life."

Based on my observation, I can say that Starbucks leaders strive to demonstrate morality in their actions by making deposits in their stakeholders' reservoir of trust. This is accomplished by:

1. Empathetically looking at business decisions through the lens of humanity

2. Communicating straightforward intent, acknowledging shortcomings, and keeping promises
3. Balancing the competing interests of stakeholders
4. Creating operational systems and quality improvement processes to deliver a consistently reliable product
5. Establishing training and empowering partners to deliver service recovery

The first three items in this list relate to expansive leadership behaviors that affect diverse stakeholders and can be exemplified at Starbucks by a single, albeit significant, leadership decision: the retention of employee health-care benefits and the Bean Stock equity rewards program. The latter two items (systems and training and empowerment) will be addressed later in the chapter in the context of operational excellence and the predictability of products or services.

INTEGRITY DURING CHALLENGING TIMES AND LOOKING THROUGH THE LENS OF HUMANITY

In 2008, in the midst of making difficult decisions about the financial future of Starbucks, Howard Schultz was being encouraged, and in some ways pressured, to do away with health-care benefits for those who work at Starbucks. Openly, Howard and his leadership team took a strong stand for these and other benefits. In his communications at the time, Howard reaffirmed the leadership's commitment to partners, acknowledged uncertainties where promises couldn't be made, and ultimately delivered on his word in a way that balanced the needs of investors and partners. As Howard reflects, "Significant change was about to occur, and our people would want to know what it meant for them and their jobs. . . . We made it clear that no one employed by Starbucks would lose their health-care coverage or stock in the company. For me, that would never be an option. As for the security of their jobs, that was a decision I could not predict, a promise I could not make." Howard and the leadership team anguished about needing to scale back on jobs for the greater good of the organization. They also could have withdrawn employee benefits as part of that preservation effort; however, based on his promise, they trimmed jobs as necessary, but they did not cut into the partners' stock benefits and health-care coverage.

Difficult decisions that affect both people and the bottom line garner respect when they reflect corporate values, demonstrate compassion and sound judgment, and reflect a unity of words and deeds. Corey Lindberg, senior accounting manager, notes, "My trust in leadership starts at the top. I came here many years ago, and I have watched how leaders genuinely care for people and know what this brand stands for. It is often the case that leaders lose trust with time and with familiarity, but by balancing the demands of being a profitable company with a willingness to make decisions from the perspective of caring for people, my respect for leadership has grown. Because leaders do what they say and openly communicate their intentions, partners do the same, and most of us aspire to our leader's level of integrity." When people hear your words and see you take actions to support those words, when they have transparency into your efforts to balance competing interests, and when they know that you care about them and also care about the long-term sustainability of your business, they extend their trust.

I have suggested that integrity, like every important component of leadership, must be thought of on both an operational and a personal level. In essence, your integrity helps your people profit other people. Adrian Levy, founder of the performance improvement company RLG International, draws out the significance of the human element as it relates to the people inside an organization by noting, "People are not a company's most important asset. People are the company. Everything else is an asset." In Chapter 5, "It Must Thrive Inside to Be Experienced Outside," we will examine the many ways in which Starbucks leaders commit to the *people* they call partners. Furthermore, it will explore how those people foster the love and profitability of *people* called customers. A willingness to make tough choices on behalf of your employees can make all the difference for your employees, your customers, and even your shareholders.

In the book titled *The SPEED of Trust: The One Thing That Changes Everything*, Stephen M. R. Covey cites a number of studies that show how employee trust and brand reputation even create financial benefits for stockholders. According to Covey, research by "Watson Wyatt shows that total return to shareholders in high-trust organizations is almost three times higher than the return in low-trust organizations. That's a difference of 300 percent!" As is the case with any publicly traded company, the trust of investors is essential to Starbucks, and the company's leadership places shareholder value among its guiding principles. In keeping with the Watson Wyatt research, Howard Schultz suggests that employee trust and shareholder value are inextricably connected at Starbucks. Howard indicates, "There are 200,000 people who work for Starbucks. The equity of the brand has been defined by the relationship we have with them and the relationship they have with our customers. I think the success we have enjoyed, which is linked to shareholder value, has a great deal to do with whether or not people are proud of the company they work for and feel as though they are part of something larger than themselves.... Shareholder value has increased significantly, in large part because management has made the right kind of decisions that are in the best interest of the entire company. We have multiple constituencies . . . and we have linked shareholder value to the communities we serve and to our people."

Irrespective of the stakeholder, leaders need to understand that integrity and trust come from the conjunction of words and actions. They must communicate their intent, mistakes, and

REFLECTION ON CONNECTION

1. Based on the hierarchical stages of customer engagement (competence, integrity, pride, and passion), how do most of your customers and employees perceive your business? Are you a "competent" employer, or is your staff "proud" to work in your organization? Do customers see you as a brand with "integrity" (you do it right and make it right when things go wrong), or are you a "passion" brand that is perfect for your customers?

2. Are most of your business decisions made solely for profit, or do those decisions also reflect "morality of action" and a desire to make "deposits in the reservoir of trust" for your stakeholders?

3. Give yourself a letter grade as a leader in each of the following areas. What is the rationale for each grade?

   - Empathetically looking at business decisions through the lens of humanity
   - Communicating straightforward intent, acknowledging shortcomings, and keeping promises
   - Balancing the competing interests of stakeholders

   Are you content with your grades? What actions will you put in place to improve them?

victories while acting in accordance with their values and promises. A consistent and enduring commitment to do the transcendent "right thing," despite competing interests, is essential to developing a high-trust organization that pays rich interpersonal and financial benefits. In addition to having the company be viewed as one that is governed with integrity, leaders must inspire employees to earn the trust of customers every day and in every interaction through excellent product delivery. At Starbucks, the product promise most often occurs through a consistent deliverable: achieving excellence and consistency one cup at a time.

TRUST IN A CUP

People come into your business to address a need. Customers don't engage in service transactions simply to see how friendly a service provider will be. They want to have a functional need met, and if you treat them in a way that engages them emotionally, you will be providing a differentiating bonus.

So how do you make sure that you are addressing functional needs in as consistent a manner as possible? At Starbucks, that answer includes the use of cross-functional teams in product and implementation design as well as a willingness to solicit and act on input received from those who have the task of delivering the product consistently. Kevin Petrisko, director of business operations, Evolution Fresh (an acquired brand I discussed in Chapter 3), a 16-year Starbucks partner who has spent most of his career working on product rollout and consistent product delivery at Starbucks, notes, "From the consumer side of trust, they want to know that they will get the same beverage if they go to Starbucks in San Antonio, Honolulu, or Paris. Because of our team approach to product creation, implementation, and testing, we've done a pretty good job at earning trust through consistency."

By bringing cross-functional teams together early to develop and improve products and implementation protocols, Starbucks anticipates and resolves many rollout challenges long before new products arrive in Starbucks stores. Field-testing encourages barista input on how to improve the consistency, efficiency, and quality of product delivery. This, in turn, ensures that swift and effective execution will occur when the product is launched across the brand. All of these efforts culminate in consistent product presentation that strengthens customer trust.

Kevin offers an example of how a new product was conceptualized from a customer experience perspective, how that product was created, and how implementation was improved by frontline input. According to Kevin, "We had iced tea at Starbucks, but it really wasn't a finished, handcrafted product like a beautiful latte. In previous versions, we poured the tea from a pitcher directly into a cup, and its presentation was rather ordinary. So the original goal was to combine tea with juice or lemonade to see if we could create something very different and explore if we could also provide a more enriched experience in the process." In order to deliver the shaken tea product, implementation teams had to design a beverage shaker, establish the optimal product build process, and establish training tools for ease of product introduction in the stores.

Kevin notes, "As we tested the product, we were hearing from customers about noticeable variation. We'd given the partners the tea shakers and said, 'Mix the tea with the lemonade, add syrups as appropriate to the recipe, and shake the blend for 10 seconds. You will then pop the lid off the shaker and then pour the hand-shaken drink in the cup; it's going to be a beautiful beverage.'" In an attempt to increase consistency and make the product easy to deliver, the team of Starbucks partners that was observing the product test also asked questions of the baristas who were preparing the beverages in the test-market stores. The baristas were asked, among other things, about the ease of drink preparation, the functionality of the newly designed shakers, and the baristas' perception of the preparation process.

According to Kevin, an unsuspected issue emerged through the evaluative process. "What we learned was that the inconsistencies came from our partners not knowing how to shake the beverage," he explains. "It sounds kind of silly, but 10 seconds allows for considerable variability, as some partners were shaking it for closer to 20 seconds and others for 5 seconds. As it turns out, that time difference in shaking made a big difference in how the beverage tasted. So we changed the protocol so that partners are to shake the tea 10 times. As a result, now you walk into our stores and you can still see partners shaking the tea (and counting to themselves 1 through 10). That adjustment has made a big difference in product consistency." To achieve trust in product reliability, Starbucks leaders begin by leveraging teams of talented people and encouraging them to steward new ideas and concepts in the direction of repeatable and effective delivery systems. These teams coordinate to test those ideas with customers and with in-store partners in strategic ways to refine aspects of the product or delivery method to remove product or service variations.

CONSISTENT AND BEYOND EXPECTATIONS

Since consistency is critical to consumer trust, how do Starbucks leaders drive reliable and emotionally engaging service that not only meets but also exceeds customer expectations? In short, leaders at Starbucks train and develop partners to create inspired moments by defining those service behaviors that should "always" or "never" occur at Starbucks. In addition, training materials communicate the impact of service basics and the expectations that leaders have for consistent service delivery. For example, as part of the Starbucks service basics, leaders have set the expectation that baristas will connect with customers to understand their needs before making a product recommendation. Leadership identifies the rationale for this service expectation and the "always/never" behaviors that emerge from it as a matter of customer trust, noting that customers form trust when the intent behind product recommendations is linked to the customer's best interest and not the business's interest. The leadership at Starbucks asserts that inspired moments begin for customers when partners exceed customers' basic service expectations—many of which have to do with being proactive in delivering personalized service even before customers have to ask.

WAIT—THIS IS NOT WHAT I EXPECTED

In circumstances in which products do not live up to consumers' expectations, a critical moment of truth occurs. From the perspective of the customer, the internal dialogue usually goes something like this: "Should I let the business know that this isn't right, or should I leave bad enough alone?" "Will the business blame me by saying something like, 'That's what you ordered'?" "Will the company stand behind this product, or is it my problem now?" or, "How much hassle will I encounter in an effort to get this remedied?" From the company's side of the interaction, the internal dialogue *should* be, "What can we do to increase the likelihood that people will let us know when they encounter a problem?" "How can we ensure that every employee knows how to handle service recovery?" and "How do we use this breakdown as an opportunity to demonstrate integrity and facilitate greater levels of customer engagement?"

Since complaints are opportunities to both reengage customers and demonstrate integrity, strong leaders look for ways to encourage customers to share their concerns. At Starbucks, this begins with offering a customer-facing promise displayed in Starbucks stores and on the company's website that reads,

"We want you to be completely satisfied. If for any reason you are not satisfied with your purchase, you may return it for a replacement or refund of the purchase price." While it is easy to make such a promise, it is much more difficult to stand behind it. John Hargrave, founder of the humor site zug.com and author of *Sir John Hargrave's Mischief Maker's Manual*, decided to put the Starbucks promise to the test. John writes, "But would Starbucks really replace *anything*? To find out, I decided to buy the most perishable item on the menu, keep it in my garage for several weeks, then attempt to exchange it."

While I will spare you the details concerning the condition of the cup at the point when John elected to return it, suffice it to say that John had to place the residual components of the cup in a plastic container. John adds, "I entered the Starbucks, feeling faint from the smell, and handed the Tupperware container to the barista. 'Could I get a replacement?' I asked, 'I think this one has turned.'" According to John, after the barista got past his confusion as to what he had been handed, the barista said, "'All right, man. No problem.' He tossed the drink in the trash, then added, 'But . . . aaaahhhhhhhh!!' He moaned, his eyes watering, as the Starbucks filled with the stink of the drink. Another barista quickly ran over to bag the trash, then carried it outside, retching. . . . But I have to say: *they didn't even ask to see the receipt*. They made me up a new Steamy Creamy, and served it with a smile." So how do leaders help employees smile and accept the type of return John offered? This can be accomplished, in part, by making sure that your staff is well trained in service recovery tools and expectations.

From the earliest phases of training, Starbucks partners are provided with the resources and the autonomy to resolve customer complaints or concerns. In the context of customer service basics, partners are encouraged to assess the need state of the customer as it relates to the complaint. For some, that may involve simply apologizing that the drink did not meet their expectations and offering to remake the beverage; for others, it may involve those components and also offering a service recovery tool like a beverage coupon. From the initial barista training through ongoing career development, the leadership's message to Starbucks partners is clear: assess the customer's need, own responsibility, avoid the "blame game," make it right with urgency, and loop back with the customer to ensure that your resolution left him highly satisfied. Starbucks leaders help staff members understand that customers whose reaction to their Starbucks Experiences is "highly satisfied" (in the course of either ordinary service experiences or service recovery) are substantially more likely to repurchase and recommend Starbucks compared to those who are simply in the satisfied range. You can think of highly satisfied as equaling the perception that you both are competent *and* have integrity; whereas satisfied equals the conclusion that your customer will stay with you until she gets a better offer.

REFLECTION ON CONNECTION

1. Do you have a publicly stated service guarantee like Starbucks? If not, why is one not in place?
2. If someone were to go to extremes to test your organization's service skills (hopefully not quite to the level of John Hargrave), what situation might that person craft? How likely is it that you would respond with service recovery efficacy in the most extreme of circumstances?
3. How much time do you spend setting expectations and providing training on what service recovery should look like in your organization?

IT'S TIME FOR PASSION AND LOVE

So your customers are highly satisfied, and they view you as competent and worthy of trust. Now how do you get them to be fully engaged? Part of this question has already been answered in Chapters 2 and 3. If you select people with genuine talent for serving others, give them opportunities to become more knowledgeable and passionate about your products, and insist upon product and customer experience excellence, you are well on the way to gaining the pride and passion of customers. Furthermore, if you define your optimal customer experience, train staff to deliver it, reduce clutter, and enhance sensory elements during the customer journey, you are even closer to reaching beloved brand status. So what's missing? Often, it comes down to the leadership's commitment to communicating the importance of emotional value and a willingness to set a goal of becoming a beloved and not just a strongly liked brand. It may be that effective business leaders are accustomed to making very practical and tactical moves to achieve success. To that end, they may view emotionality as an unwelcome aspect of their own business decision making. Or possibly they may not be well versed in the burgeoning research on emotional value. Irrespective of the reasons for the resistance, it is clear that if you communicate the importance of emotional value and you set "beloved" or "passion brand" status as your destination, you can derive a significant business advantage.

Graham Robertson, president of the brand strategy and coaching firm Beloved Brands Inc., notes, "A few brands like Starbucks and Zappos become beloved brands, and, sadly enough, they are unique. Those brands that break through like Starbucks have a certain magic to the work that they do."

To help leaders assess their journey on the continuum to brand love, Graham developed a brand love curve where leaders self-assess consumers' emotional connection in the context

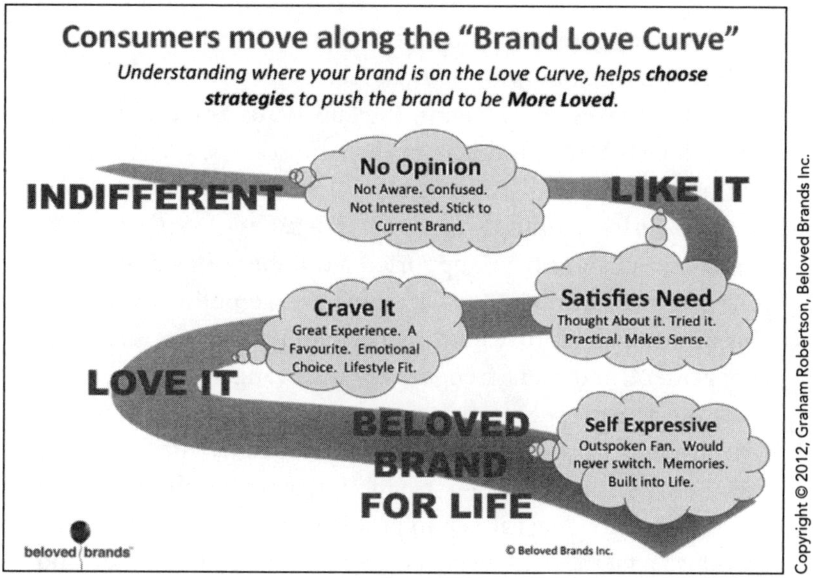

Brand Love Curve

of one of four categories ("indifferent," "like it," "love it," or "beloved brand for life").

From Graham's perspective, as businesses move to beloved brand status, they gain greater power in the marketplace. He notes, "Love is a source of power. So if I have a customer base that loves me, I am actually more powerful. As I exercise that power, I become more profitable. So if I have a following, I'll likely be more attractive to vendors and other business partners. I will have greater ease in getting neighborhood and government support when needed. I'll even have power in the context of the media because people will be more likely to report on things I do. If I launch a new skinny vanilla coffee, it will actually make the news in a way it wouldn't for a nonloved brand."

Even economists have shifted in their appreciation of the role that emotionality plays in consumer behavior and customer loyalty. Through much of the history of economics, theorists and researchers have evaluated consumer decision making through the lens of "unbounded rationality"—essentially connecting why we buy what we buy with rational factors like the functionality of our purchases. However, in the late 1970s and early 1980s, psychologists Daniel Kahneman and Amos Tversky began a revolution in economics by focusing on the role of emotional factors in decision making. The ensuing decades of exploration of customer behavior have supported a number of intuitively interesting findings about the way reason and emotion affect purchase patterns, improve customer retention, increase employee engagement, and even strengthen brand evangelism.

Even though people may claim to make purchases based on objective factors like a product's benefits and attributes, we know that those decisions are often strongly influenced by the emotional value that individuals attach to products or brands. Emotionality is also a factor in aspects of customer loyalty, frequency, and spending patterns and is manifest in a willingness to refer a business to friends and associates. Customers who make extremely strong emotional connections with a company actually perceive their preferred brands as extensions of their personality and integrate the brands into their rituals, lifestyle, and identity.

Kate Newlin, author of *Passion Brands: Why Some Brands Are Just Gotta Have, Drive All Night For, and Tell All Your Friends About*, has captured the benefit of having people identify with your company by suggesting that a passion brand is "a brand you recommend to friends wholeheartedly, even evangelically—so much so that if they don't embrace it as vigorously as you do, you perceive a cloud over *their* heads, blocking the sunshine of the brand. . . . The cloud moves on and the friendship remains. But still. What is going on?" Kate's test is fairly simple: if your customers would feel disappointed if their friends aren't as excited about you as they are—you are a passion brand.

Starbucks leaders have not been reluctant to talk about love, passion, or the romance of the brand. But they have also been very clear that the only way to become beloved is to be loving.

From the perspective of the leaders at Starbucks, love is a bi-directional phenomenon—it is enjoyed when it is authentically given. So, how about you? Are you perceived as being competent and acting with integrity? In essence, have you earned the trust of your customers? Where are you on Graham Robertson's brand love curve? Are your customers recommending you with such zeal that they would be disappointed if their friends did not share their excitement? Short-term success may be achieved through operational excellence and satisfaction alone. However, if you want to fully engage your customers, it may be time to authentically lead the human connection from a foundation of trust and set your course for belovedness.

CONNECTING POINTS

- If customers view your company as being competent and having integrity, you have created the environment for consumer trust. Trust is a gateway emotion on a journey to greater levels of emotional engagement.
- Brand integrity is the result of leaders authentically striving to align expectations and actions.
- Seeking to do "the right thing" is at the core of leadership excellence, and in today's interconnected world, it involves both your public and your private behavior.
- Success should be measured not only through short-term profitability, but also by whether you consider the betterment of others.
- Difficult decisions that affect both people and the bottom line garner respect when they reflect corporate

values, demonstrate compassion and sound judgment, and offer a unity of words and deeds.

- Integrity, like every important component of leadership, must be thought of on both an operational and a personal level. In essence, your integrity helps your people improve the lives of others.
- Leaders must inspire employees to earn the trust of customers every day and in every interaction through excellent product delivery.
- Complaints are opportunities to both reengage customers and demonstrate integrity; strong leaders look for ways to encourage customers to share their concerns.
- If you communicate the importance of emotional value and you set "beloved" or "passion brand" status as your destination, you can derive a significant business advantage.
- Customers who make extremely strong emotional connections with a company actually perceive their preferred brands as extensions of their personality and integrate the brands into their rituals, lifestyle, and identity.

CHAPTER 5

It Must Thrive Inside to Be Experienced Outside

Treat employees like partners, and they act like partners.

FRED ALLEN, *American radio personality*

Words matter! Therefore, many leaders have moved away from using the word *employee* because it connotes a power dynamic in the work relationship. The term suggests that there is a more powerful person (the *employer*) and a less powerful one (the *employee*). Additionally, *employee* describes a financial or transactional relationship—if you employ me, I work for you and you pay me. In lieu of *employee*, two popular alternatives have become part of business-speak—*associate* and *team member*. While these words are a softer way to describe the connection between people in an organization, they also imply a more affiliative or collaborative environment. Sadly, at some businesses, words like *associate* and *team member* ring hollow. In some settings, team members are not afforded the respect, trust, and appreciation that would indicate members of a true interdependent group. As for associates, frequently there is very little "association" between the leaders and the led. So why is the word *partner* used at Starbucks? And does that word describe reality or a good-feeling intention?

PARTNERSHIP? REALLY?

Business definitions of partnership typically involve a number of elements:

- An agreement between two parties to pursue common objectives
- Shared investment to realize those objectives
- A distribution of the risks and rewards emerging from pursuit of the objectives

Most business owners enter into a work agreement with new hires that hopefully has both parties seeking a shared goal. Typically, those who have been hired invest their time and talents alongside the time, talents, and financial resources of the owners. However, there is *no* true partnership because employees do *not* receive a distribution of the rewards from the business's profitability beyond a predetermined wage agreement. The employees, if you will, are definitely not partners because they have no access to the upside or any liability for the downside of the business relationship. So is the Starbucks "employee" relationship a business partnership? Well, in the most technical sense of the word, no. Starbucks "partners" face no financial liability from their working relationship, but they do enjoy a functional partnership in that they are granted Bean Stock.

By 1991, Starbucks was starting to enjoy healthy enough levels of profitability for Howard Schultz to ask for the support of the Starbucks board of directors in creating an equity reward program for employees. Since Starbucks was a private company at the time, the proposed plan was designed to grant stock options company-wide, calculated as a proportion of the employees' base pay. Howard believed that such a program would establish a direct connection between the contribution of employees and the overall market value of Starbucks. Though the board members expressed concern that this type of program might dilute the value of the shares of the investors who were funding the business, the plan was unanimously approved. When the Bean Stock program was presented to employees in 1991, Starbucks stopped using the term *employees* and began calling everyone *partners*, since even part-time staff members could become eligible for the program after six months on the job.

Through the years, the Bean Stock program has continued to evolve to increase the benefit to partners. In November 2010, Starbucks began to grant Bean Stock in the form of restricted stock units (RSUs) instead of stock options. In addition, Starbucks expanded eligibility to more than 115,000 partners in 19 markets, with a recent addition being Rwanda. Howard and the board shortened the vesting period and allowed partners to receive actual shares of Starbucks stock when they vest, as an alternative to realizing the market gain from the time of the grant to the time when they exercise their stock options. Bean Stock and the company's Future Roast 401(k) program, coupled together, constitute key components of Starbucks forward-looking compensation plan.

In fiscal year 2012, Starbucks delivered more than $214 million in pretax gains to partners from vested RSUs or from the exercise and sale of their Bean Stock options and more than $55 million to 401(k) participants in the form of the employer match, which demonstrates a guiding philosophy of leadership that success is best when it's shared. Through a steadfast commitment to this philosophy in good years and in bad, Starbucks leaders set themselves apart from those in most businesses. Communicating with partners in 2011, Howard noted, "For the past two decades, Starbucks has been one of the only retailers with a stock program that includes part-time hourly partners. This truly sets us apart from other organizations by making us not only a preferred place to work, but a business whose partners' pride in ownership undeniably contributes to the authentic connections you make with your customers. Bean Stock grants fulfill our long-standing promise to you: that if we succeed as a company, you succeed with us. . . . I have been touched personally by the many letters I have received from partners sharing how the company's performance is helping them care for their families. These are difficult times for many people, and we have to continue earning the trust of our customers and partners in all aspects of our business."

While I certainly don't have access to Howard's mail, I have encountered my share of partners who are eager to talk about how the Bean Stock they have saved over time has changed their lives. Kaycee Kiesz, a 20-year partner and program manager, Global Diversity, reports, "I went on a YMCA volunteer trip to Thailand and to Bali for a yoga retreat thanks to Bean Stock. The program also helped me put 20 percent down on my house. I wouldn't have been able to come up with the amount I needed for the house if it hadn't been for the generosity reflected in the Bean Stock program. The dollars are fantastic, but I also feel taken care of." One partner indicated that he had used Starbucks Bean Stock on three occasions, once to remodel his home, once to purchase land, and once to purchase dental implants, noting that Bean Stock had essentially given him his smile back. Volunteer trips, houses, remodeling, and the ability to regain one's smile—not bad rewards for partnering with Starbucks to drive shareholder value.

At the Global Leadership Conference in Houston in 2012, approximately 5 percent of the district managers and store managers in attendance had not activated their Bean Stock accounts. The goal was to have every one of those individuals stop by a conference booth to complete their activations. What a pleasant surprise for those partners who found out for the first time that they had an account balance of $13,000, or better yet, a long-time partner who had more than $50,000. Some business owners would say that they don't have the profit necessary to create a program like Bean Stock. I wonder if part of their problem with profits might not result from a failure to provide incentives to those who could have helped them earn more.

BEYOND THE MONEY— CARING ABOUT WELL-BEING

In the United States, the first forms of workplace insurance occurred in the mid-1800s, when employees received policies covering them in the event that they sustained disabling injuries from steamboat or railroad accidents. While employer-sponsored health insurance popped up in the 1920s, such plans didn't truly proliferate until World War II, when the federal government placed stringent wage controls on businesses but exempted health benefits from counting against salary caps. Enriched health-benefit plans were a way for companies to attract the best employees possible in a challenging wartime labor market.

Now fast-forward to 1961. Although many employers provided health insurance at that time, Howard Schultz's father was not lucky enough to work for such a company. That year, Howard personally experienced hardship because of the uninsured health costs his family incurred as a result of his father's breaking his ankle at work. Jump with me one last time to 1987. Howard Schultz, along with a group of investors, purchased Starbucks from Howard's former employers. Within one year, the company had grown from 17 to 55 stores, and Howard was in front of his board of directors making a pitch for health-care benefits for full-time and eligible part-time employees. Since Starbucks wasn't profitable at the time (unlike when Howard sold the idea of Bean Stock in 1991), he experienced considerable resistance from the board. Howard argued that the cost of providing health-care benefits was 50 percent less than the cost of hiring and retaining a new employee. He made a case for part-time employee coverage on the grounds that two-thirds of the workforce at the time were not full-timers. In addition to the fixed costs of replacing employees, Howard addressed the impact of high turnover on the customer experience by indicating that regular customers form relationships with baristas that are disrupted when employees churn. Howard's reasoning was compelling, and the board approved the Starbucks health-care benefit. As a result, Starbucks became among the first companies in the United States to provide comprehensive health insurance for all eligible employees, including people who worked just 20 hours a week. What some would see as an unnecessary expense, Howard saw as an investment in people and in Starbucks future. Toward the end of this chapter, we will look at the return on that investment from the standpoint of partner engagement and retention. Furthermore, we will explore the impact of high levels of employee engagement on innovation and customer loyalty.

The provision of health-care benefits in the quick-service restaurant sector was revolutionary in 1988, as was the extension of health-care benefits to part-time workers. In 1994, U.S. president Bill Clinton even consulted with Howard as the president explored health-care policy. To date, most employers still do not offer health benefits to part-time employees, and many of those that had provided them dropped the offering during the recent economic challenges. According to the 2012 Kaiser Family Foundation's Employer Health Benefits Survey, "In 2012, 28% of all firms that offer health benefits offer them to part-time workers, a significant increase from the 16% reported in 2011 but similar to the 25% reported in 2010."

I started this chapter by saying that *words matter*. In the words of Starbucks partners, concern shown through widespread health-care benefits *matters more*. Posting on a blog, one barista wrote, "I can also say in all seriousness that I owe Starbucks my life. If it weren't for the OUTSTANDING health coverage Starbucks provides to its employees, I wouldn't have been able to spend 90 days at a residential treatment center for a life-threatening eating disorder. The health insurance I had through my part-time job at Starbucks paid for a major portion of my treatment and aftercare, neither of which I would have been able to afford on my own." Juan, a Starbucks shift supervisor, puts it this way: "It's really amazing to me that we can just start out for a few months working 20 hours a week and get quality health insurance and its good benefits. I've had some health problems recently that required hospitalization. My insurance was my saving grace. It seems like a gift. Health insurance is but one example of how I feel valued and appreciated. In essence, leadership is saying my work means something, and that's a large part of why I have such a strong love for this company."

Throughout this chapter, I will be discussing a variety of ways in which Starbucks leaders demonstrate appreciation of, respect for, and investment in their people. My intent is not to say that this is "the" way to make the connection or to imply that the way Starbucks connects is perfect. I am, however, asserting that Starbucks leadership is dedicated to employee engagement and that concerted effort is needed to sustain a substantial workforce advantage.

INVESTING IN GROWTH AND DEVELOPMENT

In a blog article posted on the website for CollegePlus, a company that creates customized dual credit and bachelor's degree programs, columnist and blogger Caitlin Muir explains that the title of her article *33 Companies That Can Save You From College Debt* was not her initial choice. "Originally, this article was going to be 'Why I love Starbucks.' As a former barista, the company was good to me. Not only did I get cheap health insurance, great hours, and a flexible schedule but I got something that really helped me. *Tuition reimbursement*." Caitlin goes on in the article to explain how this Starbucks benefit, along with other resources, allowed her to graduate without having student loans hanging over her head.

The "ability to grow and develop" is a key factor in securing employee engagement. To make that growth happen, leaders must attend to workplace opportunities and seek educational opportunities outside of the workplace. "Starbucks U" is an example that merges on-the-job training with formal academic offerings.

Starbucks U refers to a recently created program for U.S. partners, wherein they are eligible to receive college credits for training provided as part of their job (for example, the barista training course described in Chapter 3, shift supervisor training, and so on). Starbucks leaders have secured college-credit eligibility for partners by working with the American Council of Education (ACE) to accredit select training offerings. Similarly, the leadership has collaborated with City University of Seattle and Strayer University to amplify the impact of the company's existing tuition reimbursement program for eligible partners in the United States and Canada. The City University program, for example, provides eligible Starbucks partners with the opportunity to have their application fee waived, a 25 percent reduction in all undergraduate and graduate tuition, and exclusive scholarships, among other benefits. Similarly, the Strayer University program offers 20 percent tuition discounts, free academic tutoring and advising, and the flexibility of 24/7 online courses. One partner noted, "I decided to go back to school last year. . . . I enrolled at Strayer University and received an initial $1,000 scholarship from Strayer as well as a 20 percent discount on tuition and credit for Starbucks training. A few months after I started school, I received a $2,500 fall scholarship from Starbucks U. All of this is because I am a Starbucks partner. Starbucks has made a difference in my life, a girl from Haiti who barely spoke English when I started working here. It has been the best time of my life." Leaders who are interested in growing their people find ways to collaborate with other businesses and with learning institutions like Strayer University and City University to offer benefits that they might not be able to provide alone. By finding strategic alliances, these leaders stretch and extend their employee benefit budgets and serve to answer an important question for their people: "Do you care enough about me to help me achieve personal as well as professional development objectives?"

UNITING PARTNERS IN CRISIS AND IN COMMUNITY

In addition to supporting partners through the Bean Stock program, retirement funds, health-care coverage, and educational benefits, Starbucks leadership oversees a program that encourages partners to help one another. The CUP (Caring Unites Partners) Fund began in 1998. It emerged when a group of partners worked with Starbucks leadership to establish a mechanism for raising and distributing funds for partners who encounter a disruptive hardship. Funding for the program comes from voluntary contributions by partners and the proceeds of fund-raising events that they sponsor. Starbucks administers the fund. An applicant may receive up to $1,000 if that partner is determined to have encountered an uncontrollable, financially unmanageable, catastrophic circumstance—such as the impact of Superstorm Sandy, which affected many partners in the northeastern quadrant of the United States in 2012. Eligibility for funding is independent of a partner's ever having made a contribution. While employee-to-employee funds have become more prominent since the late 1990s, the CUP Fund at Starbucks is noteworthy on several levels: sustainability, infrastructure, ongoing leadership support for the fund, expansion into international markets (more on this in Chapter 6), and how the CUP Fund connects partners to one another and to organizational pride.

People have a natural tendency to want to help those with whom they work. Many of those helping efforts, however, are ad hoc or poorly organized. Since employee engagement is connected to peer cohesion as well as employer support, leaders at companies like Starbucks offer the infrastructure and systems to maximize a caring community (this is evidenced not only in the CUP Fund program, but also in the Partner Access Alliance Network, which will be addressed later in the chapter). The company's participation in the program is largely administrative, but it also takes the form of financial contributions such as those from the busy Starbucks store located on the eighth floor of the Starbucks Support Center in Seattle, Washington.

Starbucks partners express appreciation for the opportunity to give to and receive from the CUP Fund. Partner Shao Wei, a student at Tianjin University in Tianjin, China, experienced two tragic events in rapid succession shortly after becoming a part-time employee at the Starbucks Baisheng store: her father was diagnosed with advanced liver cancer, and six months later, doctors needed to operate to remove a tumor from her mother. Shao notes, "For a poor family like ours, the huge medical cost is an extremely heavy burden. The store manager found out about the sudden blow to my family. He was very accommodating in terms of shift arrangement. Later, I had to work at several different stores. The store managers and partners at each store were both helpful and supportive. They even helped me apply for the CUP Fund. The aid from the CUP Fund is more than just money. It's more of a mental support."

Thanks to the support of her peers, Shao Wei is looking to make a career at Starbucks. "This June, I will graduate from college. I plan to stay at Starbucks for further professional development.

Starbucks gives me energy. Starbucks makes me stronger. In my future work, I will pour my passion into every cup of coffee and serve every customer with a smile." Even those who have not needed assistance from the CUP Fund find value in it. Alison Edwards, program manager, Global Learning at Starbucks, adds, "The CUP Fund is about taking care of other partners. They are part of my community. Given all the challenges in the world today, we all need a community that cares and offers a security blanket, like the CUP Fund. When I go home each day, I am proud that I work for a company where people can feel loved and I can give and receive support."

While you may or may not be able to help create or administer a program that allows your team members to support one another in times of crisis, clearly there are low-cost aspects of your infrastructure that can be leveraged to care for your team members. Often the returns to your company (in the case of Shao Wei, an interest in going from a part-time job to pursuing "professional development" as she serves "every customer with a smile") are far in excess of the resources you will expend.

The Starbucks Partner Networks are yet another example of a low-cost/high-return investment on the part of the leadership. Partner resource groups are provided meeting space at Starbucks and opportunities to work with senior leaders.

Starbucks Partner Network Groups

(Groups are voluntary and open to all partners.)

- **Starbucks Access Alliance Network** promotes equal access to physical locations, product, communication tools, and information for all partners and customers.

- **Starbucks Armed Forces Network** supports Starbucks military partners, their families, and transitioning veterans, and creates a military-friendly culture in the workplace.
- **Starbucks Black Partner Network** works to cultivate, enhance, and share the African American experience at Starbucks, one partner and one customer at a time.
- **Starbucks China Club Network** develops a global community driving business acumen, nurturing culture, and developing leaders through the lens of the China/Asia-Pacific partner network and the growth agenda.
- **Starbucks Hora Del Café Network** is a Hispanic affinity group dedicated to creating an environment for partners to develop professionally, build cultural awareness, and celebrate Hispanic culture while affecting the community in a positive way.
- **Starbucks Pride Alliance Network** works to produce positive change and increase awareness of the LGBT community within Starbucks. It strives to cultivate an equitable, dynamic, and supportive environment for LGBT partners, allies, and customers.
- **Women's Development Network** focuses on the professional and personal development of its members. The network focuses on three established pillars: community, education/development, and networking.

Kaycee Kiesz, program manager, Global Diversity, notes, "The company regularly leverages our networks to derive full value from new business, drive innovations, build relevance in new markets, and reinforce the humanity of our brand in the global communities we serve. The senior leadership team listens to concerns and supports the efforts of the members. The Access Alliance Network, for example, consulted with our Legal department to update our service dog policy. The network was also instrumental in creating our Starbucks Braille and large-print menus and Braille Starbucks Card. The Armed Forces Network partners closely with staffing/recruiting to help veterans make the transition into Starbucks careers. Our networks are often called upon to provide translation services, offer feedback on marketing materials, and help in product development."

According to Carolina Morales, senior financial analyst at Starbucks, one project of importance to the partner group Hora Del Café was to connect with partners in Brazil. "Our group focuses on kindling connections to Hispanic heritage. We share our love of Hispanic culture, food, music with one another and with all interested partners and leadership. We also want to be able to help our leaders look at Starbucks business through the lens of our culture. Recently, our executive sponsor helped us arrange a videoconference with our Brazil office, and we explored their aspirations for the Brazil market and began a conversation as to how we could help. We had a packed house here at the Support Center in Seattle, with so many people wanting to know more about Brazil and what the opportunities are there. It was such a powerful start to our relationship; our partners in Brazil seemed so inspired that we were enthusiastic here in the United States about them. The love was there." Often caring for other team members involves a critically important yet not costly investment: logistics support. When a business makes meeting space, business infrastructure, and organizational abilities available to employees who seek to care for one another and/or create positive communities, its team members engage one another in pursuits that fortify a dynamic and healthy workplace.

REFLECTION ON CONNECTION

1. What are your employees saying about your level of financial support for them in terms of their physical, emotional, educational, and financial well-being?
2. Have you looked for strategic partnerships that could allow you to extend your employee benefits budget (for example, an academic institution that will work with you to accredit your training classes for college credit)?
3. How might you leverage your business infrastructure to produce high-value/low-cost opportunities to support your team members logistically?

LISTENING AND EMPATHIZING

President Woodrow Wilson once said, "The ear of the leader must ring with the voices of the people." This is easily said, but less easily done! In fact, systematic and authentic listening may be one of the most economical and differentiating investments a leader can make. Many leaders either are too busy to listen or are more interested in speaking. As a result, listening intently, regularly, and respectfully to team members separates the great leader from the good one.

At Starbucks, effective listening takes many forms. While leaders listen informally at an individual or team level, Starbucks also has formalized a department that consistently listens for the needs and engagement level of partners. Virgil Jones, director, Partner Services, at Starbucks, notes, "Our team conducts surveys, focus groups, and continuously takes a pulse on our partner population. Within that department, the most important thing I do on a daily basis is listen to our partners. The second most important thing I do is continue to touch base with our partners and adjust, because with the way technology is advancing, the things that are hot, interesting, and engaging with our partners today is going to be completely different 18 months from now." By routinely asking questions and listening to partner input, Starbucks leaders are able to anticipate, tailor, and shift their employee-related resources for an ever-changing workforce. Virgil adds, "If you look at our total pay, we have many traditional buckets—401(k), health-care benefits, compensation—and my group is the X-factor group where we consistently look at our demographic and we try to come up with new, innovative programs that will appeal to our partners. For example, health and wellness and college-related needs are important to our demographic. Included under health and wellness is our Partner Connection program."

According to Virgil, Starbucks has about 400 different teams and clubs in the United States, with 30,000 partners participating. For sports teams, Starbucks typically offsets approximately 50 percent of the fees that participants incur and welcomes non-Starbucks partners to participate. Since approximately 60 percent of Starbucks partners are technology-savvy students, many partner-engaging services involve discount programs with computer and phone companies.

Michelle Gass, president, Starbucks EMEA (Europe, Middle East and Africa), like many other Starbucks senior leaders, demonstrates a different kind of regular and personal listening that fuels partner engagement. Her approach comes in the form of "listening tours." According to Michelle, "I travel across the EMEA region regularly and conduct listening tours and roundtable meetings. These are informal meetings where we spend about 90 minutes paying attention to the thoughts, needs, and ideas of those we serve. While listening is important, taking swift action to elevate experiences is essential. These tours are an ongoing process of connection and discovery, not an event." Starbucks senior leaders deploy a variety of processes to connect, discover, and respond to the needs of partners.

For many leaders, one of the earliest forms of empathy building they encounter comes in the form of store immersion. Clarice Turner, senior vice president, U.S. Business, arrived at Starbucks with a solid background in food and beverage service. She had worked with PepsiCo and Yum! Brands for 16 years, and immediately prior to coming to Starbucks, she had been president and COO of Papa Murphy's Pizza. Despite her varied and established experience in the industry, she was sent to a four-month immersion program that began with working behind a Starbucks counter. Clarice reports, "At that time, I thought, 'Okay, I've been in this industry for a long time. Surely I can get up to speed quicker than four months.' But those experiences are something I now credit as having the most impact on me being able to hit the ground running and truly embrace the essence of Starbucks. That time was such a gift. I did every job in the store, from taking out the trash and cleaning the bathrooms to actually training to be the store manager. I also trained to be a district manager, regional director, and regional vice president before I assumed my role at the time as division senior vice president. From the onset, it was clear that my role as a leader involved immersing myself into and empathizing with our partners."

It is common for Starbucks leaders to talk about the significance of their initial immersive experiences. Cliff Burrows, president, Americas, indicates, "I worked for six weeks at our Queen Anne store in Seattle. I am sure I wasn't the best barista ever, but I enjoyed every moment of my store immersion. That was over 10 years ago, and I will never forget the people and experiences I had there. It was an immediate, profound, and personal introduction to our work and to the world of partners who make it happen one cup at a time every day." At Starbucks, the practice of immersion was initially introduced for leaders at the level of vice president or above. Now new managers and leaders throughout the organization are afforded opportunities to gain a deeper understanding of the life of barista partners by spending time in the store and behind the bar.

Often leaders see listening as a passive pursuit. At Starbucks, listening is synonymous with connecting, discovering, understanding, empathizing, and responding. The benefits of this listening fuel the entrepreneurial and adaptive spirit of a brand that could easily have lost its nimbleness as a result of its growth and scale. In many ways, when leaders demonstrate formal and informal listening, they not only engage employees but also gain access to information that helps them stay relevant to the needs and observations of their team members. Of course, listening is a skill that parallels another critical leadership behavior: observation. When it comes to employee engagement, observation often comes in the form of acknowledgment and recognition programs.

THE POWER OF AN ACKNOWLEDGING LEADER

While most of us intend to recognize the achievements of our team members regularly, those intentions often get lost amid the deluge of challenges and demands that we face every day. By creating effective reward and recognition programs, leaders at Starbucks develop recognition excellence as a core competency within the organization. In their book *The Carrot Principle: How the Best Managers Use Recognition to Engage Their Employees, Retain Talent, and Accelerate Performance*, Adrian Gostick and Chester Elton suggest, "In response to the question 'My organization recognizes excellence,' the organizations that scored in the lowest fourth overall had an average return on equity (ROE) of 2.4 percent, whereas those that scored in the top fourth had an average ROE of 8.7 percent. In other words, companies that most effectively recognize excellence enjoy a return that is more than triple the return of those that do so the worst." Similarly, Gostick and Elton found that managers who were rated highest on recognizing employee contributions also typically produced the highest levels of employee satisfaction, employee retention, and even customer satisfaction.

Because of the importance of recognizing excellence, Starbucks leadership has developed a broad array of recognition and award programs, which include, but are not necessarily limited to, the following:

Performance Award Programs

M.U.G. award

Bravo award

Team Bravo award

The Green Apron program

Spirit of Starbucks award

Team Spirit of Starbucks award

Manager of the Quarter

Manager of the Year

District Manager of the Year

A detailed review of all of the Starbucks awards and recognition programs is beyond the scope of this book, but the diversity of offerings affords a number of important teachable lessons, including the following:

- The value of peer-to-peer recognition
- The need to scale rewards at both the individual and team levels

- Reliance on social aspects of recognition
- The enterprise-wide importance of awards

Many of the reward programs offered at Starbucks involve nominations from peers (Bravo awards, Spirit of Starbucks awards) and/or direct and immediate recognition by peers (M.U.G. awards, the Green Apron program). Rather than relying only on managers or leaders to catch people who meet the criteria for recognition, the entire organization is mobilized to immediately, or through nomination, bring those acts of excellence to light.

Similarly, excellence is recognized in terms of both individual effort and team collaboration at Starbucks. In the course of my function as a professional speaker, I have attended a large number of sales conferences, award banquets, and even service recognition events. It is rare to see awards provided to groups at these events. At Starbucks, an award like the Team Spirit of Starbucks "is presented to teams or groups of partners who work together to contribute well beyond their day-to-day responsibilities, making a significant and positive difference at Starbucks. The Team Spirit of Starbucks Award recognizes a team of partners for a single, exceptional achievement." According to the criteria for the award, that exceptional achievement must also reflect the Starbucks mission. While individual awards can foster healthy competition within an organization, they can also undermine collaboration. Balancing individual and team recognition allows both independent and interdependent excellence to be acknowledged at your company.

While some businesses get caught up in high-cost extrinsic rewards and bonuses, most of the awards offered at Starbucks do *not* involve items with substantial tangible value. In the case of M.U.G. awards, Bravo awards, or Green Apron recognition, partners receive pins, handwritten notes, or certificates to acknowledge their achievement. These pins often carry a social value among baristas, who typically wear them on their aprons. Consistent with trends in social psychological research showing that extrinsic rewards can extinguish intrinsic motivation, the emphasis at Starbucks is much less on prizes and much more on acknowledgment.

Kay Corio, a former Starbucks partner and a recipient of the Spirit of Starbucks award, shared her views of recognition at Starbucks. "I was honored to win the award. I appreciated that leadership let us know what excellence looks like and that I would be in a position to garner acknowledgment for my effort. I believe that recognition at Starbucks plays an important role in offering us uplifting moments in acknowledgment of the work we do." Providing uplifting moments for those who uplift customers—that is the role of leadership at Starbucks.

REFLECTION ON CONNECTION

1. Do you conduct "listening tours" with your people? What are your systematic approaches to leadership listening (for example, formal surveys or regular roundtable sessions)?

2. In addition to your direct observation of behavior that demonstrates excellence, what peer-to-peer recognition programs have you developed?

3. How are you balancing individual and team awards? Do you emphasize acknowledgment or rewards of substantial financial value?

THE RETURN ON PARTNER INVESTMENT

So why invest so much in your people? While it feels good to generously encourage the growth, development, and well-being of your team members, does it make good business sense? Let's address this issue at a macroeconomic level and then examine the specific benefits that Starbucks derives from its partner engagement efforts.

Across industries and continents, companies with highly engaged employees have been shown to produce improved sales, profits, and shareholder value. One such example comes from the Kenexa Research Institute's WorkTrends report. According to the findings, "Organizations with highly engaged employees achieve seven times greater 5-year TSR [total shareholder return] than organizations whose employees are less engaged." Other research groups have found that as employee engagement increases, workplace errors and lost-time accidents decrease. Elevated employee engagement is also linked to increased repeat customer purchases and strong customer advocacy.

As you will recall, Howard Schultz initially appealed to the Starbucks board of directors for health-care benefits based on his projection that it would ultimately save the company money in turnover-associated costs. From a research perspective, such an argument is sound, given findings like those of the Corporate Executive Board, which state, "By increasing employees' engagement levels, organizations can expect an increase in performance of up to 20 percentile points and an 87% reduction in employees' probability of departure." However, do investments in programs such as health insurance for eligible part-time employees at Starbucks actually result in retention rates greater than those of competitors in the quick-service sector? Typically, Starbucks reports a voluntary annual turnover rate for *full-time* partners of around 12 to 15 percent (meaning that 12 to 15 percent of full-time partners voluntarily elect to leave the company for other options); however, this percentage does not reflect the entire picture of turnover, since a large number of employees are *part-time*. Analysts who have taken into consideration both the full-time and part-time employees suggest that the actual turnover rate is somewhere around 65 percent. For many of us, 65 percent seems remarkably high, but author, broadcaster, and journalist John-Paul Flintoff puts it in perspective: "While other fast-food retailers lost staff at rates as high as 400% a year, Starbucks' turnover was a relatively low 65%."

Assuming that your turnover costs exceed your cost of benefits and you turn over one-sixth as many employees as your competition, your business will be well positioned for long-term success. This is particularly true if your engaged employees help you innovate new processes or help you reduce waste. Given the size of Starbucks, a simple act performed by an engaged partner can result in phenomenally large benefits to the company. Such is the case of Joe Young, a barista in Hutchison, Kansas, who was engaged in his job and developed a process improvement that also eliminated waste of an expensive Starbucks product, namely, whipped cream. Cliff Burrows announced the accomplishment at the 2012 Global Leadership Conference, noting, "Joe found a way in his store to improve the quality of the partner experience, the quality of the beverage, and he saved the company between 5 and 10 million dollars within the year." Are your employees engaged and generating solutions that produce savings (albeit probably not on the scale of Joe Young's) in your business? Are they seeing the business from the perspective of an owner?

At Starbucks, the ultimate value of employee engagement occurs in the millions of interactions that take place every day in buildings carrying the Starbucks brand. Since managers can't monitor all of those interactions, the care and concern leaders extend to partners is reflected in the loving discretionary effort partners show in their moments with customers. A highly engaged workforce consistently contributes to remarkable service experiences for customers, much like the ones reported by Starbucks customers.

In a blog post written by a member of the My Starbucks Idea community, one customer writes about her visit to a store she had not previously visited. Her father had died the night before, so she and her sister were getting the arrangements made for the days to come. They stopped at a Starbucks for drinks, and the barista could see that she had been crying and asked what was wrong. The customer described what happened after she told the partner that her father had died: the barista "reached onto the counter and patted my hand, extending her sympathy and telling me the drinks were on them. It sounds so trite but it was such a comfort. . . . I will always remember that kindness." The barista who served that customer went off task to give comfort to the deeply saddened person, and in the process was fully engaged in the Starbucks mission of producing uplifting moments.

Having an engaged workforce means that employees can do what is right for customers without having to be told. They can rise above the rules, processes, and procedures inherent in doing a job to make purposeful connections with the people they serve. In the end, employee engagement produces memorable kindness, profitability, sustainability, and customers for life. As an added benefit, it is much easier to manage a fully engaged workforce when the work culture is a pleasant and enjoyable one. What steps will you take to drive greater engagement within your team? The engagement of your customers relies on the engagement *you* produce for your employees, partners, team members, associates, or whatever you choose to call the people you serve.

CONNECTING POINTS

- The ability to grow and develop is a key factor in securing employee engagement.
- Leaders who are interested in growing their people find ways to work with other businesses and learning institutions to offer benefits that those leaders might not be able to provide alone.
- People have a natural tendency to want to help those with whom they work. Consider overseeing a program that encourages employees to help one another.
- Listening is not a passive pursuit; listening is synonymous with connecting, discovering, understanding, empathizing, and responding.
- Good leaders provide uplifting moments for those who uplift customers.
- Rather than relying only on managers or leaders to catch people meeting the criteria for recognition, the entire organization should be mobilized to recognize individuals and teams that perform acts of excellence.
- Across industries and continents, companies with highly engaged employees produce improved sales, elevated profits, and increased shareholder value.
- Having an engaged workforce means that employees do what is right for customers without having to be told.
- Employee engagement contributes to memorable kindness, profitability, sustainability, and customers for life.
- It is much easier to manage a fully engaged workforce when your work culture is a pleasant and enjoyable one.

PRINCIPLE 3

REACH FOR COMMON GROUND

Cultural anthropologists have been engaged in a long-standing debate between two conflicting perspectives: universalism and cultural relativism. While the words sound daunting, the concepts are rather straightforward. Universalism suggests that the underlying similarities among all people are greater than their cultural differences. By contrast, cultural relativism asserts that cultural differences have a profound effect on people, making it difficult for "outsiders" to fully understand the relevant context of behavior. While anthropologists may argue for universalism or cultural relativism, most business owners and leaders are not interested in winning a debate. Instead, they need to scale their business to maximize commonalities while making local adjustments to assure market acceptance.

Chapter 6, "Assume the Universal: Serve the Unifying Truths of Humans," examines how Starbucks leaders create connection with maximum global appeal. Conversely, Chapter 7, "Respect, Celebrate, and Customize: Listening and Innovating to Meet Local, Regional, and Global Needs," looks at how leaders localize certain aspects of their products, environments, and service delivery to forge relationships that are relevant to local customers throughout the world.

Starbucks leaders have made their share of mistakes in attempting to strike a balance between the universal and the cultural. In the process of their setbacks and victories, Starbucks serves as a helpful guide on how to make powerful and respectful connections in new markets. Whether you are considering customers in the next town, in an adjacent state, or through online delivery in this global economy, or even if you are opening a location in a country that is half a world away, this is your opportunity to "reach for common ground."

CHAPTER 6

Assume the Universal: Serve the Unifying Truths of Humans

All things are the same except for the differences, and different except for the similarities.

THOMAS SOWELL

Do you believe that people want similar things from a service experience in two different boroughs of New York City (say, Manhattan and Queens)? Do people in New York and New Delhi want the same things from service experiences? A number of research groups have looked at what customers want when they are being served. These studies segment customers by industry, nationality, age, gender, income, and a myriad of other demographic distinctions. While some differences surface across this breadth of variables, a number of service universals remain, regardless of time and place. This consumer research intersects closely with the work of theorists and researchers concerning overall human similarity.

Michelle Gass, president, Starbucks Europe, Middle East and Africa (EMEA), states, "The balance between the universal and the local is much more an art than it is a science. We have global brand standards, and my expectation is leaders who are making decisions have the Starbucks brand in their blood, so they can provide good judgments. I think you have to create an experience where it's undeniably Starbucks." Upon assuming her position as president of EMEA, Michelle toured her region, sitting down with partners and customers to understand their views on the company and its offerings. Michelle reported that she had expected to hear more of a desire for local relevance in Starbucks stores, but instead she had heard quite the opposite. Customers want to connect with the key elements that led to brand growth and love in the United States.

Whether the issue is wide cultural differences among employees, customers, or regions, your "love story" or underlying brand value proposition has to translate and your actions have to connect with those you serve. Starbucks has a fundamental service platform and leadership approach that fuels global connections because the company operates from an understanding of universal needs.

For the sake of our exploration, let me guide you through a discussion of universal human needs with insights into how Starbucks leadership is addressing them. Furthermore, I will examine how you can connect to transcendent human service by focusing on attention, appreciation, and community, as well as comfort and variety.

ATTENTION

Jean-Marie Shields, director, Brand Strategy, at Starbucks, notes, "The number one request or desire of every human around the world is to be seen and heard. The magic of the Starbucks brand comes from a willingness to actively see and hear our customers on many levels." At the individual service level, for example, the "seeing" and "hearing" aspects to which Jean-Marie refers come with an initial greeting that acknowledges a customer's presence and starts a human connection. Karen Joachim, a customer from Albert Lea, Minnesota, notes, "Quite often when I buy something, I feel invisible. Starbucks is a different story. They actually make a momentary but noticeable connection." Diala, a customer in the Mall of Emirates in Dubai, puts it this way: "I want to feel acknowledged whenever I am in a human interaction. Much more of the time at Starbucks than at many other businesses, I feel like I am noticed as a person, not viewed as a transaction."

Clearly, it is a challenge for the leader of any business with high levels of transactions to help employees see the uniqueness of the next customer. Barbara McMaster, district manager, Starbucks Northern Ireland, notes, "As a leader, I am responsible for keeping a spotlight on the next customer. Each customer needs to be recognized in the same manner as our first customer of the day. It's a lot about empathizing and thinking about how I would want to be treated. It's more than eye contact; with time, it is a matter of actually coming to know your repeat customers. Who is this is in front of me? What are their needs? What can I do?" Going beyond an initial greeting that connects, Barbara's comment ratchets up the idea of authentically "knowing" and acknowledging those whom you serve. A greeting may signal that you have seen your customer, but to feel known, those customers have to experience you as having taken the time and interest to connect with their uniqueness.

Names and Controversy

Michelle Gass reports that upon being appointed president of Starbucks EMEA, she and her leadership team sought to strengthen the Starbucks "knowing" or personal connection in her region. "We went back to our universal principal around human connection. What does every person walking the planet have? They have a name. As such, we started considering whether we should ask each customer for their first name and place their name on their cup. We certainly had lots of debate around the possible risks with doing it." Those risks included the possibility that cultural differences might produce resistance in parts of the region. Michelle notes, "We concluded that the benefits were worthy of the attempt, since a loyal customer might now be 'known' as a tall, skinny mocha, but would feel much better walking in our door and having us really 'know' them by saying, 'Hey, Jane, how's your day going today?'"

In the United States, asking customers for their names and placing the names on their cups has not consistently been a required standard, and partners had never been required to place their names on their uniforms. However, in March 2012, Starbucks launched its "names on cups and names on partners" campaign in EMEA. In addition to asking for customers' names, Starbucks baristas began wearing name tags on their aprons. An online video and paid advertisement content introduced the United Kingdom to this concept:

> Have you noticed how everything seems a little impersonal nowadays? We've all become user names, reference numbers and IP addresses. That's why at Starbucks we've decided to do things differently. From now on, we won't refer to you as a 'latte' or a 'mocha', but instead as your folks intended: by your name. Ok, we know it's only a little thing but hey, why don't we buy you a coffee . . . and you can introduce yourself. We're Starbucks. Nice to meet you.

To see the actual commercial, point your web browser to http://tinyurl.com/lecr7d2 or direct your QR reader here:

As predicted, some people in England were skeptical about the "first name" approach to personalization. For example, Chris Hackley, professor of marketing at Royal Holloway, University of London, told the BBC, "Some people might like being called by their first name, but I think many will be indifferent, and some might feel awkward—like it's over-familiar, or a bit of an intrusion into privacy. . . . It's a bogus personalisation of an economic relationship. Friendship needs to be genuine."

While I certainly agree that privacy is paramount for customers and employees today, providing a first name that will be written on a cup or that is placed on a barista's apron is not perceived as a threat by most people. Additionally, customers are free to choose the name they provide or to elect not to offer a name at all. Typically, in cases of resistance, customers will provide playful names or baristas will simply draw something like a smiling face on their cup. While Professor Hackley notes that friendship needs to be genuine, I am of the opinion that Starbucks leaders are seeking a connection that is more personal than a "hey you," but that is less intimate than friendship.

Dirk Nickolaus, Starbucks district manager in Germany, talks about the speed of acceptance for offering names in Germany: "When we first started asking our customers for their first names, it took some people by surprise, and it was a bit challenging for us. Now I hear our customers say, 'Wow! I used to walk in and the baristas would recognize me and know my drink, but now they actually address me by name. It feels welcoming.'"

Despite growing acceptance of the practice of putting names on cups, there are real downside risks, not the least of which are misspelled names or other inadvertent errors. While breakdowns can and will occur in the use of a customer's name, they happen in all aspects of human interaction. The goal of leadership is to create the right environment for human connection to occur and to help staff members manage the inevitable issues that surface. The success of name badges and name seeking in the EMEA region has had additional functional benefits. Michelle Gass notes, "Customers and partners have told me about improved handoff accuracy by having names on cups. It can be quite unsettling if a customer isn't sure if they are grabbing their cup from several on the bar. The last thing you want to do is leave the store and find you've taken the wrong drink. So now your name gives reassurance that you are getting your beverage."

The positive benefits of names on cups and names on partners in EMEA has prompted leaders in other regions to more systematically engage in a similar process. At the Starbucks 2012 Global Leadership Conference in Houston, Cliff Burrows, president, Americas, noted that he had been inspired by Michelle and her team to make names on cups and names on partners a standard practice in the United States, Canada, and Latin America. Cliff added, "It's a way we can innovate. It's a way we can differentiate. And it's a way we can strengthen that relationship between our partners and our customers." As a result of this commitment, Starbucks leadership has developed training tools to strengthen connections with customers by helping partners learn and use the customer's name and personalize the customer's cup. At the center of this training is an appreciation that baristas have an opportunity to build deeper relationships with the people they serve (particularly regular customers) by learning their names and appropriately calling them by name.

Innovation, Differentiation, and Strengthening Relationships

By taking a simple step like asking people for their first names, Starbucks leadership is systematically differentiating the brand. Karen Mishra, marketing professor at Meredith College and co-author of the book *Becoming a Trustworthy Leader*, highlights the power of differentiation through relationships. In the course of my research, I happened upon an online Twitter post from Karen in which she shared her surprise at receiving a birthday note on a Starbucks cup. During a follow-up interview, Karen added, “The partners at my Starbucks know me. Tanya is the manager. We lived in Durham years ago, left for a couple of years, and when we came back, Tanya still remembered me and my husband.” Karen notes that she is impressed by Tanya’s memory for customers’ names and how much she knows about her customers. Karen adds, “When training new hires, Tanya will say, ‘Okay, now, Justin, this is so-and-so, and they’re married to so-and-so, and this is their drink.’” Karen asked Tanya about this ability to remember people, and Tanya responded that people should be remembered and that she makes a point of learning the name of one new person every day. It is in the context of that commitment to “knowing” that Karen posted the microblog entry that caught my eye. On Karen’s birthday, her husband let her sleep in and went to Starbucks to get her coffee. When he was asked where Karen was, her husband mentioned that it was her birthday. Karen notes, “Any

time one of us isn't there, the baristas at that store will write our names and a little note like 'hi' on our cups, but this time it was a special birthday message signed by my 'Starbucks family,' and I just had to share it online."

Because a group of baristas at a single store, led by a manager like Tanya, cared about seeing, hearing, and knowing their customers, Karen was compelled to share a message about the differentiated care she received at Starbucks. Karen's status as a marketing professor and an author on brand trust was probably *not* a consideration for the barista who wrote Karen's name and birthday wish on her cup, but clearly that simple act of acknowledgment has led to a story through which Starbucks itself has been acknowledged.

Are you paying attention to your customers' need to be seen and heard? Would you go so far as to say they feel understood and known? In your business, customer knowledge may require more than remembering names and drink preferences. However, by getting to know your customers, you will probably differentiate yourself through transformative customer relationships.

APPRECIATION

Worldwide, customers want to be appreciated for their business. In fact, one of the most powerful opportunities for building loyalty occurs after the sale. Do your employees say thank you, offer a warm farewell, and invite customers into future opportunities to connect? At a leadership level, are you creating an environment of gratitude and structuring your business to demonstrate appreciation for loyal patronage?

When I wrote my first book about Starbucks in 2006, I had spent the prior two years occasionally talking with the company's leaders about the absence of a corporate loyalty card program.

At the time, the typical response I heard centered on the possibility that such a program might dilute the perceived value of Starbucks products. Like many businesses operating in the robust economy of the late 1990s and early 2000s, Starbucks leadership knew the value of repeat business, but wasn't rewarding customer loyalty. All that changed for Starbucks in June 2008, when the company made its first significant move toward a rewards program. Aimee Johnson, vice president, Digital Commerce, Loyalty and Content at Starbucks, established the rationale for the program by noting the brand was unveiling "bold consumer-facing elements to further enhance the Starbucks Experience and deepen the relationship with our customers." By creating an account, loading a Starbucks Card with funds, and paying an annual membership fee of $25, a customer could participate in the Starbucks rewards program and receive, among other benefits, a 10 percent discount on most purchases, a complimentary birthday beverage, and two hours of free wireless internet (at the time, Wi-Fi was a paid service that was available only at some Starbucks stores—more on that in Chapter 8). Ron Lieber reviewed Starbucks initial effort at loyalty rewards in a 2008 *New York Times* article and noted, "We all want to be recognized for our loyal patronage. . . . Starbucks is a company that others look to as a model. What it does with this program will influence plenty of businesses that deal in higher-dollar products. And that is why I'm glad to report that Starbucks is indeed considering some sort of elite status. It is also studying ways that card use can speed up your visit and is looking for ways to make the giveaways more generous. Big, ambitious loyalty programs evolve over many years. So it will be fascinating to see what Starbucks adds to the mix." As Ron predicted, Starbucks has continued to refine its loyalty reward concept to include special status and streamlined ease of use. Starbucks also did away with paid subscription as a point of entry and expanded the perks associated with membership. As a Gold-level member, I routinely receive announcements and member benefits that complement the free food or beverage item that I receive with each twelfth purchase.

What's noteworthy about the evolving Starbucks reward program, now called My Starbucks Rewards™, is how it addresses not just a need in the United States, but a global desire to be acknowledged as a valued customer. Since launching the program in the United States, Starbucks has progressively rolled out similar reward programs around the world. In 2010, a blogger in Singapore noted, "After many years of not having any sort of rewards/loyalty program . . . [Starbucks] finally launched a card! . . . It's definitely good to be rewarded after being a regular customer for many years."

In announcing its first-quarter results for 2012, Starbucks leadership reported that the company had gained 413,000 new members of its loyalty program in December 2011, increasing total membership to more than 3.7 million. The reward program in China demonstrated exponential growth, with 250,000 participants enrolled since its inception approximately 10 months earlier. In North America, the purchases made under the My Starbucks Rewards loyalty program represent almost 20 percent of Starbucks Card purchases.

Ying, a customer from Bangkok, Thailand, says it best: "I notice when employees say thank you for my business, and I also notice when managers appreciate their employees and leaders appreciate their customers. I see all those things happening at Starbucks. Nowadays, I particularly feel valued and appreciated for my purchases by the loyalty rewards I receive in return." In a world in which so much investment is made in marketing and advertising goods and services, the simple act of saying thank you or rewarding customers for their loyalty can go a long way toward securing their repeat business and emotional engagement.

REFLECTION ON CONNECTION

1. What universal needs for service is your business addressing?
2. When it comes to seeing, hearing, and knowing your customers, what are the strengths and opportunities for your business? Are you connecting with each customer verbally and nonverbally upon first contact? Do you go from listening to customers to customer knowledge on which you can act?
3. Do you have an appreciative business culture? Is that appreciation demonstrated in service interactions through the way managers treat frontline workers and the way leaders craft customer rewards and recognition?

COMMUNITY

John Donne's classic poem "For Whom the Bell Tolls" begins with an observation of the human condition relevant to most business leaders. In it, Donne says, "No man is an island, entire of itself; every man is a piece of the continent, a part of the main." In essence, people may enter your business individually, but many of them seek the opportunity to connect with like-minded individuals to experience the benefits of community.

Some business leaders have a heightened awareness of the human craving for community, while others have failed to help connect customers to something larger than themselves. I vividly remember sitting in a *Fast Company* magazine "Circle of Friends" group in Las Vegas, Nevada, in the late 1990s. In 1997, the founders of the magazine created an opportunity for regular readers to get together to talk about the ideas raised in each issue of the magazine. While that community building at *Fast Company* was fairly innovative at the time, online groups and discussion boards have since proliferated.

Similarly, Starbucks leadership has demonstrated innovation in building a community that consists of customers and partners; in addition, it has added a key element of social activism. Community service involvement occurs year-round at Starbucks, and the leaders set ambitious goals to motivate partners and customers to contribute 1 million hours per year in support of causes that have a meaningful impact. Starbucks has dedicated a website to helping partners and customers connect (community.starbucks.com), giving listings of upcoming projects and blogs and stories of past activities. In addition, the website confers virtual community service badges as a way of recognizing those who progress from being a new volunteer up through the level of community change maker.

In addition to its year-round efforts, for the past several years, Starbucks has declared April to be the Global Month of Service. In April 2012, nearly 60,000 Starbucks partners and customers, local organizations, and community members provided more than 700,000 individual community service acts that made a difference in more than 34 countries. More than 230,000 hours of service were donated, and 2,100 community service projects were completed in the one-month time frame. The global resonance of a program that builds purposeful community is reflected in the 50 percent increase in projects completed and 45 percent increase in volunteered hours when compared to prior-year levels.

Clearly, the level of participation in the Starbucks Global Month of Service is high and growing, and the projects are producing substantial positive benefits. For example, the 2012 Global Month of Service included projects such as 250 volunteers in Vancouver, British Columbia, building pathways, storage shelves, and cubicles in support of the Strathcona Community Centre to assist inner-city youth programs and 395 volunteers in Shanghai, China, sprucing up the Gumei community in the Minhang District while assisting local residents to reuse waste material and engage in organic gardening.

In addition to mobilizing direct opportunities to serve in the community, Starbucks leaders have engaged customers to determine who should receive a portion of Starbucks grant money. A 2012 program referred to as "Vote.Give.Grow" allowed Starbucks Card holders to register at www.votegivegrow.com. Once they were registered, customers could vote weekly throughout the month of April concerning the recipients of $4 million in grant funding from the Starbucks Foundation. While other forms of direct corporate giving will be discussed in Chapter 11, suffice it to say that Starbucks leaders continue to look for ways to partner with customers to do "good" in the world.

In Asia, for example, customers were able to connect with members of their community through purchases of Muan Jai®, a mix of arabica coffees from Thailand and other Pacific island countries. By purchasing this coffee blend, customers in Thailand and elsewhere helped improve the environment and the socioeconomic conditions of hill-tribe coffee farmers and their families in northern Thailand. A portion of the proceeds of the Muan Jai blend was contributed directly to the farmers. Not so coincidentally, in the Northern Thai language, Muan Jai means "wholehearted happiness."

One additional example that had reach both within the United States and across international borders was an alliance forged between Starbucks leadership and the HandsOn Network to create the "I'm In!" campaign. After U.S. president Barack Obama was inaugurated for his first term, Starbucks offered free beverages to individuals who pledged five hours of volunteer time through the HandsOn Network. The HandsOn Network is a subsidiary of the Points of Light Foundation, with 250 volunteer action centers in 16 countries worldwide. The response to the "I'm In!" campaign was more than 1.25 million pledged volunteer hours worldwide.

Jeremy Tolmen, a customer in San Diego, California, reports how he connects with Starbucks through its commitment to community. "I was in Starbucks at a launch party for a non-profit I work with, and I had my non-profit's shirt on. I started talking to a Starbucks partner named Kate. She asked about our non-profit and if we needed coffee for our event. It turns out Kate was the store manager, and she ended up donating all of the coffee for our event, along with five or six boxes of Tazo tea, and all the additional supplies we needed for our coffee bar. She even put together a Starbucks basket to raffle off; it had a pound of coffee in it and two mugs. I think it's amazing that a humongous corporation like that can be so generous and connect on such a small community-based level." *Amazing*, *generous*, *connection*, and *community*: Jeremy's words capture the unique and powerful opportunity that leaders have to forge special relationships with customers by community building. All leaders have the opportunity to look at their businesses as offering more than products or services. With good stewardship and a willingness to think beyond the tangible benefits and attributes of their product offerings, leaders can create places of belonging and purposefulness for their customers.

COMFORT AND VARIETY

It seems that humans have contrary needs for both predictable comfort and variations from the predictable. In other words, we want our comforts to remain stable and yet to have sufficient variety to avert boredom. In a social context, irrespective of where people live, they want to manage the inconsistencies of life by having what Starbucks offers, namely, a pleasing physical location where they can relax, unwind, and savor their favorite beverage. It is a place of comfort for locals and travelers alike.

Helen Wang, author of *The Chinese Dream: The Rise of the World's Largest Middle Class and What It Means to You*, notes that even in countries like China, where the historically preferred beverage has been tea, Starbucks has deployed staff training and inviting physical locations to foster aspiration, comfort, and success: "The chic interior, comfortable lounge chairs, and upbeat music are not only differentiators that set Starbucks apart from the competition, but also have strong appeal to younger generations who fantasize about Western coffee culture as a symbol of modern lifestyle. Starbucks [also] understands the value of its global brand and has taken steps to maintain brand integrity. One of Starbucks best practices is to send their best baristas from established markets to new markets and train new employees. These baristas act as brand ambassadors to help establish the Starbucks culture in new locations and ensure that service at each local store meets their global standards."

Uniformly executing against brand standards and consistently creating a welcoming physical environment allow people to develop daily habits and rituals that comfort them. One blogger noted, "I suppose I'm a creature of habit. . . . I just run through Starbucks on my way to work. . . . I do have to admit, as a single person, it's nice to start your morning with a friendly face that actually knows you. A few of us have developed a strange little Drive Thru window friendship."

While many of us lead companies where customer contact is not a repeated daily occurrence, rituals can still be created around seasonal product offerings or even annual events. For Starbucks, these seasonal rituals include such things as the global rollout of Starbucks® "red cups" to coincide with the Thanksgiving and Christmas holiday season in the United States. The worldwide appeal of the red cups is evidenced by a website titled countdowntoredcups.com, which is not affiliated with Starbucks.

Even before there is an announcement of the cup's release date, the website posts wording like "we're still waiting for official confirmation from Starbucks, but our guess is that it starts November 2nd." As a result, a countdown clock clicks away based on the website owner's best guess.

In addition to the countdown to red cups website, the internet is flooded with photos that people share when they hold their first red cup of the season, as well as with tweets and blog posts like, "Today is the day! . . . we stopped by our favorite neighborhood Starbucks and there. . . low and behold . . . the Mother Ship . . . Red Cup Day. That alone just makes me happy. I don't know what it is about those happy red cups but for me it marks the beginning of the holiday season and just puts me in the mood for cookie baking, snuggling by the fire and enjoying your family and friends. . . . I did a happy dance with the baristas, (my husband tried to hide and pretend he doesn't know me)." When you have people doing happy dances with your team members, you know you have produced a comforting ritual.

The allure of the red cup not only results from its seasonal presence but emerges from the changing design of the cup from year to year. It is the combination of the predictable and the anticipation of change that strengthens interest. Surely you have grown tired of brands that provide predictable products but fail to add new or exciting offerings. Or, by contrast, maybe you have lost your interest in a company when it removed an iconic product to accommodate an endless parade of "just arrived" or "new this year" items. Thanks to a strong core set of offerings, seasonal introductions, and a small set of enticing new products, Starbucks leadership drives customer loyalty, comfort, and enthusiasm. Tracy Olsen, a U.S. citizen teaching in Korea, notes, "I love Starbucks. It's the only place I can get a chai tea latte in Daegu. It's the place where I can get a comforting experience of home and enjoy new and interesting products. I can also enjoy some products that are unique to the culture of which I am a part." While Chapter 7 will look at how Starbucks adds unique elements to product selection, environment, and service delivery, Tracy's comment reflects the comfort derived from the right mix of predictable and varied offerings.

REFLECTION ON CONNECTION

1. What do your employees and customers value? What causes, events, or educational opportunities might serve to bring together a community of customers or a unity of customers and employees? How might you play a facilitating role in building social connections among like-minded people?
2. What aspects of your products or services create comfort or a sense of stability for your customers? How can you enhance the comfort aspects of your business? What products at the core of your business should remain constant?
3. What brands do you view as striking an effective balance between consistent delivery of legacy items or services with a mix of new product or service offerings? What percentage of stable to new items best suits the needs of your customers?

THE PROOF IS IN THE CAFÉ

Let's assume you have identified ways in which you can serve underlying human needs through your products, services, and community involvement. Furthermore, let's assume that you have just launched a branch of your business in a new setting (possibly on the other side of your state or even on another continent). How do you know whether your brand will be well received? Moreover, how will you know whether you are creating a sustainable connection?

For Starbucks leaders, initial acceptance in a new market can often be seen in the enthusiasm of people who anticipate a store's opening or by the lines that occur at its launch. In October of 2012, for example, Starbucks, accompanied by its joint-venture partner Tata Coffee Group, made its long-awaited entrance into India with a flagship store in Mumbai.

Starbucks store in Mumbai, India.

Approximately a week and a half after the opening, Shyamantha Asokan wrote the following in an article for the *Guardian*: "During the past 10 days, sweaty queues of up to 50 people have formed outside an old colonial building in downtown Mumbai, while a security guard operates a one-in-one-out policy. These hopefuls are not trying to get into an edgy new nightclub or shake hands with a visiting politician. They are waiting for up to an hour to go to Starbucks." No celebrities and no edgy entertainment venue; just the first Starbucks to come to India.

Customer Hazel Hardijzer understands the eagerness with which people anticipate a Starbucks opening in markets around the world. According to Hazel, "Starbucks opened at [Amsterdam's] Schiphol airport around 2007. I remember that getting our 'own' Starbucks was something very special for us. Having traveled quite a bit by that time, I had experienced Starbucks in other countries and could report that I had 'been there, done that' and enjoyed the unique treat of the Starbucks coffee experience." When customers are eager to get "their" own new store or are willing to wait an hour to get through the line at a store opening, you know that your product has appeal. But as the hype and novelty wear off, will you be able to sustain the enthusiasm and keep the cash register ringing?

For Starbucks, international success is validated by the company's financial sustainability or growth in many regions of the world. Much like the story of Starbucks success in the United States, growth came fairly swiftly during periods of global economic prosperity and positive brand reputation (although there have been exceptions in an occasional market; see Chapter 7). Even during sustained global economic challenges, Starbucks has been experiencing stability throughout North America and Europe, with strong growth noted in Latin America and Asia. For example, in 2012, Starbucks launched its first store in Costa Rica as a joint-venture partnership with Corporación de Franquicias Americanas and also opened a Farmer Support Center in Colombia. Latin American growth plans also include hundreds of new stores in Brazil and more than 300 new openings in Argentina and Mexico by 2015. Pan Kwan Yuk, a reporter and commentator who specializes in emerging markets, suggests, "As in the U.S. before Starbucks came along, there are few places in Latin America where one can just sit with a book or a laptop and while the day away." From the standpoint of stability in the rest of the Americas, Starbucks achieved the landmark of 25 years in Canada in 2012. Canada is Starbucks oldest and largest international market. In 2013, Starbucks marked 42 years of operation in the United States, with nearly 11,000 stores across all 50 states.

Some of the greatest growth of the brand is occurring throughout Asia, with 500 new stores planned to open in fiscal year 2013. More than half of those openings are in China alone. Also, 2013 marks the opening of Starbucks 1,000th store in Japan, the first international location of the brand outside of North America.

According to a report in *MSN Money* in August of 2012, Asia was contributing approximately 13 percent of Starbucks profits. At the time, John Culver, president, Starbucks China and Asia Pacific, noted, "With high-store margins and low-store penetration, given the size of the country we are in the very early stages of what we think this market can ultimately reach." China will probably eclipse Canada as Starbucks largest market outside the United States in 2014.

Overall, at the start of fiscal year 2012, Starbucks anticipated 1,200 new store openings (representing growth of approximately three stores per day), with the bulk of them likely to occur outside of the United States. These numbers suggest that the Starbucks connection is robust and thriving globally, thanks in large measure to the leadership's ability to position the brand to meet the product and the universal emotional, social, and lifestyle needs of customers from very diverse backgrounds. Even with that strong universal platform, however, Starbucks leaders, like those in every successful broad-sweeping company, have had to find ways to enhance the local relevance of their offerings—which happens to be our exploration in Chapter 7.

CONNECTING POINTS

- Customers want to be seen and heard.
- While cultural difference may affect how you demonstrate it, a willingness to seek personal connections with customers will help your business stand out from your competitors.
- A goal of the leadership should be to create the right environment for human connection to occur and to help staff members manage the inevitable challenges that emerge during human interactions.
- By getting to know your customers, you are likely to differentiate yourself from the many brands that try to sell without listening.
- One of the most powerful opportunities for building loyalty occurs after the sale, with your employees saying thank you, offering a warm farewell, and inviting customers into future opportunities to connect.
- Leaders must create an environment of gratitude and structure the business to demonstrate appreciation for loyal patronage.
- All leaders have the opportunity to look at their businesses as offering more than products or services. Leaders can create places of belonging and purposefulness for their customers.
- Demonstrate innovation in building a community that consists of both your customers and your

employees; in addition, consider adding an element of social activism.

- Human beings want their comforts to remain stable, and yet to have sufficient variety to avert boredom.
- While many of us lead companies where customer contact is infrequent, rituals can still be created around seasonal product offerings or even annual events.

CHAPTER 7

Respect, Celebrate, and Customize: Listening and Innovating to Meet Local, Regional, and Global Needs

Our Similarities bring us to a common ground; Our Differences allow us to be fascinated by each other.

TOM ROBBINS

Market expansions are challenging, and companies often overreach or fail to understand the local needs of their new market. While this chapter will explore the challenges that Starbucks has faced as it has attempted to ensure its relevance on a global stage, let's take a quick glimpse at major lessons learned from Intuit, the company behind the very successful U.S. product Quicken tax preparation software, which was started in 1983.

In the 10 years following the product's U.S. launch, Intuit successfully expanded into the Canadian and British markets. Shortly thereafter, the firm's leaders launched the product in other European countries, South America, Mexico, and Japan. Despite considerable media attention at its introduction in those countries, Intuit's sales dropped after the initial orders were filled. As a result, the company pulled back its operations in all countries except the United Kingdom, Canada, and the United States. In explaining the failed expansion efforts, the founder of Intuit, Scott Cook, noted, "The root cause was baked into our early decision where we didn't build these products based on a deep study of the countries. We built them based on what we had in the U.S. . . . The reason we succeeded in the U.S. was because we studied the potential customer better than anyone else. We knew them cold and built a product so native to the way they worked. . . . We didn't do that overseas; we gave them the product we had built in the U.S." Upon pulling out of these markets, Intuit avoided global expansion for more than a decade. As Scott Cook notes, when Intuit renewed its global growth plan, it benefited from the lessons it had learned during its first large-scale foray, this time "doing it the right way, hiring people locally who can go in and understand the customer cold and design what the solutions should be, not what they are stuck with from the US." Since Intuit revised its approach, the company has successfully expanded into Singapore, India, South Africa, and New Zealand.

This chapter takes you through a series of key approaches and adjustments that Starbucks leadership has deployed to maximize the local relevance of products, services, and physical environment. The journey begins with a regionalized model of operations. The chapter also explores the role of local business partnerships and outlines specific methods for customizing products and services to address culturally specific wants and needs.

DECENTRALIZATION AND REVITALIZATION

Prior to July 2011, Starbucks operated as two centralized business entities, Starbucks U.S. and Starbucks International, both of which were led from Seattle, Washington. In 2011, a dramatic shift in operations took place to address the mounting challenges and to seize emerging global opportunities. Starbucks senior leaders decentralized and separated into a three-region model. Earlier in this book, I've shared stories from the leaders in each of these regions, but for clarity, the leaders and regions are as follows:

> *China and Asia Pacific Rim*; president, John Culver. Countries included in this region are Australia, China, Hong Kong, India, Indonesia, Japan, Macau, Malaysia, New Zealand, Philippines, Singapore, South Korea, Taiwan, Thailand, and Vietnam.
>
> *Europe, Middle East and Africa*; president, Michelle Gass. The countries in EMEA include Austria, Bahrain, Belgium, Bulgaria, Cyprus, the Czech Republic, Denmark, Egypt, Finland, France, Germany, Greece, Hungary, Ireland, Jordan, Kuwait, Lebanon, Morocco, Netherlands, Norway, Oman, Poland, Portugal, Qatar, Romania, Russia, Saudi Arabia, Spain, Sweden, Switzerland, Turkey, United Arab Emirates, and the United Kingdom.
>
> *Americas*; president, Cliff Burrows. The region includes Argentina, Aruba, the Bahamas, Brazil, Canada, Chile, Costa Rica, Curaçao, El Salvador, Guatemala, Mexico, Peru, Puerto Rico, and the United States.

The impetus behind this Starbucks restructuring was to create a model that was less U.S.-centric but that still leveraged the best of Starbucks in ways that are relevant in global markets. This restructuring gives regional presidents a geographic area for which they are responsible and gives them full authority to develop strategic plans that address business objectives in their areas. Michelle Gass, president, EMEA, demonstrates the regional nature of business strategy development: "It's fair to say that the

EMEA business is the lowest profit unit of the three, whether you are calculating profit on an absolute or percentage basis." After spending a considerable amount of time traveling around the region, Michelle and her leadership team created a strategy based on observations and perceived needs in their geographic area, including such things as exploring the local relevance of coffee offerings, building inspirational store environments, and attempting to increase the "daily ritual" of coffee by enhancing access and availability consistent with the lifestyle of customers across the region. Later in the chapter, we will look specifically at changes made to espresso drinks in EMEA, store redesign approaches, and the enhanced availability of Starbucks products and beverages for people on the go. However, for the purpose of this discussion, senior leaders like Michelle are no longer attempting to manage a global business from the Starbucks Support Center in Seattle, Washington, and are better positioned, with full independence, to do what is needed in their regions. Certainly, the challenges faced by John Culver in the China and Asia Pacific market are quite different from those faced by Michelle in Europe, the Middle East, and Africa. For example, John has to help Starbucks be viewed as an employer of choice in China and skillfully steward expansion and distribution opportunities in India and greater China while also exploring many opportunities in emerging regional markets like Vietnam.

In addition to having a new leadership structure in the regions and creating autonomous business planning, this reorganization continues to afford leaders like Michelle, John, and Cliff the ability to share best practices that can prove helpful in other areas of the world. We saw how well this worked in Chapter 6 when Cliff Burrows, president, Starbucks Americas, adopted the "names on partners and names on cups" approach that Michelle had deployed in EMEA.

While repositioning the leadership to generate local oversight has its advantages, it is not a panacea for global success.

Each business leader at Starbucks must still balance relevant cultural needs with a recognizable Starbucks brand connection. The objective is not to subsume the Starbucks brand beneath cultural differences, nor is it to deliver an Americanized Starbucks Experience that overpowers the needs of the customers in a local market. In fact, researchers have suggested that brands like Starbucks both shape communities and are shaped by local cultures. Craig Thompson and Zeynep Arsel, writing in the *Journal of Consumer Research*, note, "In recent years, anthropological studies have built a strong empirical case . . . [that] consumers often appropriate the meanings of global brands to their own ends, creatively adding new cultural associations, dropping incompatible ones, and transforming others to fit into local cultural and lifestyle patterns. . . . From this perspective, the interjection of global brands into local cultures paradoxically produces heterogeneity as global brands take on a variety of localized meanings." In essence, all successful brands must realize that they need to be shaped by local culture and, in turn, that they are a force that shapes the cultures of those they serve.

FINDING LOCAL PARTNERS

In the beginning of this chapter, I highlighted the initial challenges Intuit faced in its global expansion efforts. In repositioning the brand for success, founder Scott Cook suggested that getting global growth right means "hiring people locally who can go in and understand the customer cold and design what the solutions should be." At Starbucks, hiring is extremely important in each market, but so is the selection of joint-venture business partners. Starbucks often must carefully vet and rely on business allies to bring an awareness of difficult-to-discern cultural subtleties as well as operational knowledge of needed business practices, optimal real estate positioning, and even local consumer behavior.

In 2007, while I was speaking and consulting across India, I repeatedly faced questions like, "When is Starbucks coming to India?" My typical response was, "I suspect when the company finds the right local business partner to assure its success here." Given that India has a young population (median age around 25 years) of 1.2 billion people who have been exposed to a growing café culture in local coffeehouses, it has long been an attractive market for Starbucks. In January 2011, Starbucks leadership deepened this exploration through a nonbinding memorandum of understanding with Tata Coffee. Ultimately, this relationship resulted in a joint-venture partnership arrangement.

Tata is a public company that is traded on the Bombay Stock Exchange. It is part of the Tata Group, a multinational conglomerate operating in seven business sectors in more than 80 countries across six continents. Tata Coffee was founded in 1922 and has been described as the "largest integrated coffee plantation company in the world." The partnership with Tata not only provides Starbucks with an opportunity to leverage cultural relevance but also created a sourcing and roasting platform with supply chain opportunities for procuring green arabica coffee beans from Tata Coffee plantations and roasting those beans at existing Tata roasting facilities.

After Starbucks opened its first store in Mumbai (followed a week later by the opening of three additional stores), Howard Schultz was also asked why it had taken Starbucks so long to enter India. His answer echoed the importance of waiting until it had secured an arrangement with Tata to warrant the substantial risk and investment: "[India] is a very complex market to enter. At one point we thought we could come here alone and we underestimated the complexity. But once we met the people from Tata, we realized overnight that the assets were so complementary between Tata and Starbucks that together we could co-author a very unique strategy—bring Starbucks in India and over a time build a very substantial significant business together."

Howard's answer not only highlights the role of partnership selection but also suggests the importance of the patient, long-term commitment required to achieve success in a global setting. John Culver, president, Starbucks China and Asia Pacific, shares, "Success in the global marketplace is not instantaneous. Your global partners and the communities you enter need to know that you are committed to their long-term growth and development. They want a good corporate citizen who will make them better and who will go through ups and downs to achieve sustainable success and positive outcomes. If you consistently provide these things, those partners and communities will make you better over the long term." As it specifically relates to the Starbucks joint venture in India, Howard Schultz adds, Tata and Starbucks "are bringing an unparalleled experience to India customers. We are investing for the long term and see great potential for accelerated growth in India." Careful selection of business partners, decentralized leadership, patient execution of strategy that integrates your brand essence with locally relevant needs, and a commitment to the long term is quite the formula for success beyond your hometown.

STRIKING A BALANCE THROUGH THE PHYSICAL ENVIRONMENT

Many brands enter communities and appear "out of place" simply because they either do not understand or have not attempted to integrate the physical properties or history of the new community. Kimberlee Sherman, program manager, Global Design and Construction Support Services, acknowledges that for a time Starbucks was not adapting its store designs to provide local relevance. "We were becoming very ubiquitous, and independent coffeehouses were able to distinguish themselves in local communities by providing interesting spaces. Their locations were more contemporary and relevant to the communities they served. We had to admit that we needed to update our design approach. After the economic downturn, we started to really reevaluate the uniqueness and fit of our design concepts."

As a result of this reevaluation process, Starbucks design leaders crafted a more customizable approach to store design. During its high-growth period, Starbucks did benefit from consistency of store presentation and economies of scale. By replicating store designs, Starbucks could purchase tables, chairs, and other fixtures in a cost-effective way; however, the stores began to look more similar and local relevance was minimized. This cookie-cutter approach to design probably detracted from the specialness of the Starbucks Experience and had an impact on customer loyalty. More freedom for unique design has been a component of the turnaround strategy. As a result, Starbucks has developed a scalable, malleable, and innovative solution that began with store design concepts referred to as heritage, artisan, and regional modern.

Kimberlee adds, "We take what we learn from concept store tests and harvest the great ideas, baking those key learnings into standard offerings for our core stores. Within each of those concept styles, there is a lot of variety in the furniture and fixtures that a local store designer can select. We have a design resource center website which is a one-stop shop for designers anywhere in the world. At that site, designers can find design guidelines and also select store elements to fit and inspire the community to be served. Then they can provide more uniqueness with local custom artwork, finishes, and the like." From Kimberlee's perspective, this blended approach, with standard items and opportunity for local variation, serves a central objective. Kimberlee continues, "We wanted to be locally relevant. We want the design to work for the customers who use each individual store. Designers need to understand the architecture of the store, the neighborhood, the customer base, and the competition. They look for anything historical or interesting about the architecture that they can use versus eliminate. Just like our baristas customize the drinks for our customers, we're customizing solutions for our regions and our markets to make the third-place environment suit them."

To better understand how Starbucks designers make stores fit with local communities, we need only look at the redesigns made prior to the 2012 Olympic Games in England. Thom Breslin, director, Design, Starbucks UK, suggests that a redesign process can sometimes be disruptive for both partners and customers. Thom sees this process as needing to drive functional, financial, and creative returns that will justify this disruptive investment. Thus, he suggests that local use patterns must first be addressed: "Considering local cultural influences is an important layer of our design process to ensure market relevance. For us, it starts with listening and observing the needs of our partners and customers. It's about communicating up front, talking to customers, listening to partners, and it's also seeing things through the lens of that collective experience. Our partners spend a great deal of time in this environment, so if we fail to design a relevant experience for them, it's hard to create a physical space that allows them to effectively connect with our customers. Design is about supporting neighborhoods with great-looking stores that surpass community ambitions and needs where people are able to develop an emotional connection with our brand."

There are many examples of Starbucks integrating brand connection with local building design; however, for our purposes, let's look at the Dazaifutenmangu Ometesando store in Dazaifu, Japan. The space was designed by Kengo Kuma and Associates; it integrates aspects of traditional Japanese and Chinese architecture (piling small items from the ground up) and uses more than 2,000 wooden batons to create a woven lattice. According to an article in *Dezeen* magazine, the "location of this Starbucks is somehow characteristic, as it stands on the main approach to the Dazaifutenmangu, one of the most major shrines in Japan. Established in 919 A.D., the shrine has been worshiped as 'the God for Examination,' and receives about 2 million visitors a year who wish their success. . . . The project aimed to make a structure that harmonizes with such townscape, using a unique system of weaving thin woods diagonally."

While store design must have functional and local relevance to the communities being served, often the products served in those settings must also change to fit with local preferences. At Starbucks, product variations typically occur with food offerings and in some cases through beverage innovation.

INNOVATING AND EVOLVING PRODUCT

Have you had a black sesame green tea or a mooncake at Starbucks? If not, you probably don't live near or haven't visited a Starbucks in China. Belinda Wong, Starbucks president, China, noted, "Our customers can definitely expect to see more locally relevant innovations across our food and beverage offerings." The company's local food and beverage innovations are far too numerous to list here, but they have included items like Murg Tikka (chicken cooked in a tandoori oven) in India, Azuki Matcha Frappuccino® blended beverage (matcha green tea, sweet red beans, and a sprinkle of kinako or soybean powder) in Japan, pão de queijo (traditional cheese bread) in Brazil, and Mozaik Pasta (a favorite local chocolate cake) in Turkey.

Barbara McMaster, district manager in Northern Ireland, shares how customized items can fit an important taste preference in a region. "We're doing work to constantly evolve our food offerings and to provide choices that make sense in England and here in Northern Ireland. One example is our evolution of the bacon butty, a sandwich that people often enjoy with a cup of coffee and which serves as a comfort food. We originally positioned it as a morning item, but as a result of customers' requests, it is now available all day. It made sense to add the bacon butty to our lineup, and we did consumer research to assure we are providing the taste experience our customers are looking for."

While many of Starbucks localized products are items that are unique to the preferences of a region, Samantha Yarwood, director of marketing, Starbucks Switzerland and Austria, adds, "At times we simply need to make a few adjustments to our traditional offerings to accommodate local appetites. Customers in Switzerland and Austria often come to us for an American-style experience and are looking for high-quality American-style beverages and food categories like muffins, donuts, and cheesecake. In our region, and in others throughout Europe, American pancakes are served with honey, syrup, or fruit, even if pancakes aren't part of a typical menu in Starbucks in the United States."

Clearly there are trade-offs in seeking local relevance. For all the gains derived from connecting with local preferences, customers have many other choices for local fare. Brands like Starbucks

REFLECTION ON CONNECTION

1. Are you seeking to sell your same products to customers in new markets, or are you understanding the needs of those markets and tailoring your solutions to be relevant to them? How far can and do you go to achieve local relevance?
2. How effectively have you sought partnerships and repositioned your leadership structure to achieve relevance in new markets?
3. Have you created a "sense of place" in your new markets such that you can blend your brand with local needs?

must also consider whether they can execute local offerings at a level of quality consistent with that of their core products.

HOW FAR CAN YOU GO?

The localized food and beverage items discussed thus far involve either new market-specific product innovations or adjustments of important but not core products. While those changes are guided by consumer research, certainly some products, like the recipe for Starbucks lattes or Starbucks® Espresso Roast, can't possibly be changed, even if local consumer sentiment favors a modification. Or can they?

Kris Engskov, managing director, Starbucks UK and Ireland, addresses a rather historic change in lattes in his region: "People drink Starbucks lattes throughout the world, and it's our top-selling beverage. Historically, we've held to the notion that our latte, like all of our core coffee offerings, should be the same everywhere all the time." Despite that traditional view, Kris notes that Starbucks in the UK and Ireland were hearing from customers that they wanted a "stronger" latte, and over a five-year period, stores in the region had noted an approximately 60 percent increase in customers adding an extra shot of espresso to their lattes. Kris continues the product evolution story by noting, "We considered making our latte stronger by defaulting to an extra shot of espresso. We test-marketed that idea, and that recipe was a success—a success not only in the taste tests with our customers, but also in tests with a key competitor's customers; 60 percent of the competitor's customers liked our latte better than the latte being prepared by the competitor. So at no extra charge, we changed our tall latte to a two-shot espresso drink." Shortly thereafter, a headline in the London *Telegraph* read, "Starbucks' UK sales boosted by extra shot of espresso." The article added that a 9 percent increase in latte and cappuccino sales occurred even in "cash-strapped" and "difficult economic times."

PRINCIPLE 4

MOBILIZE THE CONNECTION

Up to this point in the book, we have primarily examined the bond that Starbucks forges with its customers in the context of Starbucks stores. While "brick-and-mortar" connections tend to be terrific opportunities to develop personal face-to-face relationships, much of today's commerce is happening outside of a traditional retail building. People are making purchases while they are sitting in front of a computer or are engaging with brands through their mobile devices. This business principle, "Mobilize the Connection," looks at how Starbucks strengthens the relationships formed in Starbucks stores and extends them into the home, office, and supermarket experiences of customers. Moreover, it examines how Starbucks leaders leverage technology to integrate a multichannel relationship with their customer base.

Many business leaders have a love/hate relationship with technology. On the one hand, technological advances offer great business opportunities. On the other hand, the infrastructure costs associated with technology shifts and the rapid pace of technological change pose strategic and operational challenges. Although some business leaders fall in love with technology for technology's sake, Starbucks love of its customers and its appreciation for the relationship that those customers have with technology leads to a functional use of digital, social, and mobile tools. In the words of Howard Schultz, you have to "run with people in the way they run their lives." Chapter 8, titled "Growing the Connection Through Technology," explores how the leadership has improved the in-store experience through the use of technologies such as the Starbucks Digital Network. It also examines the comprehensive digital strategy that Starbucks deploys, including internal assets like mobile apps and external resources like social media.

Chapter 9, "Personal Relationships Translate: Sharing the Love from People to Products," explores the multichannel strategy adopted by Starbucks leaders that has resulted in Starbucks products being available for customers not only in Starbucks stores but also in their homes, their offices, other businesses, and virtually anywhere they go. Building on concepts from the prior chapter, "Personal Relationships Translate" looks at how technology and marketing can interface to encourage customers to explore offerings across product channels. Chapter 9 is also designed to assist you as you consider ways to present products to your customers in as many locations as you can reasonably manage. Starbucks is no longer just a coffee brand or a company limited by its brick-and-mortar footprint. Just as the Starbucks logo was redesigned to release the siren from the circle that confined her, the Starbucks connection has emerged beyond the boundaries of the Starbucks store.

CHAPTER 8

Growing the Connection Through Technology

Information technology and business are becoming inextricably interwoven. I don't think anybody can talk meaningfully about one without talking about the other.

BILL GATES

In a 2012 *Time* magazine survey, people were forced to choose one item to take to work: their wallet, their lunch, or their mobile device. The result: 66 percent chose their mobile device over their lunch, and 44 percent chose their mobile device over their wallet. In the same study, 68 percent of adults report that they sleep with their mobile phone next to them, and 89 percent say that they couldn't make it through a single day without using their mobile device.

In my 2006 book *The Starbucks Experience*, I spent little time talking about technology or the future of mobile communication and interconnectivity. Instead, I shared how Starbucks leaders positioned their coffeehouse as the "third place," an environment that provided a desired alternative to customers' first place (home) and their second place (work). In the intervening years, Starbucks leaders have widened their focus to engage customers in the first and second places (more on that in Chapter 9), as well as to innovate connections in a mobile world that essentially encompasses all the places where customers find themselves other than work, home, or Starbucks stores. While I was discussing this evolution with Howard, he shared, "We started out before there was a digital revolution; the third place was our stores. Our mobile focus has evolved to the point where everyone is getting primary information and communicating in a way that was nonexistent before. I don't think any enterprise or organization can exist in the future without having a primary relevant position in the minds and hearts of people through these mechanisms, whether it is technology or software. I think we are off to a very good start, but we also recognize it could be fleeting. As such we must continue to make the investments and understand what is relevant. Many brands will come and go in terms of relevancy and trust in the digital world, as trust and relevance will be harder to maintain digitally than through a physical presence."

Starbucks has become a recognized leader in digital platforms, social media engagement, and innovation. For example, Starbucks was selected by *Forbes* as one of the top 20 innovation companies in 2011 and was recognized by General Sentiment's QSR MediaMatch report in 2012 as having the highest impact value ($111 million) among the quick-service restaurant sector. Impact value assesses the reach of a brand and determines a monetary estimate based on the broad discussions and overall exposure garnered by a company. Additionally, the Starbucks Card mobile app received the Wireless Application and Mobile Media (WAMM) award as Best Retail, Shopping and Commerce Application in 2011.

At the core of Starbucks successful digital strategy are several interrelated areas that all business leaders should consider when they are attempting to connect with customers from the broad mass market to the one-to-one. The five key components of this digital strategy are (1) commerce, (2) company-owned web and mobile channels, (3) loyalty/customer relationship management (CRM)/targeted database, (4) social media, and (5) paid digital marketing.

COMMERCE, STARBUCKS WEB AND MOBILE CHANNELS, AND LOYALTY/CRM/ TARGETED DATABASE

One of the largest components of Starbucks current mobile strategy is anchored to commerce and connects through the Starbucks Card. Even before Starbucks initiated the loyalty card program discussed in Chapter 6, the leaders had created a Starbucks gift card. To understand the dimensionality of the card business, let's assume that you buy a $10 Starbucks Card as a gift for a friend. Your friend can use the $10 and simply throw the card away. Alternatively, he might add value to the card while he is in a Starbucks store and continue to use it as a prepayment card. Finally, he may register the card online (thus becoming part of the Starbucks loyalty program). Once the card is registered on the Starbucks website, your friend can either manually or automatically replenish the Starbucks Card from a credit card that he places on file or add value to the card at the register. Given these options, the Starbucks Card itself represents a multibillion-dollar business, with half of Starbucks Card customers using it solely as a gift card and the other half using it as their own loyalty and prepayment mechanism.

As of January 2011, customers in the United States with an iPhone, iPod touch, or BlackBerry were able to download the Starbucks Card mobile app, add their Starbucks Cards, track rewards, and reload their cards through either PayPal or a credit card. Subsequently, Starbucks enhanced the app's capability to include phones with Android-based operating systems, merged it with an existing app so that it includes a store locator and other features, and expanded its availability outside of the United States. Adam Brotman, chief digital officer, offers a sense of the importance of these enhancements and the challenges involved in them: "It was hugely important for us to extend our mobile pay app to Android and integrate functions of our existing apps into one seamless app experience. Android took off fast as we were developing our original iPhone and BlackBerry apps, so we worked as quickly as possible to produce a well-integrated app for this exploding population of mobile phone customers."

Through these efforts, Starbucks leaders produced a complex, yet easy-to-use, mobile payment and social app that also offers a rich value-added experience for Android and iOS mobile platforms. From the standpoint of ease of mobile payment, a customer simply selects "touch to pay" and positions her phone for a Starbucks barista to scan. In addition to ease of payment, customers can track purchases and see their progress toward rewards, receive messages in a mobile inbox, garner information on food and beverages, and select e-gifts.

The Starbucks mobile app was the first widespread mobile payment program of its kind in the United States, and it reflects the leadership's willingness to take a practical and innovative step into the mobile arena. Starbucks leaders did not attempt to declare a technical standard in mobile payment, as they believed that future standards would probably emerge from credit card companies working with businesses like Square, Google, Amazon, PayPal, Microsoft, and Apple. Instead, Starbucks leaders took a pragmatic and adaptable approach, utilizing the most readily available technology at the time—the 2D barcode. As part of a large-scale upgrade of the company's Point of Sale system (POS), Starbucks leaders purchased 2D scanners and integrated them into the POS.

After extensive testing prior to the initial launch, Adam Brotman notes, "Mobile pay is the fastest way to make a purchase at Starbucks. Not only is the transaction quick but the line isn't slowed down with customers reloading their cards. It's better for everybody. Our customers are voting with their hands and they want mobile payment." Within approximately a year and a half of starting to accept mobile payments, Starbucks had captured more than 100 million transactions, and by late 2012, it was capturing more than 2 million mobile payment transactions per week. Adam adds, "Mobile pay is accelerating, but we also realize that not every customer is going to be a member of our loyalty program. Not everyone is going to have a Starbucks Card and want to pay with it." Although Starbucks Card transactions are 25 percent of Starbucks tender, leaders wanted to give customers more choices. In essence, they wished to reach a larger segment of their customer base through the mobile momentum that they achieved with their mobile payment app. As a result, they looked for a mobile wallet that would give customers the ability to make purchases directly from a debit or credit card using their mobile device.

In August 2012, Starbucks announced a strategic alliance with and a $25 million investment in Square Inc. to achieve a mobile wallet solution. Square gained widespread attention in 2009 when it launched a mobile credit card capture solution geared primarily to small business owners. That solution involved placing a small credit card capture device into the headphone jack of an iPhone. Square's leadership in mobile payment technology served as the foundation for the Starbucks leadership's choosing Square's existing wallet software for expanded use in Starbucks stores. Curt Garner, Starbucks chief information officer, notes, "There are a large number of Starbucks customers who pay with traditional credit and debit cards. That may be because their visit frequency is low or they prefer not to use prepaid cards. Square is an option for those people so that they can enjoy the convenience of mobile and all the benefits of tracking their purchases, along with getting digital receipts. Additionally, their mobile wallet provides a directory of businesses near them that accept mobile pay tender on their platform." At full functionality, the Starbucks and Square collaboration is expected to utilize geotracking technology that will facilitate not only mobile payment but mobile ordering as well.

Within three months of the announced alliance between Starbucks and Square, the Square Wallet mobile payment option went live, with initial mobile payment benefits at 7,000 company-operated U.S. Starbucks stores. At the time of the launch, Marcus Wohlsen, a staff writer for business at *WIRED* magazine, predicted that a mobile payment revolution would be initiated at Starbucks: "Because of its openness and seamless approach, Square at Starbucks is better positioned than any other technology to become the gateway drug that could finally make mobile payments mainstream. . . . Paying with Square at Starbucks is simple. People will start using it because of little perks like getting your receipt via text. Soon you'll also be able to add a tip just by tapping. Multiply that usage by even a few dozen customers at each of 7,000 Starbucks stores, and the network effect starts to ripple. You use Square next at a merchant nearby because you see it in the app. Merchants near Starbucks start using Square to get into the directory. A virtuous cycle ensues, and Square—which is to say your phone—becomes just another way you pay."

Both the Square Wallet and the Starbucks Card mobile app afford customers convenience in the purchasing process. These apps also provide valuable information to customers. In the closed-loop system of a loyalty program (one where you can track the effectiveness of marketing efforts through the sales information obtained during loyalty card or loyalty app use), a merchant can also learn from and refine its offerings for its customers. Adam Brotman, Starbucks chief digital officer, gives a specific example of the power of integrating customer analytics, customer relationship management information, and a targeted database approach. According to Adam, there are more than 10 million members in the Starbucks loyalty program, of which about 5.5 million have opted in to receive communications, marketing messages, and offers from Starbucks. On average, those 5.5 million opt-in customers receive a weekly e-mail from Starbucks (although the frequency is higher for those who purchase merchandise from the StarbucksStore.com website and separately opt in for communications through that platform). The frequency of e-mails also tends to increase around the holidays.

Adam addresses the targeted nature of these e-mails by noting, "We tend to create about five or six different groups of emails so that we can make sure that people get an offering that is highly relevant to them. For example, we looked at our database of My Starbucks Rewards members and isolated customers who buy food regularly. We then started examining other characteristics about this group such as what drinks they were buying, when they were coming in, and other demographic or psychographic variables. We then did predictive modeling by looking at the rest of our My Starbucks Rewards customer database." In essence, Adam notes that his team found other individuals in the rewards customer database who were similar to the regular food customers in behavioral and demographic characteristics, with one exception: they were not buying food at Starbucks. Adam's team then crafted a message targeted at these individuals, encouraging them (without making a discount offer) to consider Starbucks food offerings. The e-mail also featured attractive pictures of Starbucks food. Several hundred thousand of these customers who had behavioral characteristics that resembled those of regular food customers received this targeted e-mail. According to Adam, "Customers who received the food email purchased food seven times more often than they ever did before. We had an initial sales lift with a sustained tail effect and this targeted group performed 700 percent better than the control group performed."

While Starbucks is utilizing data gathering, analysis, and data modeling approaches to better forge relevant messages to and connections with customers, Adam and other leaders at Starbucks readily admit that they are still working to create more tools to automate these processes. Additionally, the leaders are looking for ways to communicate more efficiently and personally into the mobile inbox that is part of the Starbucks Card mobile app. Rather than targeting their communications to traditional e-mail, the future holds great opportunities for Starbucks leaders to send messages through the mobile app, thus utilizing the app as a one-to-one connection platform. Eventually, Starbucks leaders will also be able to personalize the look and feel of the company's website and mobile app based on their knowledge of the individual user. The Starbucks website and app can be presented differently depending on the characteristics of the customer.

Before we leave our discussion of the capabilities and importance of the Starbucks Card mobile app, let's take a moment to understand how the app engages customers through "gamification" strategies. Amish Shah, chief product officer of the mobile apps company Bitzio, Inc., describes gamification as "using game-type mechanics in non-game businesses to increase efficiency, customer loyalty and engagement." As it relates to Starbucks, Amish notes, "Starbucks has incorporated game mechanics and design into its popular loyalty program. Through multiple reward levels and a progression tracker, Starbucks coffee lovers are continually given incentives to engage with the brand." From a visual perspective, this "progression tracker" takes the form of virtual gold stars falling into a virtual cup on the Starbucks Card mobile app, and it is just one example of the company's deployment of gamification principles.

Conversations with Starbucks leaders who are involved with digital technology often focus on the mechanics of popular online games. Beyond acknowledging the fun and theatrics of games like World of Warcraft, Zynga Poker, and Rovio's Angry Birds, common drivers behind the success of these games include factors such as achievement, rewarding frequency, and being able to publicly show advancement. With this awareness, leaders at Starbucks are integrating emotional drivers from game theory into the ways they engage customers through their mobile devices. One example of how Starbucks deploys gamification came in the form of a two-week, seven-round scavenger hunt in collaboration with the American pop singer and songwriter Lady Gaga. Each round involved customers decoding clues by going into Starbucks stores, using mobile QR readers, and visiting Starbucks digital properties and blogs. The scavenger hunt was designed to get customers to want to work in teams and share their experiences. The venture was a win/win for both Starbucks and Lady Gaga, as she released a new album during the hunt and customers gained exclusive access to it on the Starbucks Digital Network. The winners of each round received Starbucks and Lady Gaga prizes. The Starbucks/Lady Gaga marketing and gamification example reflects the power of working with individuals or organizations that have the ability to generate social media interest, followed by welcoming customers to gain special access or playfully interact.

REFLECTION ON CONNECTION

1. How would you assess your success in forging a digital connection of trust and relevance?
2. Do you have a multipronged and integrated strategy concerning digital and mobile solutions?
3. Are you using game-type mechanics to increase efficiency, customer loyalty, and engagement? How can you deploy common drivers behind popular games more successfully in your digital strategy, such as by rewarding achievement or frequency and enabling public displays of achievement?

GIVING CUSTOMERS SOMETHING TO TALK ABOUT—IT'S A SOCIAL MEDIA WORLD

In many ways, Starbucks, by the nature of its culture, was well suited for social media. After all, Starbucks leaders value emotional engagement and connections with customers and community. Yet in other ways, a full commitment to digital and social strategy took a mind shift for its leaders. For example, Chris Bruzzo, senior vice president, Channel Brand Management, was charged with launching Starbucks in the social space. Chris notes that the social connection is authentic to the Starbucks brand and that coffeehouses by their nature facilitate social meeting networks: "In a sense, coffeehouses have served as the original social network. That said, Howard called me around Christmastime in 2007 and shared, 'We need to be in the social and digital space. I know people have been giving me that message for a while, but now we've got to move. We are struggling to hear our customers, and we must address this digitally.' Howard propelled us to launch the My Starbucks Idea customer idea site in 2008, and shortly thereafter to move into Twitter."

In Chapter 3, I shared the benefits of the MyStarbucksIdea .com site from the perspective of hearing the voice of the customer. It is important to note that the site has also helped change the Starbucks culture in a way that is necessary for future social media success. Prior to the customer idea site, messages to and from customers were mainly routed through the brand communication division at the Starbucks Support Center. My Starbucks Idea created a much broader and more immediate dialogue between customers and Starbucks subject-matter experts. Against that backdrop, Starbucks could next launch onto the highly interactive microblog platform of Twitter. Chris Bruzzo notes that Starbucks Twitter (@starbucks) launch was greatly aided by having the right person approaching the right leader at the right time: "This young technical guy knocked on my door one day and said, 'Chris, I want to grow and I want to help develop the business through social. I think Twitter could be the place.' This was before Twitter was a well-known concept, and frankly, I didn't fully appreciate what it had to offer or how it would effectively work for us. But since this partner had a background as a barista and he envisioned Twitter as a 'way to extend the barista connection online,' I thought we should give it a chance. Starbucks engaged Twitter before any other social media thanks to that partner because he perceived it to be the place for brands. Facebook was not getting a great deal of traction for companies at the time. On the first day the account was created, Starbucks had 600 followers; 1,500 the second day. Starbucks has over 3 million followers as of mid-2013."

From the perspective of outside analysts, the Starbucks approach to Twitter is praised on the basis of its direct engagement with customers and responsiveness to customer service issues. Kylie Jane Wakefield, writing for *The Content Strategist*, notes, "Checking out Starbucks' Twitter page, it's visible that most of the tweets are directed at users. . . . In fact, many of its tweets start with 'sorry about that!' or 'sorry to hear!,' offering dismayed customers solutions to their problems. Instead of losing disgruntled customers, Starbucks directly responds, solving the issues and making sure that customers are, in the end, satisfied. . . . By responding to customers directly and doing its best to fix the problem, Starbucks shows that it cares about the people who buy its products." From a social media perspective, Twitter fits well with the Starbucks focus on "uplifting moments" and personal connections. As a result, the Starbucks Twitter strategy is to speak directly with customers as opposed to microblogging "look at us" or marketing-type messages.

While Starbucks had an easy entry into Twitter, the company's Facebook page required initial groundwork. Alex Wheeler, vice president, Global Digital Marketing, and the first person to be hired to address social and digital issues as part of the Starbucks brand team back in 2006, notes, "It took a little effort for us to establish our official presence on Facebook. In order for that to happen, we connected with the Facebook page owners of about a dozen existing fan pages. All together there were probably about 30,000 fans across those dozen pages. We let those page owners know that we wanted to consolidate their pages to have an official presence. Everybody was very receptive and excited about that consolidation and that was the beginning of our Facebook journey."

Two of the key elements in the Starbucks Facebook strategy are authenticity and interesting content. Starbucks is committed to making friends, not offers. In essence, the Starbucks social media team wants to generate credible interest, not to give people incentives to follow the company. Using that test, Alex and her colleagues on the social media team have helped steer the Starbucks page away from "baits." A bait is where you get someone to "like" your page so that he can see additional content.

In addition to authentic and high-quality content, Starbucks leaders seek to deliver frequent and consistent messages. For example, the social media team tweets daily and posts on Facebook with regularity, but not in an overwhelming fashion. Specifically, the team believes that its Facebook feeds should engage the appetite of Starbucks followers without overwhelming them with content. The social media team also reads posts that people place on the Facebook wall and engages with them actively. A significant challenge for this team is managing the scale of activity on these sites. For example, there have been threads that had 30,000 comments on a status update. From a strategic perspective, managing scale is a good problem to have. Twitter posts and Facebook feeds should engage the appetite of your followers without your bombarding them with messages. Twitter and Facebook are about connecting. There are more appropriate settings for selling and closing.

In addition to Facebook, Starbucks has a strong social presence through YouTube, Google+, Foursquare, Instagram, and Pinterest. Also, the company's employment team has been actively involved with LinkedIn. With regard to YouTube, a marketing content specialist at Pardot, Matt Wesson, notes, "Starbucks is constantly expanding its content channels and exploring new formats to connect with its customers. I believe it is also one of the best companies out there when it comes to the use of video to tell its brand story. The company's YouTube channel has over 250 videos that focus on the company's values, give 'behind the scenes' insight, and share customer's personal experiences."

Despite effective expansion onto new platforms and praise from analysts, forward-moving Starbucks leaders are continuously looking for new ways to innovate their social media strategy. Adam Brotman states, "We are excited about the opportunity to do a lot more with YouTube. When we tell story through video, we're just as apt to embed those videos into the player on the home page of Starbucks.com as well as embed them within Facebook. So when we connect and tell our story through video, YouTube is only one of several different channels that we're utilizing. Given the speed of change in the digital space, complacency or a sense of contentment is not an option." Great leaders continually seek to leverage the options that are emerging through technology and to position their businesses on social platforms more effectively and strategically.

WHY STARBUCKS IS SUCCESSFUL IN SOCIAL MEDIA

In 2012, PhaseOne, a leading analytical-based marketing communication research firm, conducted a study that looked at 75 top brands across six vertical markets: automotive, dining, food/beverage, retail, services, and technology. In order to assess social engagement, PhaseOne analyzed the brands in its survey by using metrics such as Facebook likes, Klout scores, and Netbase sentiment analyses. The conclusion: *Starbucks is the number one brand when it comes to engaging social media users.* In discussing this finding, PhaseOne researchers noted, "To achieve this successful social media engagement, Starbucks focused its Web page, Facebook page and television advertisements on the individual and his or her individualized experience with the brand. For example, Starbucks Facebook page engages the visitor by speaking to his or her coffee preferences and personal stories." While individualized experiences and unique preferences are substantial components of Starbucks social media success, the company also benefits from a thoughtful and respectful approach to each social platform in which it participates. By taking this strategic and methodical approach, Starbucks ultimately draws participants on those platforms toward the brand.

Many companies jump on emerging social platforms with zeal; however, Starbucks leaders take a more calculated approach to entry. Members of the Starbucks social media team examine each new platform opportunity to determine whether there is a fit with the human connection that is the essence of the brand. Similarly, they look at whether they have the resources to engage on that platform effectively while seeking to respect the existing members of the community. Adam Brotman notes, "Considering the level of reach and engagement we have achieved, we are a pretty small team that is very thoughtful about our commitment to an emerging platform. Let's take Pinterest as an example. It is such a personal platform that we knew we should be there. As it was taking off, we saw a lot of our customers on Pinterest and we were eager to reach and connect with them but we spent about 6 months discussing our launch. Behind the scenes, we were agonizing about not getting on the platform quickly, but we also wanted to do it right. If you get into Pinterest you realize there's a way to engage and a respectful way to show up. Just like on Twitter, Facebook, and Instagram, there is an authentic approach needed to engage the community and we had to place that into the context of how we honor our brand essence. When we did engage Pinterest with a concept of Starbucks love, we tended to post and pin a lot of things that were not our own. We put considerable thought into the Pinterest boards we put up." In the context of its "Starbucks Loves" theme, Starbucks pins things like coffee, food, music, and inspiration. As a result, Starbucks boards include "real food," "coffee moments," and "inspiring places." These themes are not only at the heart of the brand but close to the hearts of Starbucks customers.

By building social media connections through individualized experiences, unique preferences, thoughtful platform selection, and respect for the platform community, Starbucks pulls customers to its content, as opposed to pushing marketing material to them. Mark Bonchek, PhD, founder of ORBIT+Co, describes this as creating "gravity." Mark states, "Where traditional companies push out messages and products, these companies pull customers in. Instead of treating customers as passive targets, they treat them as active participants. Like the sun in a solar system, they create a gravitational field that pulls customers into their orbit. They go beyond customer loyalty to building customer gravity."

Thanks to this gravity, Starbucks has done what many brands only talk about: translate social media and digital spending into ROI. Alex Wheeler, vice president, Starbucks Global Digital Marketing, notes, "One of the really important moments in our social media journey occurred in 2009 when we did Free Pastry Day. We decided to launch our new food platform through digital only, which was very unusual for us. The question was: could digital and a free food offer drive traffic? On the strength of digital/social, a million people went into Starbucks that day, and we created awareness through about a million and a half pastries." While it's one thing to see that many people in a Starbucks store for a free item, the company routinely garners hard data that show digital investment to be an efficient business driver. As Alex puts it, "We have validation of the amplifying effect that digital engagement has on the direct marketing and paid marketing investment."

BENEFITING FROM THE AMPLIFYING EFFECT OF SOCIAL MEDIA ON PAID DIGITAL ADVERTISING

On a purely strategic level, Starbucks leaders see both social media and paid digital advertising as playing important roles in creating connections with customers. Paid ads expand the brand's reach, while social media addresses reach along with engagement, fun, and brand building. Starbucks leaders are building fans and followers through social media and are deciding when to do something in that space that is directed at promotion or at engagement. If leaders are seeking engagement, they attempt to trigger "virality." Adam Brotman puts it this way: "In social, if somebody likes you or likes your comment, it shows up to their friends, family, and followers. When they retweet you in social, it literally amplifies and magnifies your brand's reach. The benefit of social is that people are engaging with us. They are telling their friends that they are checking in at a Starbucks, and they are usually telling it on Foursquare and connecting their Foursquare to Facebook or Twitter or Instagram. We integrate paid digital advertising into our social strategy. We take the viral effect of the messages we send into our regular feed and enhance them intelligently by connecting with paid digital advertising in the social space. So when we do promoted tweets and promoted stories on Facebook and Twitter, we efficiently lower the cost of each paid impression and connect with that many more customers."

Dave Williams, CEO, BLiNQ Media, who likens Facebook to the world's largest cocktail party, suggests that the goal of the medium should not be to give a hard sell on the platform, but to achieve likes—the equivalent of receiving a business card at the party. Dave notes that the Starbucks approach to the integration of social and paid media is a desirable best practice. "For me, consumer-initiated ads are the future of advertising, not only on Facebook, but across other social networks too. Facebook's Sponsored Stories—initiated by the consumer, not the brand—is one of the cleverest ways to tap into this data mine. Here the user becomes a brand champion, with micro interactions such as likes, posts, check-ins or apps used relayed to friends and turned into subtle, but promoted content. Starbucks is the obvious brand example here that has utilized Sponsored Stories well, steadily building up its fan base before using the social graph to pick up on discussions around coffee breaks and its various food and drink products, and serving up ads with a social context."

Given Starbucks thought leadership on social media strategy, I asked Adam Brotman to offer his advice directly to readers like you. His response was straightforward: "I can't imagine there is a more powerful place than digital when it comes to connecting with your customers, telling your story, or gaining reach. Digital is everything from a website to digital marketing and even loyalty. Square is a great example—for a physical retail merchant, Square gives you the ability to not just have an efficient way to accept credit card payments easily but they've created an entire operating system between the small merchant and his or her customers and you can complement that with Twitter and Facebook and a compelling website." Adam also offered the opinion that every business should have a dedicated person or team that pays attention to community management, brand building, and marketing through digital. If a business is small, those responsibilities might be only part of a single individual's job description, but they need to be addressed consistently and tactically. Adam suggests that you need someone to "commit time to thinking about the platform that fits your business and customer interface, and not just social media but your own website, your loyalty program, how you use payment as a form of communication, the nature of customer relationship management systems, and how data can guide your marketing and engagement strategy. Whether there are two people or 2,000 people in your business, you have to have a strategy. You can be scalable and customizable, but you must have someone to chart and monitor the course."

REFLECTION ON CONNECTION

1. How strategic are your decisions concerning the social media platforms through which your brand will engage?
2. Are you looking for ways to measure the ROI and amplifying effects of your social and media strategies? Are you linking paid digital advertising to your social media strategy?
3. Have you dedicated resources to "commit time to thinking about the platform that fits your business and your customer interface, . . . your own website, your loyalty program, how you use payment as a form of communication, the nature of customer relationship management systems, and how data can guide your marketing and engagement strategy"?

TECHNOLOGY THAT SERVES MISSION

Starbucks leadership has made vast investments in technology, some of which its customers and partners notice, while others operate in the background. The bulk of these capital expenditures targets the delivery of uplifting moments and enhancement of the Starbucks connection. One of the most obvious of these changes was the company's transition to having one-touch free Wi-Fi in stores. The company's former chief information officer told me he knew Starbucks was behind the times several years back when he went to the taco truck outside the Starbucks Support Center in Seattle and noticed that the truck was offering one-click free Wi-Fi, but Starbucks was giving customers only two hours of Wi-Fi a day, and only if they registered a Starbucks Card and kept a minimum balance of $5 on it. So in 2009 Starbucks made the investment needed to make Wi-Fi seamless and easy to use. At the same time, Starbucks worked with content partners to create the Starbucks Digital Network, which allows customers who use the in-store Wi-Fi network to access free curated Internet content from various partners. For example, customers can get a Pick of the Week download from iTunes, view local businesses on the Square Directory, scan a local restaurant review, or read a book through New Word City. From premium content to locally relevant information, the Starbucks Digital Network provides added value to enhance the in-store Starbucks Experience.

Another less obvious example of technology being used to improve the in-store connection is a project as mundane yet massive as the overhaul of the stores' Point of Sale (POS) system to something called Simphony. Curt Garner, Starbucks chief information officer, notes, "To take an order in our old POS, it had to be entered in a particular sequence, with size first and then drink and then any modifiers." Leaders observed ordering interactions and noticed that even regular Starbucks customers who had actually learned the correct ordering sequence for their drinks occasionally were tripped up. For instance, let's assume that someone regularly comes into Starbucks by himself, but on a particular occasion is accompanied by his child. The customer says, "I'll have a double short peppermint mocha, a hot chocolate, an oatmeal, and a turkey bacon breakfast sandwich." In that stream, the barista would be forced to remember the hot chocolate and not ring it in until she could go back and clarify the size. Obviously such a system placed a considerable cognitive demand on the baristas, distracted them from full engagement, and produced ordering errors. A new customer might come in and give an order that was not in the prescribed sequence; the barista would repeat the order in the way that was necessary to ring it into the POS, but it often sounded as if the customer was being corrected. Curt notes, "From all those observations, the idea of conversational ordering was born. That notion was we would let technology resolve the order of a drink entry. The barista could enter a drink into the system in any order consistent with the customer's ordering pattern."

In essence, the computer starts constructing the drink on the screen, and it shows the default part of that recipe in light gray and what needs to be marked on the cup in dark green. Curt and his colleagues anticipated that the conversational ordering aspects of the new POS would be of particular value to new baristas, but they were surprised to find that tenured baristas appreciated the new system as well because it gave them a visual check that they had rung the order in correctly. Curt adds, "We also took advantage when rolling out Simphony, our Point of Sale solution, to do several things from a tech perspective that tried to look around the corner into the future. One was to create a networked solution so instead of having dumb cash registers sitting on a counter disconnected from anything in the enterprise, and then dialing into them once a day to retrieve sales, every single register has an IP address on our network. We are pulling sales from those registers constantly and also sending and receiving information from them continually. The POS architecture allows us to connect with APIs (application programming interfaces) and other routines that enable us to plug and play things like scanners and afforded us a 90-day turnaround time on Square."

A great deal of technology spend at Starbucks is also occurring on behalf of streamlining communication to those within the organization. As difficult as it is to deliver consistent leadership messages in a small organization, Starbucks leaders have the added challenge of communicating to hundreds of thousands of partners around the world. As a result, Starbucks leadership is constantly working to develop integrated technology solutions to offer options other than relying on very busy store managers to see to it that all messages cascade down.

When asked what the future of technology and digital looks like for Starbucks, Alex Wheeler said it succinctly: "Technology will evolve and people will change, but our mission will guide us. Technology will serve our mission, and we will deploy our strategies to engage our partners and customers wherever they spend their time. We will seek to stay relevant to them and uplift them through human connection."

Technology is powerful when you view it as a way to enhance the human connection rather than as inevitably leading to impersonalization. In the area of leveraging technology to fuel humanity, Starbucks leaders have produced some interesting and unexpected results, even in other businesses. For example, Jack Dorsey, CEO of Square, discontinued the use of the word *users* thanks to the Starbucks leadership. According to Jack, Howard Schultz, a member of Square's board of directors, privately inquired why Square referred to its customers as users. Jack reflected, "The term 'user' made its appearance in computing at the dawn of shared terminals. . . . It was solidified in hacker culture as a person who wasn't technical or creative, someone who just used resources and wasn't able to make or produce anything (often called a 'luser')." Based on the provocative nature of Howard's question, Jack noted that Square will replace the word *user* with the word *customer*. From Jack's perspective, this simple word change reflects a shift to a more humanity-based focus on service. Specifically, he notes that Square must stop "distancing ourselves from the *people* that choose our products over our competitors. . . . We have customers we earn. They deserve our utmost respect, focus, and service."

When talking about the word *partner* in Chapter 5, I said that *words matter*. Hopefully, the lessons provided here will help you see the powerful "human connection" that you can forge with the help of technology. Technology is not an end unto itself, nor is it something that is provided for technology "users"; it is a tool for serving and connecting with your "people" and your "customers"!

CONNECTING POINTS

- While "brick-and-mortar" connections tend to be terrific opportunities to develop personal face-to-face relationships, most brands today face the challenge of building or extending personal connections outside of a traditional retail building.
- Key components of a comprehensive digital strategy include (1) commerce, (2) company-owned web and mobile channels, (3) loyalty/customer relationship management (CRM)/targeted database, (4) social media, and (5) paid digital marketing.
- Today, successful businesses look for ways to integrate their digital assets to build online commerce, brick-and-mortar traffic, customer engagement, and consumer loyalty.
- Twitter and Facebook approaches should focus on consistent but not overwhelming levels of communication, delivered for the purpose of connecting.

- When you consider engaging on an emerging social media platform, you should consider three aspects: Does the platform fit with your brand? Do you have the resources to sustain engagement? Have you spent time understanding how people prefer to interact on that platform?
- By building social media connections around individualized experiences and unique preferences, you are likely to pull customers to your content.
- No matter what the size of a business, its leaders should designate someone to be in charge of social media strategy.
- Technology should serve the mission, not the reverse.
- Technology is powerful when you view it as a way to enhance the human connection rather than seeing it as inevitably leading to impersonalization.
- Technology might be something that you should not view as being provided for "users," but instead should see as a tool for serving and connecting with your "people" and your "customers"!

CHAPTER 9

Personal Relationships Translate: Sharing the Love from People to Products

Advertising moves people toward goods; merchandising moves goods toward people.

MORRIS HITE

When personal relationships are created between employees and customers and strengthened through the use of technology, brands are given permission to transfer those emotional connections to new product offerings. Starbucks is an example of how to take in-store person-to-person connections and leverage them into consumer packaged goods (CPG) categories such as Starbucks VIA® Ready Brew (individual servings of instant coffee), Starbucks ready-to-drink beverages, bulk-packaged coffee and tea, and other Tazo and Starbucks-owned branded products that are served by foodservice providers. In a case study on relational capital (translating human connections into marketable value), Ranjay Gulati, Sarah Huffman, and Gary Neilson suggest that Starbucks has earned a license to sell consumer packaged goods: "Due in large part to Howard Schultz's careful nurturing and development of the Starbucks Experience, the company has been able to leverage its increasingly strong brand through a variety of alliances to sell Starbucks coffee and develop new products with the Starbucks name. The goal in establishing these relationships has been to continue to develop the brand outside the company's retail stores in order to reach customers through multiple points of contact . . ."

That having been said, many people are surprised to find that Starbucks started out in the bulk-goods business, *not* the brewed coffee business. The original Starbucks store dark-roasted small batches of coffee beans and sold them to in-store customers, by mail order, and to local restaurateurs. In essence, Starbucks began as a consumer packaged goods business. Leaders later strategically positioned the company as a global service experience business, delivering brewed coffee and espresso-based drinks. While the leaders built the brand into the global giant that it is through the store-based connection (the third place), they have more recently mobilized the connection to move into customers' homes (the first place) and offices (the second place). Because of the success, connection, and love they've forged in the Starbucks stores, the leaders have also developed a substantial market selling in the business-to-business space. In addition, the leadership has fostered new product innovation that serves consumers' mobile lifestyles.

Throughout this chapter, we will examine how Starbucks deploys a multichannel approach to product creation, launch, and delivery. We will explore innovation in both coffee and adjacent categories, and also look at how Starbucks positions its products to be used where customers want them—and not necessarily requiring customers to come into a Starbucks-branded location. This chapter is designed to help you see how Starbucks innovates relevant product offerings in new categories through either strategic business alliances, innovation, or acquisitions. It is intended to help you take your existing connection with customers and extend it into their highly mobile lifestyles.

RECLAIMING COFFEE MERCHANDISING—IN STORE

While most customers look at a Starbucks store as a place to grab a cup of coffee or to share a conversation while enjoying a beverage or food item, each store also has a limited amount of prime merchandising space available. As you will recall from Chapter 2, in the mid-2000s, Starbucks store managers became so concerned with their year-over-year comps that the merchandise shelves in Starbucks stores were filled with non-coffee-related products. This prompted Howard Schultz (who was functioning as the chief global strategist for Starbucks at the time) to write an e-mail memo to then–chief executive officer Jim Donald, with copies to the Starbucks senior leadership team, on February 14, 2007. That e-mail, which somehow was leaked to the media, was titled "The Commoditization of the Starbucks Experience." In it, among other things, Howard wrote, "I am not sure people today even know we are roasting coffee. You certainly can't get the message from being in our stores. The merchandise, more art than science, is far removed from being the merchant that I believe we can be and certainly at a minimum should support the foundation of our coffee heritage. Some stores don't have coffee grinders, French presses from Bodum, or even coffee filters."

Merchandising in Starbucks stores has certainly changed since Howard crafted his cautionary memo. In my nearest Starbucks store in St. Petersburg, Florida, and probably in a store close to you, there are normally two seven-feet-tall by four-feet-wide displays with seven shelves of merchandise in each. This merchandise usually includes the Bodum French Press pots that Howard wanted to see in 2007. In addition, the shelves contain various hot and cold Starbucks-logoed mugs and cups, canisters of full-leaf Tazo tea, boxes of Tazo tea bags, and Starbucks VIA instant coffee and tea packages. These shelving units are supplemented by four or five wicker baskets that sit in containers on the floor and typically hold various coffee blends and occasionally packaged food items like potato chips or gourmet popcorn. Complementing these baskets are packaged food and beverage items in or around the display case, including Starbucks Refreshers™ beverages, Evolution Fresh juices, milk products, fruit cups, yogurt cups, Starbucks ready-to-drink beverages, Ethos® water (a Starbucks subsidiary), and Starbucks branded nuts and fruit snacks. At various locations around the café, there are specialty merchandise tables displaying items like the Starbucks at-home espresso brewing machine, the Verismo® system by Starbucks, and espresso and milk pods used in that machine.

The presence of coffee-related items in Starbucks stores is congruent with a broader business strategy that includes diversifying the company's sales mix well beyond the products that baristas handcraft for customers. This enhancement of Starbucks consumer goods follows a path that has been successfully traveled by foodservice brands like Ben & Jerry's ice cream, which was once a small ice cream store in Vermont and is now a powerful brand that is owned by Unilever. Ben & Jerry's now operates a vast global network of ice cream shops and enjoys widespread distribution of its packaged ice cream in supermarkets and convenience stores. Jeff Hansberry, president, Starbucks Channel Development and Emerging Brands, notes, "Starbucks captures only a small portion of the $100 billion coffee, tea, and ready-to-drink beverage market globally. . . . We are working to build a greater share of that global opportunity with our [consumer packaged goods] business by growing across channels, categories, and countries where our products are sold."

Annie Young-Scrivner, president, Starbucks Canada and former global chief marketing officer and president of Tazo, places the scope of this retail opportunity in the context of the four Starbucks location models: "We really want to make sure we're earning the connection with the customers no matter where they are. Our future is based on selling coffee and related products for customers to use at home, at work, in our stores, and on the go. We have great opportunities for gaining market share and expanding our business out through consumer channels that stretch well beyond our vast store footprint." The evolution of this Starbucks channel strategy offers lessons for us all—namely, define an initial channel of delivery, master execution in that channel, then direct your efforts more broadly to other channels of distribution that meet your customers' needs wherever they are. As you look at your business, how are you performing on the "four-place" model that Starbucks uses? Are you engaging your customers with your products, services, or communications in their home, at their work, in your building, and at all the places in between? To achieve this breadth of presence in its customers' lives, Starbucks must rely upon and serve the needs of other businesses that wish to either sell or distribute its products. Given this reliance on other business entities, let's take a moment to understand the business-to-business side of Starbucks.

DELIVERING THE BUSINESS-TO-BUSINESS CONNECTION

Starbucks is not exclusively a business-to-customer (B2C) company. In reality, the company engages in several types of business-to-business (B2B) relationships that support an ever-widening sales mix. Most notably, these include foodservice customers, licensed stores, and joint-venture partnerships.

On the foodservice side, Starbucks offers training, marketing, and merchandising expertise along with equipment and a portfolio of beverage products (including brewed coffee, hot and cold espresso-based drinks, syrups, cocoa, and Tazo tea) to business customers in retail settings such as fine dining, travel, recreation, universities, government offices, lodging, and healthcare facilities. In addition, Starbucks sources companies' internal beverage needs, including those for cafeterias, public spaces, meetings, and catering. When you attend a conference and the break station has a sign that says we "proudly brew" Starbucks coffee or when you see Starbucks coffee being served at a restaurant at which you are dining, you are experiencing the Starbucks brand extension into the foodservice space.

In the case of licensed stores, businesses like Kroger, Vons, and Safeway (large supermarket chains) own, staff, and operate the physical store or kiosk locations under a Starbucks-approved license. In addition to a strong licensed store position in supermarkets (a favorable affinity placement for leveraging sales into supermarket aisles), licensed stores are also frequently located in airports, general merchandise retailers like Target and Meijer, and other compatible settings.

In some cases, Starbucks goes beyond a licensing agreement to a full-fledged joint-venture alliance with a distribution partner. In fact, Starbucks longstanding relationship with other companies in consumer goods began in 1994 with its North American Coffee Partnership agreement, which involved collaboration with PepsiCo North America. Through this agreement, Pepsi manufactures, markets, and distributes ready-to-drink coffee beverages in a joint-venture arrangement. Currently these ready-to-drink beverages carry either the Starbucks or the Seattle's Best Coffee brand. (Seattle's Best Coffee is a company that started roasting coffee on a Seattle pier in 1970. It was a rival company that Starbucks purchased in 2003.) Specific coffee beverages made available through this joint venture include Starbucks® bottled Frappuccino® coffee drinks, Starbucks Doubleshot® espresso drinks, Starbucks Doubleshot® Energy+Coffee drinks, Starbucks® Iced Coffee, Starbucks Discoveries, Iced Café Favorites, and Starbucks Refreshers.

In these joint-venture arrangements, Starbucks leadership must ensure that both parties are carrying out their responsibilities in a reciprocal relationship where both companies gain from the other's efforts. In Chapter 7, we discussed how choosing the right collaborative business partner is critical to success in new markets, particularly international ones. Similarly, partner selection is of great importance when it comes to extending the breadth of your offerings. Gary Stibel, founder and CEO of the New England Consulting Group, notes, "The key is choosing a partner. . . . Everybody thinks most licenses succeed—it's absolutely the opposite. The vast majority of all licensing arrangements or attempts to enter [consumer packaged goods] by restaurants fail." To appreciate the complexity of the challenge of CPG licensing, food and travel writer Robert Lillegard notes, "Even long-standing relationships can grow sour. Starbucks and Kraft had a very ugly public split in 2011 after the coffee giant claimed that the distributor wasn't doing enough to promote its products." Robert adds that Kraft sought to enjoin the 13-year partnership from dissolving, "but was ultimately unsuccessful. Now the two companies compete for shelf space, with Kraft's Gevalia and Maxwell House going up against Starbucks' offerings." The Kraft relationship notwithstanding, Starbucks leaders have enjoyed strong licensed and joint-venture partnership arrangements, largely because of the way Starbucks leaders perceive themselves as serving their business partners.

Whether it is selling through a foodservice customer, a Starbucks licensed store, or a joint-venture partner, Starbucks leaders expect business-to-business service experiences to reflect Starbucks mission and values while producing strong connections and relationships like those forged in the café environment. Starbucks seeks to provide solutions and partnerships that improve outcomes by connecting with and anticipating the needs of business customers. Beyond products, Starbucks leaders want the company's business customers to experience personalized care based on a deep understanding of where their business is going and the goals they wish to realize from working with Starbucks. In essence, business customers should enjoy a Starbucks Experience marked by personalized attention and a commitment to a lasting relationship.

For Starbucks, serving business customers and business partners takes on added significance for brand equity. Andrew Linnemann, vice president, Green Coffee Quality and Engagement at Starbucks, notes, "When a customer is served in a licensed store, for example, our name is on the cup. We need to care for our business customers and select our business partners carefully because their actions reflect on the way Starbucks is perceived through the customers they serve. When it comes to licensed store partners and joint-venture partners, we are looking to not only understand their operational competencies but we want to know who they are as a company and a culture. Do they share and demonstrate similar values as us?We will walk away from a licensee or joint-venture partner if it's not the right fit."

In the mind of the end consumer, a Starbucks is a Starbucks, whether it is a licensed store in an airport or a company-owned store down the street. From the perspective of the leadership, the service experience at Starbucks should be uplifting, personal, and relationship-focused, whether a Starbucks partner is serving a customer in a Starbucks store or a Target employee is serving Starbucks products to a customer in a Target location. In the end, a business is not buildings or brand names; it is a collection of people who should share like-minded objectives. While the delivery of a business-to-business experience has to vary based on the needs of the business being served, this is equally true for the delivery of experiences to individuals.

Ultimately, the principles that define great customer experiences are extremely similar, no matter whether your customer is an individual consumer or a group of individuals from different departments within a business. With the right partners in place and a rich understanding that the needs of your business partners have similarities to those of your individual customers, you should be positioned to present your offerings to connect with your customers across all settings. For Starbucks, a key strategic opportunity exists in serving customers in their first place—their homes.

REFLECTION ON CONNECTION

1. With whom do you partner to magnify the scope of the customers you can serve?
2. Do you view business partners as customers of your business? How do you see your relationship with your partners affecting your service to your end customers or to those that they serve?
3. Have you earned a "license to sell" other services or products to your customers through the strength of the connections that you form in the delivery of your current slate of offerings?

SERVING CUSTOMERS AT HOME

While it initially partnered to distribute its packaged coffee products, Starbucks has taken over the manufacturing, distribution, and sale of those items, and the leaders at Starbucks continue to innovate ways to place their coffee products in settings other than their stores. This has led critics to warn that Starbucks is grabbing for profit in mass retail in a way that will compromise its in-store sales. For example, when Starbucks launched its single-serve instant coffee product VIA in 2009, Steve Toback, managing partner of Invisor Consulting, noted, "Starbucks is positioning VIA against its own fresh brewed coffee, challenging people to see if they can taste the difference. So, why should customers pay a premium for Starbucks fresh brewed coffee when they can get VIA for a buck a cup? If the campaign is successful, won't VIA potentially cannibalize fresh brewed coffee sales?" While these outsiders' concerns are reasonable, Starbucks leaders have not experienced cannibalization and in fact have grown sales by combining in-store and in-home coffee options. Ultimately, the leaders' ability to see and seize opportunities across channels is what drove the decision to expand the company's offerings. The decision emerged largely from the leadership's acute sensitivity to the different need states and rituals that surround coffee consumption. Some customers may visit Starbucks regularly for their morning coffee, but still have times when they want to make high-quality coffee at home. Similarly, some might have a morning ritual in which they routinely make coffee at home, but also stop at a Starbucks store during a morning break. In essence, coffee consumption is not a zero-sum game where customers choose to either brew at home or go into a Starbucks store, and this is something of which the leadership team was acutely aware.

Because of the complexities and the dynamic nature of the consumer packaged goods marketplace, Starbucks leaders are constantly facing tactical challenges. For example, Starbucks worked with a competitor, Green Mountain Coffee Roasters (GMCR), to craft a partial partnership. GMCR, a Vermont-based specialty coffee company, acquired Keurig Incorporated in 2006. Keurig is the market leader in single-cup brewing machines for the consumer market. The Keurig machines offer ease of coffee brewing by requiring coffee drinkers to simply place a mug under the brewing mechanism, add water to a reservoir, insert a single-serving coffee packet (referred to as a K-Cup pack), and push a button. Through the acquisition of Keurig, GMCR positioned itself as the exclusive supplier of K-Cup packs. In addition to providing its own coffee brand, GMCR purchased the

Quebec-based coffee company Van Houtte and added K-Cup packs with the Van Houtte name. Other brands like Newman's Own and Folgers have entered into licensing agreements with GMCR for manufacturing and distribution of their coffees in K-Cup packs for use in Keurig brewing systems.

So what could Starbucks do in terms of positioning its products in K-Cups? Starbucks had previously endorsed the Tassimo coffee brewer (which is a direct competitor to Keurig) and sourced coffee in a different single-serving format (t-discs) needed for use in the Tassimo system. Given the termination of Starbucks agreement with Kraft Foods Inc., the Tassimo system, which was created by Kraft, was less integrated into Starbucks existing distribution system. Many coffee consumer analysts speculated on the course Starbucks would take with its historic rival GMCR and the Keurig system. Some suggested that Starbucks would acquire GMCR; others indicated that Starbucks would create its own alternative to both Tassimo and Keurig. But in March 2011, Starbucks and GMCR announced a K-Cup agreement. Since that time, Starbucks has expanded its license with GMCR to include products for Green Mountain's Vue™ brewer (which is a newer system that produces stronger, hotter, and larger beverages). Through their collaboration, Starbucks is the exclusive licensed super-premium brand for GMCR's traditional Keurig and Vue brewers. In addition, GMCR distributes Starbucks K-Cups and Starbucks Vue packets to department, specialty, and mass retail stores. In discussing the decision to engage with GMCR, Andrew Linnemann, vice president, Green Coffee Quality and Engagement, notes, "In the United States, the growth of the coffee sector has been refueled by single-cup brewing systems, and it makes sense to offer our highest-quality coffee to those looking to enjoy the convenience and consistency of delivery through their Keurig." Imagine that one of your competitors creates a platform on which you can sell your goods. You know that selling on that platform will be good for you from a distribution standpoint, but will also fuel the strength of your competitor. What would you do? While Starbucks has found a way to collaborate with GMCR, that does not imply that healthy competition has ended.

In 2012, Starbucks released a home-brewing single-serve system. The Starbucks brewer creates not only drip coffee drinks, but espresso and latte beverages as well. The Verismo system features Swiss-engineered high-pressure technology to create Starbucks-quality drinks through the use of milk and coffee pods. From the perspective of Starbucks leaders, Verismo offered a variety of important opportunities for customers and for Starbucks. These included such things as (1) an at-home brewed coffee option, with an adjustable high-pressure system specific to your drink selection, (2) an opportunity to release a product that goes beyond brewed coffee and also creates Starbucks signature espresso beverages, and (3) a chance to create a proprietary coffee-brewing platform for Starbucks that fits nicely as a merchandise item in Starbucks stores. The tactical decisions made in the highly competitive coffee brewer world demonstrate key lessons for leaders. Specifically, leadership requires skill in collaboratively positioning products in the context of competitors' proprietary delivery systems while constantly innovating proprietary delivery systems of their own through strategic relationships with manufacturing and distribution partners.

COFFEE IN THE SECOND PLACE: THE WORLD OF WORK

A 2012 Reuters survey suggests that about 10 percent of the world's workforce works from home. The remainder may find themselves at the mercy of the oft-maligned world of office coffee. Through the years, companies like Starbucks have been elevating the experience of the office coffee brewer and providing solutions to meet their customers at work. Companies with between 20 and 50 employees can select a Starbucks coffee service that provides brewing equipment, ground Starbucks coffee, and regular service. Additional items like Tazo tea, napkins, and cups are also available. Larger companies can enjoy the same coffee service or upgrade their brewing system to the Starbucks Interactive Cup® brewer, which grinds and brews individual cups or carafes of coffee with the push of a button. To see the Starbucks Interactive Cup brewer demo, go to http://tinyurl.com/bovsqhm or point your QR reader here:

The success of Starbucks efforts to win the second place can be demonstrated through examples such as an alliance between Starbucks and Selecta. Selecta, Europe's largest vending services company, is working with Starbucks in Switzerland to deliver three solutions to address the needs of businesses of all sizes. These brewing/dispensing options range from small tabletop products to large integrated coffee corners. Selecta provides its customers with a swath of Starbucks products, including Vanilla Latte, Espresso, Doppio Espresso, Cappuccino, Café Crème, Caffè Latte, Chai Tea Latte, Latte Macchiato, Espresso Macchiato, and Hot Chocolate, and a variety of Tazo teas, including Calm™, China Green Tips, Earl Grey, English Breakfast, and Refresh™.

According to Frank Wubben, managing director, Starbucks Switzerland and Austria, "I met the CEO of Selecta and we created the vision of how the two market leaders in coffee, Selecta in office coffee and Starbucks in retail, could bond together to build an exciting office customer proposition through Starbucks coffee. In about 5 months' time, we were able to develop our scalable office coffee concept. For me, the most important part is customers who come to our stores will have the opportunity to enjoy their favorite beverage at their office desk. Conversely, people who have not entered our stores may now do so thanks to the quality of Starbucks coffee they are enjoying at work." The leaders are banking on the fact that, rather than detracting from the in-store Starbucks connection, a product must be available in the context of both a customer's work and home life. This availability increases customer contact with the product and embeds it more deeply into the customer's rituals, lifestyle, and identity.

CREATING ON-THE-GO SOLUTIONS

While much of life is experienced at home or at work, Starbucks has created product offerings for the grab-and-go speed at which many of us live. Whether it was testing Drive Thrus in California in 1994, collaborating with Pepsi to manufacture bottled Frappuccino beverages in 1996, or the arduous process of creating VIA, the instant single-serving coffee product that was launched in 2009, Starbucks has been constantly looking to make its products available to customers so that they can enjoy a high-quality beverage wherever they go. Howard Schultz explained VIA to Starbucks partners by noting, "We announced that Starbucks will introduce an instant coffee, providing our customers with great tasting Starbucks coffee, anywhere and anytime. Not surprisingly, this news raised some eyebrows, and some cynics are asking, 'Why go instant, Starbucks?' There are numerous logical reasons: the significant size of the instant coffee market . . . ; the increasing mobility of consumers (imagine a cup of Starbucks VIA Ready Brew on a mountaintop); and, regardless of our ubiquity, that customers continue to tell us they want more Starbucks, and more ways and opportunities to enjoy it."

Beyond market trends, Howard also emphasized the importance of sustaining the company's core values and innovating dynamic solutions that respond to the changing needs of customers irrespective of the inevitable criticism: "I know some will question our decision, and I understand this reaction. Expectations from brands like Starbucks are high, and interaction with our brand is very personal. Yet in spite of those high expectations (or perhaps because of them), we are confident we can disrupt and reinvent the instant coffee category—introducing quality coupled with value. I believe that Starbucks VIA Ready Brew is just that—and the proof is in the cup."

The proof is not only in the Starbucks cup, but in the profitability of products like VIA, which had global sales of $100 million in its first 10 months. That represented approximately 30 percent of the $330 million premium single-serving (or pod) category. Domenick Celentano, an entrepreneurial food executive, chose Starbucks VIA as one of the "most memorable new product launches" based largely on how effectively Starbucks partners sampled the product in stores and across channels (in-store and supermarket), as well as how effectively the leadership embedded the product launch through social media strategies like those discussed in Chapter 8. As far as sampling is concerned, Domenick notes, "Sampling is a time proven method for facilitating consumer trial. Starbucks having ultimate control in their own stores orchestrated sampling customers with free VIA coffee. To control their sampling effort they waited to introduce the product in grocery stores until sometime in 2010. Even though they were not in retail groceries initially, they used the brand presence of their regular line of coffee and dispatched baristas to retailers such as Safeway and Target stores to give out VIA samples to shoppers."

Annie Young-Scrivner, president, Starbucks Canada, echoes Domenick's view concerning sampling. Talking about the rollout of Starbucks Blonde Roast, Starbucks light roast coffee, Annie notes, "What is different here than at other consumer package companies is our sheer ability to drive awareness and trial in a very cost-effective way. So as an example, after two weeks we had exceptional awareness on Starbucks Blonde Roast, which is incredible." Annie suggests that those extraordinary levels of awareness are achieved with an absolute spending rate that is only 10 percent of what competitors often need to spend to achieve similar results. She explains, "We have been able to efficiently gain awareness and trial due to the excitement and enthusiasm of our fantastic 200,000 partners across the globe who engage nearly 70 million consumers every single week. In order for other CPG companies to get a trial, they typically have to go through a third-party grocery sampling or a dry sampling. We, however, can get a fresh cup of coffee right in front of our customers as they walk through the door and create excitement around the new product launch, while also soliciting helpful feedback." By training Starbucks partners in how to sample new products, collect feedback, and share it with the leadership, Starbucks has a distinct in-store advantage. In the case of VIA, as Domenick Celentano noted, Starbucks baristas were then deployed in the shopping aisles of Target and Safeway. This approach demonstrates the genius of leveraging human assets to maximize effectiveness in cross-channel efforts. Once baristas had mastered sampling VIA in the Starbucks store environment, the expertise and the overall acumen of those baristas was used to drive the product's success across channels.

From the perspective of integration with social media and cross-channel promotion, Domenick observes, "You just can't get away from the fact that social media in food [promotion] is powerful and Starbucks being marketing geniuses know this. . . . Social media gave them viral publicity and very little cost to the company. . . . They promoted their VIA Taste Challenge through Facebook driving people into their stores comparing

VIA against freshly brewed Starbucks coffee. The Facebook promotion offered a free coffee in-store for trying." Using social media to drive customers into your business so that your people can enrich the connection and engage increased customer awareness, trial, and product adoption—that sounds like a formula for success, doesn't it?

GETTING CUSTOMERS TO CROSS THE CHANNEL

In addition to the cross-channel promotions mentioned previously, Starbucks has explored and engaged both low- and high-tech ways to drive customers from one channel to the next. On the low-tech side of the equation, Starbucks has provided customers with a free in-store tall coffee when they bring in an empty one-pound. bag of coffee beans purchased outside of a Starbucks store (such items had a coupon that was not present on coffee bean packages purchased in Starbucks stores). Similarly, early in the launch of the Verismo system, purchasers were provided with a Gold-level membership in the My Starbucks Rewards program, which ordinarily would have required the customer to buy 42 beverages before receiving special loyalty rewards on in-store beverages and food.

On the higher-tech side of integration, Starbucks is working with some supermarkets and other distributors to enable purchases of Starbucks bulk coffee or related Starbucks consumer products to count toward loyalty rewards on the Starbucks Card and is exploring packaging materials that will interface with the Starbucks mobile app. Annie Young-Scrivner shares how technology and Starbucks packaging have merged: "Caffè Verona is one of our dark roast coffees and we actually call it our coffee of love. On Caffè Verona bags we have placed a QR code that links to stories of the coffee. One such example is of a couple's engagement story. The man had a first date with his girlfriend at Starbucks and later proposed to her in a forest that he staged to look like a Starbucks. He took pictures of the engagement scene and posted them on Facebook. We found that couple and asked if we could re-create his engagement experience and make the story available through a QR code on our bags. So if you're in the supermarket aisle or drinking your coffee at home, you can click on the Caffè Verona bag and experience a true love story about our customers and Starbucks. That's an example of how we seek to share our story, leverage technology, and engage with customers across channels. It is our effort to reach for the magical." Since you may not have that particular Starbucks bag available, you can experience that story by directing your browser to http://tinyurl.com/clu9bmm or using your QR reader here:

Suffice it say that Starbucks leadership is perpetually seeking magic and exploring synergies that will encourage customers or give them incentives to widen the array of Starbucks products that they purchase or consume and the settings in which they purchase and consume them. Often the magic can be achieved in rather subtle ways, including simple e-mails like one I received announcing that I would receive a holiday Starbucks Card if I bought three qualifying Starbucks or Tazo products. The e-mail depicted consumer products and indicated that qualifying products had to be purchased outside of a Starbucks store. Redemption required the original grocery register receipt and the universal product code (UPC) from the qualifying products' packaging.

Starbucks and Tazo holiday e-mail promotion.

REFLECTION ON CONNECTION

1. Have you outlined the key contact points you have with customers? Have you identified strategic opportunities that might enable you to connect with and serve your customers in more settings?

2. What methods do you use to drive awareness, trial, and product adoption cost-effectively? How can you allow customers to sample your services or products?

3. How are you encouraging your customers to experience the breadth of your product or service offerings, so that they are not siloed into one channel of your deliverables?

INNOVATING AND ACQUIRING STRONG PRODUCTS IN ADJACENT CATEGORIES

In Chapter 3, I shared how Starbucks leaders tactically moved into adjacent beverage categories through the acquisition of Tazo and Evolution Fresh. In that chapter, we focused specifically on how those products allowed Starbucks to migrate the brand's core competency of creating in-store experiences onto other product platforms. Through those types of acquisitions, combined with non-coffee-based innovation, Starbucks has also been able to strengthen its consumer packaged goods footprint. For example, bottled Evolution Fresh juices include flavors in four categories:

- Fruit (organic orange, pomegranate, and so on)
- Greens and vegetables (a wide array, including essential vegetables and vital greens)
- Refreshment (organic ginger limeade, pineapple coconut water, and so on)
- Smoothies (apple berry fiber smoothie, protein power smoothie, super greens smoothie, and more)

These beverages are being made available through select Starbucks stores in the United States. Both Evolution Fresh and Tazo are becoming more prominent consumer brands through their presence in grocery stores like Whole Foods, Albertsons, Ralphs, Vons, and Gelson's. In fact, to accommodate the demand for Evolution Fresh juices, Starbucks has had to expand from its original 72,000-square-foot manufacturing facility in San Bernardino, California, to a 260,000-square-foot building in Rancho Cucamonga, California.

Not only has Starbucks opened the Tazo Tea store concept mentioned in Chapter 3, but in late 2012, Starbucks also purchased

Teavana. Teavana has more than 300 company-owned stores and reaches customers globally through its website, www.teavana.com. As the name implies, Teavana is positioned as the "heaven of tea" and is a specialty retailer that caters to newcomers to the world of tea as well as tea connoisseurs, offering more than 100 varieties of premium loose-leaf teas, crafted teaware, and other merchandise associated with tea. While the full strategic value of the acquisition has yet to be realized, Teavana creates for Starbucks a ready-made distribution channel (given Teavana's existing store network in prominent high-traffic areas like shopping malls) and the opportunity to serve a broader base of consumers.

Starbucks has also expanded its retail opportunities through pure innovation, particularly when it comes to products like Starbucks Refreshers, a drink made with Green Coffee Extract that fits into the "energy drink" category as opposed to the "coffee" category. In announcing the launch of Refreshers in 2012, Annie Young-Scrivner, president, Starbucks Canada, suggests the importance of Starbucks entry into the energy drink sector by stating, "The energy category is the fastest-growing category within measured CPG channels at $8 billion, up 16 percent over the last year. The launch of Starbucks Refreshers beverages continues to support our growth strategy to innovate with new products, enter new categories, and expand into new channels of distribution."

Starbucks Refreshers come in three forms: handcrafted in-store beverages, canned sparkling beverages, and a VIA single-serve instant option. The essence of Refreshers across these three presentation formats is a blend of fruit juice and Green Coffee Extract. Cliff Burrows, president, Starbucks Americas, emphasizes the importance of the innovative component of Starbucks Refreshers by noting, "Innovation is at the core of everything we do. . . . The introduction of Starbucks Refreshers beverage platform, featuring Green Coffee Extract, is an innovative extension of the coffee market and is the perfect solution for customers looking for a boost of natural energy and thirst-quenching, delicious refreshment." Extending the coffee market into tea, juice, and energy drinks certainly affords more opportunities to grow the brand through both café/beverage service environments and shelf space in retail establishments, but as with all strategic decisions, there are both risks and rewards.

THE RISKS AND THE PAYOFFS

Jane Genova, a member of the Motley Fool Blog Network, eloquently identifies four key risks of Starbucks expanded consumer packaged goods approach. From Jane's perspective, these challenges include competition with established consumer packaged goods brands, competition from private-label discount brands, projections of flat packaged coffee sales, and "the fourth possible peril is this: A combination of brand fatigue (too much Starbucks distributed through too many market channels) and unbundling the beverage from the iconic ritual of carrying it around in a cup with the green logo and the cardboard wrapper." Certainly Jane raises an important question about brand fatigue and the presentation of products outside of the familiar relationship forged with customers; however, Starbucks has invested a great deal in the creation of the primary relationship with customers in the retail store environment and has created a global demand for its product offerings. Rather than people becoming tired of the brand, the company finds ways to broaden its opportunities to engage customers and expand the places where it can do so. Thus, Jane's concerns are addressed by Starbucks diversification beyond packaged coffee sales and by the return on investment generated by Starbucks channel strategy.

In 2012, Starbucks grocery revenues were growing almost three times as fast as its in-store sales. Currently, Starbucks is still deriving most of its revenue from its retail stores. However, operating revenue for fiscal year 2011 reflects that the packaged goods business was 32 percent of global revenue and 19 percent of its U.S. business. Bill Smead, portfolio manager at Smead Capital Management Inc., notes, "The company's real value and growth potential lies in its brand. . . . They sell water, milk, and coffee beans at boiling temperatures. Warren Buffett says the best companies buy a commodity and sell a brand."

Starbucks leaders definitely buy commodities, build connections, and then mobilize those connections to further strengthen the Starbucks brand. As reflected in earlier chapters, the leaders at Starbucks begin with their passion for their commodities and their people. From there, the leaders steward relationships (connections) between partners and customers. Once those connections are made, Starbucks leaders build even greater brand strength by leveraging technology and constantly exploring ways to provide wider sets of offerings in more areas of a consumer's life. In the end, the leaders elevate products to the status of brands and then leverage brand strength to deliver more products that are designed to ultimately create even greater brand equity.

CONNECTING POINTS

- When personal relationships are created between employees and customers and strengthened through technology, brands are given permission to transfer those emotional connections to new product offerings.
- To achieve a maximum presence in your customers' lives, you may have to serve the needs of other businesses in order to get them to sell or distribute your products.
- The central decision in brand expansion is the degree to which your company owns the infrastructure

through which you are growing your brand and the degree to which you can control versus influence those you entrust with maintaining your brand standards.

- A business is not buildings or brand names; it is a collection of people who should share like-minded objectives.
- The principles that define great customer experiences are extremely similar no matter whether your customer is an individual consumer or a group of individuals from different departments within a business.
- Leadership in the world of consumer packaged goods requires skill in collaboratively positioning your products in the context of competitors' proprietary delivery systems and constantly innovating proprietary delivery systems of your own through strategic relationships with manufacturing and distribution partners.
- When it comes to new product introduction, social media is an important tool for driving your customers' awareness, trial, and product adoption.
- Forward-thinking leaders find ways to encourage customers or give them incentives to widen the array of products that they purchase and consume and expand the settings in which they purchase and consume them.
- According to Warren Buffett, the best companies buy a commodity and sell a brand.

PRINCIPLE 5

CHERISH AND CHALLENGE YOUR LEGACY

As a consultant and speaker, I work with a considerable number of entrepreneurs, business owners, and corporate executives. While there are great differences among these leaders, most of them share two commonalities. First, they wish to guide their people and their businesses in the direction of profitability. Second, they want to make a substantial and sustainable difference through their work. This principle, "Cherish and Challenge Your Legacy," addresses both the success and the significant ambitions of leaders, while also examining how the leadership at Starbucks approaches these goals.

Chapter 10, "Honor the Past, but Don't Be Trapped in It," demonstrates how Starbucks leaders have renewed the entrepreneurial spirit that led to the company's success as a start-up. Additionally, the chapter explores how the leaders direct that entrepreneurship toward solutions that will meet the future needs of their partners and customers. In Chapter 10, you will experience some of the bold and experimental steps that Starbucks leaders are taking to increase the relevance and uniqueness of the brand. In addition, you will encounter some of Starbucks innovative breakthroughs and setbacks.

Chapter 11, "Taking the Long View: Building Success That Lasts," explores how Starbucks leaders make choices to achieve a lasting positive impact on partners, customers, and communities. It examines how Starbucks serves as a catalyst in areas such as sustainable building design, environmental stewardship, small business viability, and global employment. Further, it demonstrates the strength of conviction required to sustain a focus on the significance of your impact and not simply your quarterly profit and loss statements.

Ultimately, "Cherish and Challenge Your Legacy" should encourage you to define the legacy you wish to leave and evaluate your leadership performance, in part, based on your progress toward that legacy.

CHAPTER 10

Honor the Past, but Don't Be Trapped in It

The day before something is a breakthrough, it's a crazy idea.

PETER DIAMANDIS

Before we examine the adaptive and progressive strategies Starbucks designed to ensure that the brand stays relevant, let's take a moment to look at one of the biggest challenges to fostering innovation for strong brands like Starbucks: complacency and inertia born of success. One of the best examples of the liability created by past accomplishments is the Polaroid Corporation.

The glory days for the legendary Polaroid brand ran from the company's creation in 1937 through the late 1970s. During World War II, the company prospered as a defense contractor, but the pivotal innovative moment for the brand occurred in 1948, when Polaroid's founder, Edward Land, created a camera that could process a photograph in minutes. For the next 20-plus years, that single invention was the ticket to Polaroid's monopoly on the instant photography marketplace.

Despite having invested more than 40 percent of Polaroid's research and development budget in digital technology, the company's leaders never fully engaged customers in their efforts to develop digital cameras. As a result, Polaroid saw its market share drop and was ultimately forced to file for bankruptcy in 2001.

Andrea Nagy Smith, writing for the Yale School of Management, places the responsibility for the company's failure squarely on faulty "fundamental assumptions that did not allow top management to adjust to new market realities. First, Polaroid leaders believed that customers would always want a hard-copy print.... When customers abandoned the print, Polaroid was taken by surprise." Andrea further points out that the leaders at Polaroid had a history and a bias toward making money in photography through chemistry as opposed to digital breakthroughs. According to Andrea, "The sheer profitability of film sales created another obstacle to thinking about new business models.... 'Instant film had gross margins well in excess of 65%. So if you're dealing with a media change, how do you replace that with something that's almost or probably as profitable as instant film?'" Polaroid's leaders were victims of their own success. The very strengths that had brought Polaroid dominance in its market worked against the leadership's nimble pursuit of an alternative path. To a lesser degree, Starbucks leaders in the early to mid-2000s became overly fixated on a rapid store growth model.

CHANGING THE PARADIGM

When I wrote my previous book about Starbucks in 2006, I noted that the company was opening a store every four hours and that Howard Schultz suggested that Starbucks was "in 'the early stages of growth,' 'the second inning of a nine-inning game,' and the 'beginning chapters of a long book.'" In 2006, I also gave examples of Starbucks imminent growth plans, including "aggressive growth in China, in-store downloading of music on customers' MP3 players, espresso dating in conjunction with Yahoo!™ Personals, and the distribution of movies and books."

While the focus on international growth (in China and throughout the world) has been sustained since 2006, a great deal has changed. MP3 players are not as popular as they once were. In fact, drippler.com, an electronic gadget news source, reported a substantial rise in site visitors in 2012 who no longer had an interest in owning an MP3 player because of the surge in the desirability of smartphones. Yahoo! Personals shut down in 2010, and customers were migrated over to Match.com. Starbucks 2006 plunge into the movie marketing business with the release of the movie *Akeelah and the Bee* failed to deliver the hoped-for result, so the company pulled back from movie distribution. The ultimate reality was that the 2006 rate of Starbucks store growth was also not sustainable. In fact, opening six new stores a day posed such an operational and staffing challenge that Starbucks was not able to sustain the strength of its brand connection, particularly in the context of global economic challenges.

Jon Gertner, author of *The Idea Factory: Bell Labs and the Great Age of American Innovation*, describes how Starbucks leaders shifted their strategic course. He opines, "Starbucks no longer seems to perceive its future as depending on an ability to clone its essential store concept ad infinitum. . . . These days, the overarching gestalt of the company—demonstrated by its plans for redesigned stores, investments in innovative coffee machines, an expansion of its digital networks and rewards programs—is striving for every branch to be both more versatile and more artisanal."

TIGHTENING UP

In addition to reliance on artisanship and versatility, Troy Alstead, Starbucks chief financial officer and chief administrative officer, suggests that the transition was also anchored to fervent attention to operational excellence and efficiency: "It's interesting for me in hindsight to recognize that new store growth was masking problems we were beginning to experience before we closed 800 U.S. stores in 2008 and 2009. Many in the press, consumers, analysts, and even most of us inside Starbucks believed that we were great store operators." Troy goes on to note that Starbucks brand strength in attracting customers was clouding the picture, covering merely satisfactory operations. Specifically, he points to the leadership's historically marginal performance on the effectiveness of labor deployment or on using data to determine whether a store's hours should be adjusted. Troy shares, "Across many important operational elements, we were just getting by. As such we have had to innovate to exercise greater financial discipline. We still need to achieve powerful human connections, but in the process we also need to create more efficient staff deployment as well as greater management of productivity and waste."

A key element in the success of the Starbucks transformation in the area of efficiency improvement results from an alignment between leaders who are charged with driving change and those who are responsible for ensuring consistent operations. As Craig Russell, senior vice president, Global Coffee, puts it, "If you only let operators run the world, we probably wouldn't have as many stores and we wouldn't have as much innovation. If you only let innovators run the world, you'd have businesses that would be very hard to run and may not make as much money. Our challenge has been to bring both sides of this equation together so we could produce innovations that improve operations, drive growth, enhance the partner and customer experience, and increase profitability. That's a tall order, but it often occurs in the most subtle ways." Ultimate success in driving innovation hinges on the alignment of those who foster change and those who maintain stability.

One example of the subtlety of the improvements that have emerged from an "operational innovation" mindset is the Starbucks "steaming pitcher." Starbucks leaders announced the new pitcher in 2012 by noting that the innovative "design will allow Starbucks baristas to handcraft espresso beverages more efficiently and consistently, so they can continue to deliver great customer service." Specifically, the pitcher's tapered bottom not only was created in pursuit of perfectly steamed milk, but also allowed baristas to easily pour milk to lines marked in the pitcher that conformed to all Starbucks drink sizes. It also limited the space available to overfill the pitcher, thus decreasing waste. In essence, the pitcher, which was smaller than its predecessor, offered a threefold win: (1) improved product quality and consistency, (2) increased ease of use for baristas, and (3) reduced milk waste. While some innovation occurs through changing a central tool like the steaming pitcher, other breakthroughs come from reworking entire delivery systems like Drive Thru.

As mentioned in Chapter 9, the history of the Starbucks Drive Thru concept dates back to 1994, when the first Drive Thru was opened in Vancouver, Washington. While early exploration verified that many customers had the desire to buy Starbucks beverages from the comfort of their vehicle, the execution of that delivery has been a source of continued innovation and operational improvement. Clarice Turner, senior vice president, U.S. Business, indicates, "Drive Thru has been somewhat of a challenge for us at Starbucks. We pride ourselves on the third place experience, and it is often difficult to bring that to life in a Drive Thru. In fact, our customer research had shown a difference in how our Drive Thrus perform relative to the in-store experience. The core of these differences involved consistency and speed of service." One baseline assessment of success in the Drive Thru is the balking rate, or the rate at which people leave the Drive Thru line prior to ordering. Clarice notes, "Our balk rates were unacceptable, so we created a burning platform around this information and asked our partners, 'How do we fix this?' The answer involved operationalizing standards, making the work simpler, and clarifying roles to drive consistent outcomes across our Drive Thrus." This was essential for Starbucks, since Drive Thrus are company-operated stores that contribute nearly 45 percent of U.S. retail profit.

According to Clarice, the standardization process began with an across-the-board upgrade to state-of-the-art headsets and other tools to ensure that baristas could communicate effectively with customers. Timers were later introduced as an awareness tool, with the caveat that speed of service was important, but it was not the only aspect of the experience. Subsequently, wireless 2D scanners were introduced to facilitate mobile payment in the Drive Thru lanes. Upon announcing the availability of using the Starbucks Card mobile app while paying at a Drive Thru, Starbucks leaders explained the innovation challenges they had faced: "Implementing mobile pay in the Drive Thru took a few more considerations than it did inside the store. For one, we needed something that would allow you to perform

REFLECTION ON CONNECTION

1. What are the strengths of your business that have been most instrumental to the success you have achieved? How might those success drivers inadvertently become traps that could constrain future growth?
2. How aligned are the operators and the innovators in your business? Would you say that both groups share an "operational innovation" mindset?
3. Is your organization innovating product delivery tools as well as comprehensive and integrated process improvements?

the scan yourself, rather than handing your phone over to us. Plus, we needed a scanner that would still provide a smooth experience when the weather acts up and at night when it's harder to see, and one that you could comfortably reach from various car heights." If you are using your mobile phone to pay at a Starbucks Drive Thru, the barista can easily use her wireless 2D handheld scanner to capture the bar code off your phone, irrespective of weather, lighting, or the vehicle you are driving. Obstacles overcome, innovation implemented, operational efficiencies achieved, and customer experience enhanced—that is the evolution of great advances in business.

CURIOSITY DIRECTED INWARD

While many people have offered their opinions concerning the differences between an invention and an innovation, I have always favored the view that an invention is a new creation and an innovation is a new solution that attracts a customer. In essence, innovation is an applied and marketable phenomenon. It involves taking an invention and/or an existing product or service and improving on it in a way that makes it more valuable to those you serve. Often leaders have a robust appetite for customer-facing innovation, but at Starbucks, equal attention is directed to improvements that add value to the lives of partners. At the forefront of this innovation is curiosity and a willingness to ask about and listen to the ideas and concerns of your people.

While Starbucks leaders have a long history of surveying partners, they intensified their efforts as part of the company's transformational agenda. Specifically, the leaders engaged in a 30-minute comprehensive interview approach to supplement the company's routine closed-ended 10-minute survey. That more intensive survey was geared to get to the core of the partner experience and involved a qualitative dialogue that asked probing questions. Given the size of the Starbucks workforce, involving partners in a survey that takes three times as long as the ordinary format requires a sizable investment. This was particularly true when the first wave of the survey produced a 91 percent response rate from the more than 100,000 U.S. partners. The survey also required substantial time to process, given the hundreds of thousands of open-ended comments that it garnered. Later, Starbucks rolled out the detailed survey in international markets and achieved a similar 90 percent response rate. Those responses were used to guide leadership efforts to better understand partner needs and innovate improvements in offerings that were important to partner groups, such as Starbucks U (discussed in Chapter 5).

Howard Schultz describes one such partner-focused innovation by noting, "We just did something in China that I think is one of the most innovative things we have ever done in our history—and it had nothing to do with the customer. . . . Think about an Annual Meeting of Shareholders; we had a similar meeting with partners and their parents in Beijing and Shanghai, and we had about 90 percent participation." From Howard's perspective, the benefit of this novel approach (meeting with the parents of Chinese partners) reflects the company's ability to weave Starbucks connection–based values into a family-centric event reflecting cultural and local relevance.

RELEVANCE AND RISK

By definition, the key to innovation is relevance to the audience. However, seeking relevance is not for the faint of heart or the risk-averse. At the same time, the pursuit of relevance is not a reckless pursuit. In fact, it is often a combination of small iterative improvements mixed with calculated bold—hopefully game-changing—moves. Many of Starbucks game-changing efforts have been discussed in previous chapters. They include the significant investments needed to create VIA, Blonde, Verismo, the Starbucks mobile app, and the partnership with Square. Similarly, they can be seen in the courage and capital involved in acquiring Tazo, La Boulange, Evolution Fresh, and Teavana.

While talking about relevant innovation, Howard Schultz best described the role of calculated risk and bold moves by noting, "The future of our company is based on having the kind of curiosity that is linked to the DNA of the entrepreneurial endeavors that we have had for 40 years. And that curiosity has to anticipate and understand what is coming and what will be relevant. Then you have to make a big bet." As an example of a "big bet," Howard mentioned the company's willingness to enter the instant coffee market with VIA. In essence, Starbucks leadership decided to enter a more than $17 billion category that had experienced virtually no innovation in 50 years and that was dominated primarily by a single company. Howard adds, "We decided to take the premium franchise of Starbucks and go down a road that has been linked to the bowels of quality. We had enough insight, curiosity, courage, and confidence that we cracked the code on quality by leveraging technology. We were willing to make a big bet, take a big swing, and demonstrate to our people and our customers that we had the wherewithal to take the road less traveled because this is who we are."

In the context of that "insight, curiosity, courage, and confidence," Howard is quick to caution that no company can make a large number of big bets in a year. He believes that each one has to be "highly calculated and supported. There has to be a vested interest by the leaders of the company that we are united because we have to convince an organization to follow us and give them a reason why they should do so. You have to ask and answer the question in the affirmative, 'What is in it for them for doing this?'"

By achieving alignment at the leadership level and then considering the impact of innovative changes on those who will be asked to implement them, Starbucks creates a culture of risk tolerance. Katie Seawell, vice president, Espresso and Brewed Coffee at Starbucks, notes, "What I love about this company is we're not afraid to explore new ideas. It is scary pursuing Blonde or VIA, or going into juices, but you need to be willing to take your brand and product into new spaces. If you don't, you run the risk of becoming dated, and customers and partners alike will lose interest in you as competitors claim the white space filled with new products and ideas."

While the next "big thing" or "big risk" is an essential part of business leadership, Starbucks attempts to balance a sense of urgency with due diligence. While recognizing Starbucks as being among the Top 25 Most Innovative Companies in *Fast Company* magazine, innovation author Jon Gertner describes Starbucks balancing act between urgency and prudence by pointing out that Howard Schultz (as Steve Jobs was at Apple) is "still the company's main instigator—has a kernel of an idea. . . . He then activates a team, even inviting members over to his house for pizza, if that helps to create a stir of urgency. Ideas at Starbucks are supposed to undergo a rigorous review process and 6 to 12 months in the company pipeline. Sometimes, too—as was the case of Blonde (18 months in development) or VIA instant (about 20 years)—it can take far longer." In other cases, such as launching an in-store campaign to sell wristbands in support of a Starbucks job-creation program called Create Jobs for USA (which will be discussed in Chapter 11), the process of innovation and launch was compressed to a brisk 30 days.

Overall brand innovation at Starbucks is a by-product of listening to the voice of the stakeholder, careful new idea evaluation, a timely development cycle, and a careful test-marketing phase. Troy Alstead, Starbucks chief financial officer and chief administrative officer, notes, "We've become much better at taking ideas, exploring their viability, making adjustments, and turning those ideas into profits. Part of that comes from learning as a result of our past mistakes and limiting the scope of new idea tests. One such example of an unsuccessful launch was our Sorbetto product."

Starbucks test-marketed Sorbetto™ iced beverage in a few select stores north of Seattle in the spring of 2008, and by the summer of that year had engaged in a slightly broader test market throughout Los Angeles and Orange County in southern California. Melody Overton, who writes a popular Starbucks blog titled StarbucksMelody.com (which garners approximately 55,000 unique visitors and 90,000 monthly page views), suggests that Sorbetto's failure was not a function of taste. She states, "It was absolutely delicious. Lots of people liked it." Melody goes on to highlight factors that probably led to Sorbetto's demise. Her list includes the timing of the product's release relative to both the U.S. recession and the closing of Starbucks stores. Melody viewed Sorbetto as ambiguously falling somewhere between beverage and dessert, and she noted, "The machines required to make the beverage in the store were a terrible problem. They were incredibly labor-intensive to clean. They took up a lot of precious counter space. They looked like a big Slurpee machine which created a very poor 7-11 type image for Starbucks. All in all, it just didn't add up."

While Sorbetto was not a commercial success for Starbucks, Troy Alstead suggests that the way in which the launch was handled reflects the maturation of leadership: "Sorbetto shows how our innovation strategy continues to evolve. For example, we only provided the product to some of our stores, and we were quick to reverse course when it did not make financial sense to pursue. That is different from prior years, where we would broadly launch an unsuccessful product like Chantico™ and leave it in the market for a year." Chantico was a thick, sweet, hot, drinking chocolate of a type that could be found in European cafés. Starbucks launched the product nationally in January of 2005, describing it as a "drinkable dessert." At launch, Starbucks leaders predicted that Chantico would produce a handful of beverage line extensions; however, it was removed from Starbucks stores around January 2006. Failed product tests are never a desirable outcome, but leaders who successfully drive innovation learn how to manage the speed and scope with which those products are presented to and removed from the marketplace.

THE EVER-MOVING RELEVANCE TARGET

John Kotter, a former professor at the Harvard Business School and author of *Leading Change: An Action Plan from the World's Foremost Expert on Business Leadership*, confirms what many leaders experience every day, namely, that the "rate of change in the world today is going up. It's going up fast, and it's affecting organizations in a huge way. . . . New companies spring up seemingly overnight. Products and services that were revolutionary two years ago are rendered obsolete if they don't adapt to market changes fast enough." Throughout this book, you've been exposed to many ways in which Starbucks leaders attempt to stay ahead of the obsolescence curve. For the purpose of discussion here, let's look at how Starbucks leaders approach innovation through food and beverage experimentation, new concept designs, and technological advances both inside and outside of the Starbucks store.

Food and Beverage Experimentation

From its inception, Starbucks has had a conflicted history with food delivery. In 1998, Starbucks test-marketed a full-service restaurant concept that it called Café Starbucks. Three Café Starbucks had opened in the Seattle area by the fall of 1998, serving items prepared on-site such as chicken pot pie and meatloaf. Roseanne Harper, writing at the time for *Restaurant News*, noted, "The Café Starbucks concept includes a wait staff, seating for up to 65, and a menu that covers all dayparts beginning with full breakfasts. In addition to a repertoire of espresso-based drinks, Café Starbucks serves wine and beer."

Also in 1998, Starbucks leaders were testing a brand concept, Circadia, in San Francisco, California. Mark Gimein described Circadia in *Fortune* magazine by noting, "Surrounded by San Francisco's pricey new loft apartments, [Circadia] resurrects the feel of the 1960s coffee shops of Greenwich Village. . . . Circadia may be the start of a bigger chain and a testbed of concepts for Starbucks' flagship store." Mark went on to describe Circadia as a drop-in office for prospective San Francisco entrepreneurs, complete with high-speed Internet (which required a credit card swipe for use) and a well-equipped conference room that could be rented for $50 per hour. According to Mark, the menu at Circadia included "salads, sandwiches, and 'nosh plates.' . . . Circadia's full bar features the usual and the creative." While neither Café Starbucks nor Circadia proved to be a successful venture, they reflect the long history of the brand's exploration of food and noncoffee beverages.

As discussed in Chapter 3, Howard Schultz kept prepared food items out of the morning Starbucks lineup until he could be sure that the smell of food (particularly burnt cheese) did not overwhelm the aroma of brewed coffee. By 2008, not only had Starbucks leaders found ways to allow coffee and warmed foods to coexist in the Starbucks store, but they had also championed healthier "grab-and-go" and "right-sized" food options. Erin Zimmer, national managing editor for *Serious Eats*, noted, "Starbucks pitched a new game plan . . . a 'healthier' breakfast line-up with fewer calories and more protein."

Continuing in the direction of fewer calories and ready-to-eat options, in 2011, as part of the company's fortieth-anniversary celebration, Starbucks leaders introduced eight managed-portion desserts and eight Bistro Boxes (four snack-sized and four entrée portions). The dessert items, referred to as Starbucks Petites, included Peanut Butter Mini Cupcakes, Red

Velvet Whoopie Pies, Lemon Sweet Squares, and Cake Pops. Each of these mini-desserts was less than 200 calories. The initial Bistro Box lineup included items such as Chipotle Chicken Wraps, Sesame Noodles, Tuna Salad, as well as Chicken and Hummus. All Bistro Box items were created to be less than 500 calories, and the specific items just listed were less than 400 calories. Over time, the lineup of mini-desserts and Bistro Boxes changes, but the focus remains on creating flavorful options that offer convenience and managed portion sizes.

Starbucks strategic approach to food led Christine Hall, a 66-year-old Virginia woman, to gain media attention when she reported that she had adhered to what has now been called the "Starbucks Diet." Over a period of more than two years, Christine had gone from 190 to 115 pounds by eating almost exclusively at Starbucks. On an average day, Christine purportedly would have black coffee and a cup of oatmeal for breakfast. At lunch and dinner, she would have either a Bistro Box or a panini sandwich.

As part of the continuing evolution of Starbucks food items, Starbucks purchased Bay Bread LLC, a bakery company with 20 La Boulange stores across the San Francisco Bay area, for $100 million in 2012. Upon making the acquisition, Cliff Burrows, Starbucks president, Americas, indicated, "It's a superb opportunity to bring high-quality food into Starbucks," and when talking about expansion, stated that Starbucks "will take it one store at a time. Wherever opportunity takes us." Once experimentation is engaged in or an acquisition is made, leaders must truly have the patience and the discipline to allow brands to move in the direction of their optimal success.

New Concepts

Consistent with this chapter's title, Starbucks leaders did not abandon their values or turn their back on their core competencies in pursuit of the changes needed as part of the company's

Transformation Agenda. However, some observers have expressed concern over the speed and magnitude of Starbucks leaders' appetite for innovation. For example, some commentators sounded an alarm over the possibility that alcohol would become a prominent feature in all Starbucks stores, and headlines like "Latte or Lager" proliferated when the leaders at Starbucks incorporated alcohol sparingly and strategically through an emerging concept called Starbucks Evenings. Stores that provide Starbucks Evenings offer the traditional Starbucks items throughout the day and evening, but add a menu of wine, beer, and small plates after 4 p.m. By late 2012, only five Starbucks Evenings stores had opened in and around Seattle, Washington; five more were in the Chicago, Illinois, area; four were open in and near Atlanta, Georgia; two could be found in Los Angeles, California; and one was open in Portland, Oregon. Starbucks Evenings stores are designed as neighborhood meeting spots. The Starbucks website shares the value proposition behind the Starbucks Evenings concept by suggesting that it gives customers who already love Starbucks during the day even more reasons to love the brand at night. According to the Starbucks website, "Sometimes you just want a glass of wine and a delicious bite to eat without going to a bar or making a restaurant reservation. . . . Drop in after work, with friends, after yoga, by yourself, after a long day or after a great day. The food is amazing. The wine selection is simple and smart. The chairs are just as comfortable as they are in the morning." From the standpoint of food, Starbucks Evenings locations offer items such as truffle macaroni and cheese, bacon-wrapped dates with balsamic glaze, artichoke and goat cheese flatbread, and chocolate fondue. Rather than seeing the Starbucks Evenings concept as a ubiquitous strategy to drive traffic during the evening hours, the leadership is exploring a targeted approach by making the option available only in neighborhoods where the leaders believe that Starbucks Evenings will be an excellent fit.

In a similar vein, Starbucks leaders launched a dramatically varied walk-up/drive-up store concept, the first of which was opened in Denver, Colorado, in late 2012. Mark Wilson, writing in fastcodesign.com, describes this concept by noting, "Starbucks opened a store unlike any before it. There are no leather chairs or free power outlets. In fact, there's no space for the customer at all. Starbucks has reimagined the coffee hut as a 'modern modular,' LEED® certified drive-thru and walk-up shop. The building was constructed in a factory and delivered from a truck, but its facade is clad in gorgeous old Wyoming snow fencing. As diminutive as the shop may be, its designer wants

New modular store concept, Denver, Colorado, USA.

drivers to pass by and ask 'What is that?' only to conclude that, oh, 'it's art.'"

This concept store addresses sustainable building objectives (which will be discussed in more detail in Chapter 11), while also achieving local relevance in a low-cost, easily scalable option. The walk-up/drive-up takes only 500 feet of retail space and can accommodate five baristas and all the equipment necessary to deliver the full Starbucks menu.

According to Chris Carr, executive vice president, U.S. Retail Stores, every emerging concept, whether it is Starbucks Evenings, the walk-up/drive-up store, or an idea that is just beginning to surface in the Starbucks innovation pipeline, must be "analyzed through the three filters of our retail operating model: partner, customer, and business. We have established the

REFLECTION ON CONNECTION

1. Are you willing to make potentially game-changing big bets? How would you rate your ability to drive innovation from the standpoint of your insight, curiosity, courage, and confidence?
2. What innovation risks are you presently taking? What are the risks you incur from not taking your brand into a new space?
3. When it comes to exploring innovative ideas, do you ask if the proposed solution makes sense for your customer, your business, and your staff? What other filters (for example, cost, ease of implementation, or likely reward) do you apply when you are evaluating the viability of an idea?

operational discipline to ask ourselves: Does it make sense for our partners? Does it make sense for our customers? Does it make sense for our business? When we are testing any new initiative, we hold ourselves accountable to ensure that our innovative solution will successfully pass all three filters. If the test does not deliver on behalf of our partners, customers, and business, we have developed the discipline to walk away." Innovation is only as good as the mechanisms an organization has to interpret the success or viability of the concepts. At Starbucks, leaders have clearly defined the criteria by which innovation should be advanced or curtailed.

Technological Advances for In- and Out-of-Store Experiences

In Chapter 8, we looked at how Starbucks leaders have deployed technology to enhance the customer connection. From the perspective of innovation, technology is also being advanced to create forward-looking product delivery options and experience enhancements. From the standpoint of new delivery approaches, imagine having your favorite coffee beverages prepared just for you—by a vending machine. The first prototypes for this technology were presented through the Seattle's Best Coffee brand.

As you recall, Seattle's Best Coffee is the Seattle-based coffee company that Starbucks purchased in 2003. Chris Bruzzo, senior vice president, Channel Brand Management, highlights the overall strategy behind the Seattle's Best Coffee repositioning. Chris notes, "We've struggled at times clarifying the role of Seattle's Best Coffee within our brand family. That brand is now focused on being the on-ramp to premium coffee for individuals whose lifestyle might not presently connect with the Starbucks brand. We are positioning ourselves to serve the 107 million adults in the United States with median household incomes around $50,000. For most of these people, time is precious and their coffee rituals are tied to their vehicles and/or linked to convenience and value. They're on their way to work, and they're getting their coffee at convenience stores, gas stations, or quick service restaurants like Subway and Burger King."

Given the target consumer for Seattle's Best Coffee, the brand is innovating in the direction of product positioning at convenience or QSR settings, as well as creating franchised delivery models and the Seattle's Best Coffee vending machine. In keeping with this strategy, leaders at Seattle's Best Coffee announced a franchise Drive Thru model in 2012. Melissa Allison, *Seattle Times* business reporter, noted, "In Seattle's Best Coffee's latest divergence from corporate parent Starbucks, every new location will be a 523-square-foot Drive Thru-only café. . . . The chain expects to open thousands of little red stores from which baristas will dispense brewed coffee, sweet flavored lattes, handheld pies and breakfast sandwiches. . . . If all goes according to plan, the tiny cafés will be situated mostly in empty suburban spaces. . . . The stores will be owned by franchisees who can afford multiple locations, with launch costs at the low end of Seattle's Best current startup range of $265,000 for a kiosk."

If 523 feet of space is too much for coffee delivery, how about a 9-square-foot retail "on-the-go" footprint? Leaders at Seattle's Best Coffee have worked with Coinstar Inc. (the company associated with Redbox DVD kiosks) to create a vending option called the Rubi kiosk

Seattle's Best Coffee Rubi kiosk.

that grinds and brews a 12-or 16-ounce cup of premium coffee and other beverages in just about a minute. According to Bill Mikulka, Rubi's general manager, "The coffee market is enormous . . . [and] is very much about convenience, quality and value. We've built a platform that can be in arm's length of desire." In the spirit of affordability and value, Rubi kiosks serve fresh-brewed coffee with prices starting at just $1 per cup.

Other technology explorations at Starbucks are looking to enhance the quality of the coffeehouse experience. One such example is the wireless charging spots with Duracell Powermats. As someone who has used Starbucks stores as a location for crafting the words of my books, I have often faced the challenge of finding an available power outlet for my laptop computer. In an effort to decrease the power source search, Starbucks leaders have placed inductive charging technology in some of its tabletops in select Boston, Massachusetts, locations. The purpose of this effort is to assess how customers respond to emerging charging technologies in the context of their overall utility in the café experience.

A VIRTUAL LEARNING LAB

It would be impossible to provide an in-depth review of all the product, service delivery, and experience enhancement innovations that are currently being explored at Starbucks. Such innovations take forms as diverse as a relationship with the National History Museum in the United Kingdom to offer My Starbucks Rewards members the opportunity to receive two-for-one deals and priority access to the annual Christmas ice rink near the museum. Additionally, technological innovation can take the form of a pop-up screen for computer users in Starbucks stores in Switzerland and Austria, asking them to rate the quality of their beverage so that instant service recovery can occur, if needed.

Ultimately, Starbucks benefits from a leadership team that maintains the passion for entrepreneurship that led to the company's meteoric rise. That passion was reawakened during the push for the brand's survival during the 2008–2009 time frame. The leaders have tightened up their operational discipline and diversified their delivery platforms. Howard Schultz encapsulated the necessity of innovation at Starbucks, and probably for your business as well, when he told a London British Forum, "Any company, small or large, consumer or otherwise, that is going to embrace the status quo as an operating principle is just going to be dead. . . . The need for constant innovation and pushing forward has never been greater than it is today. Every company must have the ability and the discipline to really be curious and look around the corners [to] see things and anticipate things that other people don't see. But, that is not enough. You must then have the courage to go after those things. Not to bet the company on them, but execute [that] kind of courage." If you had to reduce the Starbucks model of innovation down to a sentence it would simply be the following:

> Mix curiosity, courage, and discipline in a tireless pursuit of the ever-changing needs of your people, your customers, and the profitability of your business.

Sounds like a solid formula for any leader who wants to "honor the past but not be trapped in it."

CONNECTING POINTS

- Complacency and inertia are challenges to innovation for successful brands.
- A great deal of long-term business success is associated with innovations in operational excellence and efficiency.

- Alignment among leaders is essential to innovation. Innovators and operators must share a common vision.
- An invention is a new creation. An innovation is a new creation that attracts a customer.
- By definition, innovation must be relevant to your identified audience.
- When making potentially game-changing big bets, leaders must demonstrate insight, curiosity, courage, and confidence.
- If you're unwilling to take your brand into a new space, people will lose interest in it as others bring forward new products and new ideas.
- In order to turn ideas into profits effectively, leaders must be willing to make mistakes and learn from them.
- Innovation should be filtered through three questions: Does it make sense for your customers? Does it make sense for your business? Does it make sense for your staff?
- If you embrace the status quo as an operating principle, your business is likely to die.
- Great corporate leaders must have the ability and the discipline to look around the corners to see and anticipate things that other people can't see.

CHAPTER 11

Taking the Long View: Building Success That Lasts

You are not here merely to make a living. You are here in order to enable the world to live more amply, with greater vision, with a finer spirit of hope and achievement.

WOODROW WILSON

What are your primary responsibilities as a leader? Are they to drive profitability, maximize the potential of your people, and strengthen your brand equity? In their book *A Leader's Legacy*, James Kouzes and Barry Posner suggest that true leadership "brings with it a responsibility to do something of significance that makes families, communities, work organizations, nations, the environment and the world better places than they are today." While Kouzes and Posner's words might seem like lofty and untenable platitudes, the leaders at Starbucks view themselves as being responsible for more than business success. In fact, Howard Schultz integrates the broader social good with the overall viability of Starbucks business by noting, "Since Starbucks earliest days, I have believed in a strong link between our company's performance, our values, and the impact we have on the communities where we do business. This interdependence is at the heart of our mission. . . . Such interdependence is also right for our business, especially in the times we now live. Consumers have long rewarded brands with their loyalty when they feel a company's mission and aspirations align with their own."

In fact, at Starbucks, the leadership's aspirations regarding social responsibility are defined in one of the company's guiding principles, that involving neighborhoods. That principle reads:

> **Our Neighborhood**
> Every store is part of a community, and we take our responsibility to be good neighbors seriously. We want to be invited in wherever we do business. We can be a force for positive action—bringing together our partners, customers, and the community to contribute every day. Now we see that our responsibility—and our potential for good—is even larger. The world is looking to Starbucks to set the new standard, yet again. We will lead.

Throughout this chapter, we will look at just a few of the socially responsible areas where Starbucks sets "the new standard" and "leads." For our purposes, we will look specifically at behaviors leadership demonstrates in the course of setting goals, taking action, and measuring progress in the areas of environmental stewardship, ethical sourcing, community development, and job creation.

ENVIRONMENTAL STEWARDSHIP

If you were to Google the phrase "saddling future generations," you'd come up with more than 356,000 results. Most of these references apply to the perceived shortcomings of political leaders globally who borrow money to pay for present-day services and leave the repayment of those loans to future generations of taxpayers. While this behavior is expedient for a politician's re-election, many critics see it as myopic and irresponsible social policy. The parallel in business is a leader who achieves short-term profitability at the expense of long-term sustainability. Such a leader might consume large quantities of finite raw materials and "saddle future generations" of leaders with a supply shortfall. For example, leaders in agribusiness and commercial fishing have been accused of short-term profit taking in the form of overfarming or overfishing.

At Starbucks, leaders not only consider the short-term impact of the resources they consume, but also look for ways of doing business that decrease consumption over the near and long term. Additionally, these leaders seek to drive initiatives that will help influence other organizations to consider responsible stewardship of finite resources. This impact on other organizations is particularly evident in the areas of sustainable building design, the recyclability of Starbucks cups, and manufacturing processes (for example, the environmentally friendly changes to the Starbucks cup sleeve).

Sustainable Building Design

While I have spent time talking about culturally relevant building design (such as the Bank store in Amsterdam) and designs that offer new delivery platforms (such as the walk-up/drive-up concept in Denver, Colorado), Arthur Rubinfeld, chief creative officer for Starbucks and president, Global Innovation and Evolution Fresh Retail, indicates that the galvanizing and energizing force among Starbucks store designers is "a stake we put in the ground around 2008, when we announced our goal to lead the world in global, sustainable retail building practices in company-owned stores worldwide. Environmental considerations have long been a part of our company, but in 2008, we claimed a specific aspiration and shifted our role to not only be stewards but responsible educators. We are building stores with sustainable products by utilizing metal, wood, and stone/organics, as well as recyclable and recycled materials. As importantly, we are making sustainability more visible so people around the world might consider an environmental lifestyle. We're educating consumers about water conservation, energy conservation, and we have taken a leadership position when it comes to eco-conscious stores. There is immense satisfaction in inspiring others."

One highly visual example of the sustainable store design can be found in a Starbucks concept store referred to as the Reclamation Drive Thru, located in Tukwila, Washington.

Reclamation Drive Thru, Tukwila, Washington, USA.

Anthony Perez, senior manager, Global Store Design, was responsible for the project and shares the eco-conscious nature of its design: "Shipping containers source our coffees and teas from around the world. But many end up in scrap yards once they reach their average 20-year lifespan. Reclamation Drive

Thru was inspired by a desire to help keep items used throughout our supply chain, like old shipping containers, out of the waste stream. The result: a 450-square-foot Drive Thru and walk-up store made from four end-of-life-cycle shipping containers. One small 20-foot container holds garbage, recycling, and storage, but other than that, the whole store is contained within the shells of four containers that have been reclaimed, refurnished, renewed, and revived. And it works! . . . This small project came at a perfect time here at Starbucks as we challenge ourselves to deliver LEED certified stores across the U.S."

LEED certification refers to meeting Leadership in Energy and Environmental Design criteria. If these criteria are met, the result is a voluntary third-party verification by the U.S. Green Building Council, indicating that the building has been designed and constructed and is being operated in an ecologically sound manner. It is an approach to creating a built environment that conserves water and energy, reduces greenhouse emissions, decreases waste sent to landfills, and increases occupants' health and safety. Many business leaders have passed on remodeling or building physical spaces that meet LEED standards because they fear that building costs will be considerably higher. However, the Natural Resource Defense Council suggests, "Green building skeptics sometimes argue that it's difficult or even impossible to build green without paying a big cost premium. But real-world examples show that you can complete a LEED certified green building project for an average of 2 percent more in upfront costs, and sometimes even below standard market construction costs. Plus, any extra first costs you pay can be recovered through faster lease-up rates, rental premiums and increased market valuation."

Responsible management of capital expenditures is important, and when it comes to Starbucks stores, so are responsible sustainability efforts. Jim Hanna, director, Environmental Impact at Starbucks, notes, "Around 75 percent of our controllable environmental footprint comes from our retail operations. . . . For us to have any credibility as a responsible company in this arena, we had to tackle our stores first."

Ben Packard, former vice president, Global Responsibility, puts Starbucks leadership position on LEED in perspective by noting, "We have been working with the organization responsible for LEED certification, the U.S. Green Building Council, since 2001. Rather than setting our own standards on sustainable buildings and then going out to validate our effort, we knew it would be important to have a trust mark conferred by an independent certifying agency. LEED criteria were designed for office buildings and not retail spaces, so I became involved as chair of the retail development committee at the U.S. Green Building Council to work with other retail industry and environmental leaders in making appropriate adjustments to the criteria. Once those retail standards were established, we pursued LEED certification aggressively."

In a Starbucks LEED certified store, some energy- and water-saving elements might be noticeable by customers. These would include items like LED lightbulbs; energy-efficient equipment such as icemakers, dishwashers, or blenders; low-flow faucets; and dual-flush toilets. Non-customer-facing energy-efficient, water-saving efforts would include energy management systems, which have shown reductions of 20 percent in heating, ventilation, and air-conditioning (HVAC) energy consumption; a water filtration system that produces 50 percent less wastewater than prior systems, and a sanitizing sink that saves a substantial quantity of fresh water while adhering to all applicable health standards.

To have an interactive virtual tour of a LEED certified Starbucks store, please go to http://tinyurl.com/orvk49d.

Each year Starbucks publishes a corporate social responsibility report that serves as a report card on the company's progress toward social and environmental goals. In 2011, for example, the report validated that the company was "on track" to meet its goal of having all its company-owned new buildings make their way through the lengthy process of becoming LEED certified, noting that 75 percent of new company-owned stores had, in a year, already achieved LEED certification status.

The lessons learned from Starbucks journey to LEED include the importance of setting ambitious sustainability goals; seeking third-party criteria to validate your achievement of those goals; playing a role in refining these criteria for your industry, if necessary; executing against those goals; and transparently reporting your progress toward your objectives. In a smaller business setting, you may wish to access tool kits provided by the Office of Small Business Programs at the U.S. Environmental Protection Agency (an example of which can be found at http://tinyurl.com/m7tl7td).

In addition to receiving recognition like the Green Building Design Award from Global Green USA and a 2012 Good Design Is Good Business Award conferred by *Architectural Record* for the company's efforts toward LEED certifications, Starbucks has also been acknowledged for its overall accomplishments in energy conservation and its reliance on renewable energy. It has been recognized as a Green Power Leadership Award winner by the Environmental Protection Agency, since Starbucks is a top U.S. purchaser of renewable energy. For example, in 2011, Starbucks purchased more than 421 million kilowatt-hours of green energy through Green-e® certified renewable energy credits. Those wind-generated electricity purchases powered more than 50 percent of Starbucks U.S. company-owned stores. The company has set goals of reducing its energy use by 25 percent from 2008 levels and having 100 percent of its electricity consumption generated through renewable energy by 2015.

Merging innovation with efforts to reduce energy consumption, Starbucks has teamed up with the Bonneville Power

Administration and a collective of public utilities in the northwestern United States to explore whether changes in human behavior can result in substantial energy savings. Instead of relying solely on energy-saving technology, Starbucks leaders will challenge store partners to compete with partners in other stores to see who can create the greatest energy reductions. The leaders at Starbucks are taking responsibility for short-term energy efficiency and long-term environmental stability. In the process, they are leading others in the pursuit of more sustainable business practices. This leadership position could not be more evident than in the area of recycling.

Bringing Materials Back for a Sequel

Just as Starbucks leaders worked with the U.S. Green Building Council to establish LEED criteria for retail buildings, so too have company leaders collaborated with other experts and leaders in the area of recycling to create a solution that decreases the waste associated with Starbucks cups. As I was completing my previous book about the company, Starbucks was poised to launch the industry's first hot beverage paper cup with 10 percent postconsumer recycled fiber. By demonstrating the safety of the recycled content in its cups, Starbucks had been able to encourage the U.S. Food and Drug Administration to change its position prohibiting the use of postconsumer recycled content in paper products that came in contact with food.

While the use of postconsumer recycled content in cups was an important step, it did not mean that the cups themselves were necessarily recyclable. This was problematic for the leaders at Starbucks, who had set a goal of ensuring that 100 percent of their cups would be reusable or recyclable by 2015. Ben Packard, former vice president, Global Responsibility, notes, "Our cups are made of paper, but that paper is covered with a polymer. This means in cities where the recycling market will take that material, the cup is recyclable. In other cities, the polymer makes it nonrecyclable. This type of variability prompted us to begin hosting a meeting in 2009 which we call the Cup Summit."

The Cup Summit has continued to grow annually and brings together individuals from all areas of the plastic and paper cup value chain. These stakeholders include raw material suppliers, government officials, beverage and retail businesses, cup manufacturers, nongovernmental organizations, recyclers, and academic experts from institutions like MIT. According to Ben, "Initially, we thought our solution would come from changing materials, but we were encouraged to challenge all assumptions and map every aspect of a cup's journey. As such, we literally had a map from tree to garbage dump on which we outlined all the things that would have to change and how we would need to go about effecting those changes." Because of the knowledge gained through the Cup Summits, the leaders at Starbucks have already implemented recycling in a number of U.S. markets by developing close relationships with the leaders of various municipalities. The company has also initiated recycling pilot projects across the United States and collaborated with Canadian and U.S. paper mills to explore compatibility and ways to drive demand for cups with postconsumer content.

Jim Hanna, director, Environmental Impact, notes that Starbucks is committed to the recyclable cup issue because it is good for the environment and because it is important to customers. He offers, "Our footprint is most affected by our built environment as well as the energy and other resources that go into running our stores, but when we talk to our customers and other stakeholders, they are asking about our progress on the recyclability of our cups. The Starbucks cup is a touchable, tangible, visible icon of the company, and it symbolizes our environmental performance." When an environmental issue is salient to your customers, it has to rise on your project priority list.

A similar iconic and tangible aspect of the Starbucks cup experience is the cup sleeve. In 1997, Starbucks introduced the sleeve made of corrugated paper in an effort to reduce the waste that occurred when customers requested that their hot beverage be double cupped. The sleeve offered an insulating layer between the customer's hand and the Starbucks cup, with the added benefit that it could be constructed with postconsumer recycled fiber, since the sleeve never made contact with the coffee. At the time it was launched, 60 percent of the composition of the sleeve came from this recycled material.

The sleeve was initially intended to be an interim solution as Starbucks leaders researched alternative strategies to alter the thermal properties of the company's cups. In the end, it was determined that the sleeve was the most viable option—thus, it continues to be used today. Matt Cook, president of LDP Manufacturing, the supplier that provides the cup sleeves, suggests that the leadership at Starbucks pushed his company to improve the sleeve: "Starbucks leaders essentially asked us, 'What does the next generation of a hot cup sleeve look like? Is it possible to create a product that has less material, increases recycled content, and offers the same or even superior thermal insulation?' I can't express to you the magnitude of that challenge, but we worked with Hinkle Corporation on the chemistry around the internal adhesives and ultimately produced a groundbreaking technology. It is the new hot cup sleeve, which Starbucks calls the EarthSleeve™." Without compromising its thermal properties, the new sleeve uses 35 percent less paper and is made from 85 percent postconsumer recycled fiber (a 25-percentage-point increase from its predecessor). Certifying organizations have determined the sleeve to be fully compostable, and Western Michigan University has determined it to be repulpable. With nearly 3 billion cup sleeves produced in 2011 alone, Starbucks calculations suggest that the EarthSleeve™ will save more than 100,000 trees.

While cups and sleeves are high profile, most of Starbucks recycling efforts are not customer-facing. Many initiatives involve things like syrup bottles, milk jugs, and cardboard boxes. However, the leaders at Starbucks are never content with those behind-the-counter efforts. They understand that sustainability is not something that is done as a marketing or publicity effort; it is an authentic commitment to the future viability of businesses and to future generations of customers. While smaller business owners aren't likely to be able to support recycling research, they can take simple steps like looking for a printing company that uses recycled paper or seeking out vendors that supply environmentally friendly products. In the end, it is not enough to talk about sustainability. True leadership requires a willingness to invest in the long-term health of one's business and active collaboration with others, out of a genuine sense of responsibility.

REFLECTION ON CONNECTION

1. How are you ensuring that your leadership decisions are not "saddling future generations" of leaders with sustainability challenges?
2. Where have you not only responsibly managed energy-efficiency, recycling, or green building issues for your business, but also partnered with other leaders to advance these issues in your industry?
3. What are the most salient customer-facing and non-customer-facing environmental issues you are addressing?

CARING ABOUT THE PEOPLE THAT BRING PRODUCTS TO MARKET

In Chapter 2, I discussed C.A.F.E. Practices, Starbucks commitment to the success and sustainability of suppliers in its coffees' countries of origin. I also noted that Starbucks had worked with Conservation International in the creation of these practices so that the needs of coffee farmers would be met. To that end, the leadership has set out three specific farmer-related sourcing objectives:

- "Ensure 100% of our coffee is ethically sourced by 2015."
- "Invest in farmers and their communities by increasing farmer loans to $20 million by 2015."
- "Improve farmers' access to carbon markets, helping them generate additional income while protecting the environment."

By 2011, Starbucks was on track with each of these objectives, as 86 percent of its coffee was ethically sourced under C.A.F.E. Practices, $14.7 million in loan commitments had been made to farmers, and programs in Mexico and Indonesia were paving the way for more farmers to have access to carbon markets and environmental protection.

Starbucks has a massive supply chain challenge that extends beyond coffee farmers. At the store level alone, it requires more than 83,000 deliveries a week to enable its stores to operate when a partner opens the door in the morning. The supply chain must also address the future growth and expansion of the business across products, categories, and channels. In many ways, the Starbucks brand rests on whether the supply chain can take ideas and create a physical manifestation of them in the marketplace.

Despite those challenges, the leaders at Starbucks must ensure that their suppliers are diverse and that they are committed to business ethics and humane operations. Starbucks leaders understand that they can outsource physical activity, but they cannot outsource responsibility for the quality of their products or the way people are treated in the creation of those products.

An example of Starbucks willingness to take strong but respectful actions when its suppliers' behaviors are suspect occurred when workplace safety allegations were made concerning a supplier's U.S.-based manufacturing plant. According to Kelly Goodejohn, director, Ethical Sourcing, "In that case, we sent a message to plant management saying, 'Over the short term, we're going to stop doing business with you, but we want to understand what's happening in your facility and then want to talk about capacity building and remediation.'" After Starbucks notified the manufacturer, the leaders had a third-party monitoring company with whom Starbucks works globally go into the manufacturer's facility and conduct a three-day, in-person review. In addition to direct observations and meetings with plant leadership, the evaluation team spoke directly with employees in the plant.

In cases where third-party evaluations are required, Starbucks leaders hope those evaluations will result in verifiable remediation of the problem areas and allow for the maintenance of the supplier relationship. If that is not possible, those supplier relationships will be terminated. Kelly notes, "We recognize that the amount of money we spend with suppliers is significant and, as such, we have a responsibility to make sure that our values permeate throughout our supply chain. That is not an easy task because you're dealing with a wide array of cultures and different corporate priorities. But we tie the importance of ethical sourcing back to the fact that taking care of your people and your community produces positive business results." As Starbucks demonstrates a positive connection between humane treatment of workers and strong business growth, Starbucks suppliers are also demonstrating similar behavior for subcontractors and suppliers. In essence, being a humane and responsible company is good for business.

UPPING THE COMMUNITY PARTNERSHIP

The leaders at Starbucks have a long history of working on issues of employment opportunity, leadership development, and economic growth. For example, in 1998, Starbucks worked with former National Basketball Association star Earvin "Magic" Johnson through his Johnson Development Corporation in a joint venture, referred to as Urban Coffee Opportunities, to build Starbucks stores in underserved urban neighborhoods. Magic, who sold his stake in the 105 stores involved in the joint venture back to Starbucks in 2010, noted, "Through our partnership with Starbucks, we were able to serve as an economic catalyst in urban cities through the creation of new jobs."

By 2011, Starbucks had begun making a transition from Urban Coffee Opportunities to a new model for community stores in the Harlem neighborhood in New York and in Los Angeles's Crenshaw community. That pilot approach was designed to take financial contributions from those stores and share them directly with a community-building organization in each of those regions. In announcing the new community store model, Howard Schultz noted, "Starbucks is partnering with two organizations doing heroic work to address the economic, social and education challenges in their communities. . . . These two partnerships are intended to help us learn how our company can successfully join with change-making community organizations in a localized, coordinated and replicable way." Through these initial coordinated efforts, Starbucks shared approximately $245,000 with the two community organizations in the first year of operations. Based on the success of the initial community stores, Starbucks leaders announced that they were expanding the program to Houston, Texas, by contributing funds based on the performance of a newly remodeled Gulfgate Center Mall store to the Association for the Advancement of Mexican Americans. On a smaller scale, leaders can simply look for ways to support community activities through service organizations, schools, and community-based nonprofits. These types of opportunities forge reciprocal win/win relationships leading to business success and the overall health of the communities served.

Stewardship in Foundation Form

The Starbucks Foundation, which was created in 1997 with the purchase price from Howard's first book, *Pour Your Heart Into It*, has served as a launchpad for many of Starbucks community development projects, starting with a focus on literacy programs in the United States and Canada. Over the years, the foundation has broadened its efforts globally. At present, the Starbucks Foundation supports community development projects in coffee-, tea-, and cocoa-growing regions. These projects include such things as improving water sanitation, increasing health and nutrition, and providing microcredit and agricultural training. The Starbucks Foundation also has become involved with Ethos Water, a company started in 2001 with the simple mission, "help children get clean water." Ethos Water, which is now a Starbucks subsidiary, has made more than $7 million in grants in support of that mission, with 5 cents from every bottle of Ethos Water purchased being dedicated to clean water efforts. The Starbucks Foundation also administers community service grants to nonprofit organizations and provides funds in the form of matching grants to organizations in which local Starbucks partners actively invest their own time and money.

Since there is not enough space in this book to dive deeply into all the projects and programs supported by the Starbucks Foundation, let's look at a couple of initiatives that address the primary themes of education and leadership development. For example, the Starbucks Foundation established the Starbucks China Education Project. The project, which began in 2005, builds on the strong cultural values concerning formal education that are found throughout China. In support of this project, Starbucks committed $5 million (approximately RMB 40 million) to learning programs in China through a U.S. nonprofit organization called Give2Asia. Funds from the project are used in China to train teachers in rural areas, support scholarships for teaching college students, and aid teachers as well as students who were affected by the 2008 Sichuan earthquake.

The Starbucks Foundation is also committed to youth leadership training globally through the Youth Leadership Grants program. Leaders at Starbucks reported in 2012 that "there are more than 1.2 billion 15 to 24 year olds, the largest global cohort of young people in history. Unfortunately, a growing number of these young people are disengaged and unemployed, often referred to as NEET (not engaged in employment, education, or training). The Starbucks Foundation is interested in supporting organizations that equip young people ages 15 to 24 years old." Specifically, the Starbucks Foundation is providing Youth Leadership Grants to international organizations that assist young people in developing skills in business savvy, social conscience, and collaborative communication.

Starbucks commitment to maximizing the employability of youth goes beyond the grants extended through the Starbucks Foundation. For example, Blair Taylor was the CEO of the Los Angeles Urban League when he approached Howard Schultz with a set of concerns and a request. Specifically, Blair shared that he told Howard, "Kids in urban schools are not getting the experiential learning that kids in suburban schools receive.

They're not going away to Europe on their summer vacation or touring the Hamptons. They don't get the opportunity to see outside of their neighborhoods." Furthermore, Blair suggested to Howard "that urban school kids from inner-city schools and poor rural schools are keeping up pretty well with their suburban counterparts during the school year, but a gap emerges as a result of the differences in the experiences they have over the summer months."

Blair advised Howard that, because of this, he wanted to take a delegation of 20 to 30 kids from Crenshaw High School, a low-performing high school in the Los Angeles Unified School System, to China in the summer of 2011. In order to make this trip a reality, Blair had to line up three corporate partners. Blair's rationale for the trip to China was to give students from this inner-city Los Angeles school a view into the twenty-first-century global economy. According to Blair, Howard was the first business leader to jump in and support the effort. Blair stewarded a contingent of Crenshaw students and teachers in meetings with Chinese business leaders, entrepreneurs, and students from the number one high school in China. According to Blair, "We toured Shanghai, Beijing, and Tianjin. We rode the speed bullet train that travels at 200 miles an hour and got to see things that were life-changing for these kids. Most of these Crenshaw students had never been outside of Los Angeles County; 90 percent of them had never been on an airplane; some of them had never even seen the ocean, although they live 5 to 8 miles away." At the end of the trip, Blair asked the students in his delegation why they thought they had met with premier high school students in China. According to Blair, "One young man raised his hand and said, 'Because one day those kids are going to be running China.' Then the young man paused and said, 'And one day we are going to be running the United States, and we need to know each other.' When these kids came back, they looked at themselves as world ambassadors and future world leaders—not as kids from a low-performing school." In the next year, Blair Taylor left his position as CEO of the Los Angeles Urban League and became the chief community officer at Starbucks, helping the brand continue to provide unique opportunities to raise the expectations and skills of young people.

Starbucks efforts to promote ethical sourcing, global improvements in children's access to clean water, education grants, and support of youth leadership initiatives all share a common thread. Each effort reflects a belief that a business must leverage its size and prosperity for good. I suspect that your customers will become increasingly aware of the environmental track record of business leaders and their concern for their suppliers and the communities they serve. Those efforts are likely to be an important consideration for a growing number of consumers. Socially conscious decisions will probably result not only

REFLECTION ON CONNECTION

1. Have you set ethical sourcing guidelines and objectives?
2. How would you handle a supplier against which workplace safety allegations are leveled? Do you have an established process for evaluating, remediating, and, if necessary, severing relationships with suppliers who are not transparent or do not honor the human rights of those they hire?
3. Do your social responsibility initiatives go beyond grants and involve the active participation of your people? Have you identified key social giving targets such as clean water, education, and leadership to maximize the impact of your efforts?

in short-term sales success, but also in a brighter long-term future. Leaders must develop a perspective that considers the well-being of future generations—many members of whom may become employees or consumers.

JOB CREATION

Abraham Lincoln offered sage advice to leaders when he said, "Be sure you put your feet in the right place, then stand firm." However, like much wise counsel, Lincoln's words are easier understood than followed. Throughout 2011, Howard Schultz put his feet in a number of bold places by writing a memo to partners titled "Leading Through Uncertain Times" and an open letter to Americans that was printed as a full-page ad in publications like the *New York Times*. Howard essentially challenged readers to take swift action and stand firm for increased business involvement in job creation and decreased partisan gridlock in the U.S. Congress.

Specifically, Howard noted, "Let's tell our government leaders to put partisanship aside and to speak truthfully about the challenges we face. Let's ask our business leaders to create more job opportunities for the American economy. And as citizens, let's all get more involved. Please, don't be a bystander. Understand that we have a shared responsibility in solving our nation's problems. We can't wait for Washington. At Starbucks, we are trying to live up to our responsibility by increasing our local community service and helping to finance small-business job creation with Create Jobs for USA. Our company is far from perfect, and we know we can do more for America. But we need your help. We need your voice." Howard asked readers to share their input on blogs, offer inspiring photos on Pinterest, and provide innovative ideas on Facebook. Howard also asked readers to include the hashtag #indivisible in their posts so that Starbucks could collect and amplify the shared ideas.

In addition to taking out an advertisement and facilitating online innovation and idea sharing, Howard Schultz encouraged campaign donors to withhold funding from either political party "until the Congress and the president return to Washington and deliver a fiscally disciplined long-term debt and deficit plan to the American people." More than 100 CEOs from major U.S. companies and scores of other contributors heeded Howard's call in an effort to get government officials to focus on debt reduction and job creation. At the same time, Starbucks was in full swing with its Create Jobs for USA program.

To launch Create Jobs for USA in November 2011, the Starbucks Foundation donated $5 million to support community development financial institutions (CDFIs) through the Opportunity Finance Network, a national network of CDFIs that invest in opportunities to benefit low-income, low-wealth, and other disadvantaged communities in the United States. Columnist Joe Nocera, writing in the *New York Times*, explains, "It didn't take long for Starbucks to find the perfect financial partner. . . . Most, but not all, CDFIs are nonprofit, and their loan default rates are extremely low. . . . Opportunity Finance Network acts as an umbrella group to the best of them."

Starbucks then created and made available a red, white, and blue wristband embossed with the word *INDIVISIBLE* for those who chose to make an in-store or online contribution of at least $5 to support Create Jobs for USA; 100 percent of the donations went directly to Opportunity Finance Network to support community lending across the country. In essence, Starbucks sought to create greater access to credit for small business owners in order to stimulate job creation and economic growth. The Create Jobs for USA program not only leveraged the participation of Starbucks customers but also amplified the power of capital. Joe Nocera adds, "Here is the most beautiful part about the whole arrangement. The donations to Create Jobs for USA will not be loaned to the CDFIs. They will be turned into capital . . . that equity can be leveraged 7 to 1 . . . if 10 million Starbucks customers donate $5, that will support $350 million worth of lending. That's real money."

In June 2012, Starbucks expanded contribution opportunities for Create Jobs for USA by creating, selling, and donating a portion of the proceeds from an artisanal INDIVISIBLE ceramic mug and other INDIVISIBLE items such as whole bean coffee and merchandise. The mug was produced at one of two surviving potteries in East Liverpool, Ohio, a town that was once the ceramic capital of the United States. Ulrich Honighausen, the owner of Hausenware, a tableware company based in Sonoma County, California, and the supplier of the INDIVISIBLE mug, noted, "I am a U.S. citizen raising three children in this country, and for years I've wanted to make ceramics in the United States. A week after I heard Howard first talk about job creation in the United States, I was at a housewares conference and started asking people where could I make ceramics domestically. When Starbucks officially launched their Create Jobs for USA program, I thought I had to do my part to help create jobs in America, and that led me to contract with a small factory in East Liverpool. I was so inspired by what I saw in Ohio—the craftsmanship, need, and opportunities there—that I started another factory in the area which will compete in a more automated way against imports."

For a more detailed exploration of East Liverpool, Ohio, and the INDIVISIBLE mug, please go to http://tinyurl.com/cmzr7ds or point your QR reader to:

By April of 2012, Howard shared the initial success of Create Jobs for USA with CBS News: "We're getting money in the hands of [CDFIs], (who then) lend it to small businesses, create jobs in start-ups and existing businesses. In fact, 80 percent of the money we've raised has already been (given) out. And we can document with great transparency where the money's going and the jobs that are being created."

An example of the benefits from funding through the Starbucks jobs program is Gelato Fiasco. In 2007, Josh Davis was 25 years old when he and Bruno Tropeano, his 24-year-old business partner, opened a Gelato Fiasco gelateria in Brunswick, Maine. Because of their success in Brunswick, a town of approximately 23,000 people, Josh and Bruno had their sights set on an expansion into Maine's largest city, Portland, approximately 25 minutes to the south. Josh and Bruno found an optimal location for their new store, but they had to make a decision quickly to secure the 10-year lease. A call to their bank gave Bruno and Josh sufficient assurances of funding to lead them to sign their lease agreement. Unfortunately, after the lease was signed, their bank and several other lenders denied their loan requests.

As a last resort, Josh and Bruno went to a CDFI supported by the Create Jobs for USA program and received a $140,000 loan, allowing them to expand and add 10 new employees (full- and part-time) to their 21-person staff. Josh notes, "Starbucks turned what was going to be a truly unmitigated disaster into a real success story." Not only did Gelato Fiasco open in Portland, but the new Gelato Fiasco store was located approximately a block away from a busy Starbucks store. Oh, by the way, the Portland Gelato Fiasco serves coffee. So what was Starbucks response to a neighbor/competitor that it had supported? According to Josh, "The staff at Starbucks actually posted an article about our business in their store. Even though we were setting up shop a block away, they acted out of abundance and not competition."

Josh and Bruno were grateful for the trust placed in them and decided to take that gratitude and "pay it forward." To that end, they created a gelato flavor for their wholesale business (which distributes gelato to supermarkets throughout Maine and New England) and directed a portion of the revenues from that flavor back to the Create Jobs for USA program. According to Josh, "The motto of the city of Portland, Maine, is 'Resurgam,' which means 'I will rise again,' and we thought that motto applied well to our situation, so we named our special commissioned flavor Sweet Resurgam and gave $1 per pint back to the Create Jobs for USA program."

Few business leaders make a public call to fellow business leaders and politicians to set aside selfish differences and act in the greater good. Even fewer refocus themselves to partner with customers to generate solutions that produce tangible economic benefits, some of which might be perceived as competitive in nature. While many of Howard Schultz's actions may be outside the scope of what is achievable for you as a leader, Howard serves as a reminder to all of us that we can do more than complain about social challenges—we can (and, moreover, we have a responsibility to) be a force for constructive change.

CONNECTING POINTS

- Leadership carries with it a responsibility to make the world a better place than you find it today.
- There is typically a strong interdependence between a company's performance, its values, and the impact it has on the communities it serves.
- When it comes to sustainability, it is important that you set ambitious goals; seek third-party criteria to validate your achievement of those goals; play a role in refining those criteria for your industry, if necessary; execute against those goals; and transparently report your progress toward your objectives.

- When an environmental issue is salient to your customers, it has to rise higher on your project priority list.
- Sustainability is not something that is done for marketing or publicity purposes; it is an authentic commitment to the future viability of your business and to future generations of customers.
- It is not enough to talk about sustainability; true leadership requires a willingness to invest in the long-term health of your business and to actively collaborate with others out of a genuine sense of responsibility.
- Being a humane and responsible company is good for business.
- Leaders must develop a perspective that considers the well-being of future generations—many members of whom may be employees or customers.
- As a leader, it is essential (in the words of Lincoln) that you put your feet in the right place, then stand firm.
- You can do more than complain about social challenges—you can (and, moreover, you have a responsibility to) be a force for constructive change.

CHAPTER 12

Forging a Real Lifestyle Connection

Take a moment and think about your ideal customers. Now imagine them waking up in the morning and using one of your products in their homes. On their way to work, they stop by your store, check in on Foursquare, open your app, and purchase an item with mobile payment. At the office, they take a break and encounter your products or go online to check their Facebook page and read a post of yours in their feed. During the afternoon, they sign up to participate with your team in a community improvement project on their day off. They invite their friends to participate in that event with them. They take pictures as they help their community and post those images on Instagram, Twitter, and Facebook. They use your products at the event. They stop at the supermarket on their way home, and your offerings are on their shopping list. Okay, it's time to come back to reality.

It is important to remember that Starbucks started out as a single store and that anything is possible if we take the lessons learned from Starbucks as a nudge to think about how we can innovate and expand our products, services, social media tools, technologies, and channels. The leaders at Starbucks also demonstrate what is possible when you foster product passion, teach your people the importance of human connections, seek operational excellence and efficiency, and engage in a never-ending pursuit of relevance.

Howard Schultz puts it this way: "Any consumer brand today—whether Starbucks or a product like Tide— . . . [must] create relevancy in all aspects of your customers' lives. . . . The price of admission is not good enough if your relevancy and market position is only where the product is sold. We said to ourselves that we have to be as relevant socially and digitally as we are when the customer is inside our four walls . . . companies that don't understand [that] are going to [be] left behind."

Traditionally, marketers talk about lifestyle brands as those that connect with customers' personal identity. They are brands that "promote a lifestyle" customers value or to which they aspire. Starbucks is certainly a business that has all the traditional aspects of lifestyle branding, as its leaders have stewarded the brand to authentically project an image of product passion, concern for the human connection, and community values. However, Starbucks leaders have also taken their value proposition up a level to something I refer to as an "advanced lifestyle" brand. Not only does Starbucks "project a lifestyle," but it enters the lifestyle of its customers.

Typically, Starbucks builds its connection with customers through its primary well-distributed channel: Starbucks retail stores. In fact, some research suggests that 80 percent of U.S. citizens live within 20 miles of a Starbucks store, and that the farthest anyone would have to travel to get to a Starbucks company-owned store is 140 miles (the study did not include licensed stores, so the distance may be even shorter). Once that connection is forged through the store channel, the leaders at Starbucks have positioned their brand to meet their customer on the go, whether that be on a mountaintop with VIA, in a health food store with Evolution Fresh juice, on a train in Switzerland, or through a mobile app in Beijing. Aimee Johnson, vice president, Digital Commerce, Loyalty and Content, notes, "We are committed to understanding our in-store customers and connecting to them in ways that fit both where and who they are!"

A proliferation of your brand certainly has risk. Reuben Gregg Brewer, director of digital content at Value Line, cautions that there are "material risks to Starbucks recent expansion efforts. While going global is a great idea, moving outside of one's niche can, and often has, proven disastrous. Time and again new concepts in the quick service space flame out after coming to market. . . . Starbucks' efforts could, indeed, result in a lack of focus. . . . Moving into additional distribution channels, Starbucks' could risk oversaturation with its core brand and all of the others it has just added."

Many partners with whom I have spoken report having confidence in Starbucks future based on the ability of the leadership to adapt and transform to changing customer needs. This confidence is not limited to those within Starbucks. Jim Cramer, bestselling author and television host of the popular CNBC program *Mad Money*, noted after the release of the Verismo system in 2012, "I am going with Schultz—not against him—because it has been a horrendous bet to go against Schultz in either the first or the second iteration and I think it will be a horrendous bet once again. . . . Schultz has primed Starbucks for a third round of growth and you don't want to be caught outside looking in." From my vantage point, success always hinges on high-quality products, provided the way customers want them, offered in a caring environment that builds connections. As long as Starbucks—or any business, for that matter—is achieving those objectives, customers will offer it their sustained support. While I imagine the leaders at Starbucks will continue to guide their brand wherever the opportunities and customers take them, I am certain that they will remind partners that the ultimate future of the brand depends on connecting in "uplifting moments."

These moments are like those provided by Starbucks barista Daniel Rowe. Daniel had a relationship with a regular customer,

Kelly Dietrich. On most occasions, Kelly would also order a Tall Nonfat Latte for his wife. As Daniel shares, "One day Kelly upsized his wife's nonfat latte to a grande. I figured she might need a little extra that day, so I wrote 'Hope your day gets better' on her cup."

Kelly's wife, Gini Dietrich, founder and CEO of Arment Dietrich, a Chicago-based integrated marketing communication firm, and coauthor of *Marketing in the Round*, notes, "The fact that the barista at Starbucks knew I was in for a long day because I ordered a larger drink was pretty incredible. I took a picture of the cup and uploaded [it] to Facebook, and essentially I thought that would be the end of our interaction. To my surprise, about a month later, my husband came home with another personalized cup from Barista Dan, which asked if I was real."

Gini checked "maybe" on her cup and added, "It depends on your definition of real." Dan had never met Gini, but for months they had made a very "real" connection through Gini's husband and messages sent back and forth a couple of times a week on Starbucks cups. Gini expanded her relationship with Dan through her

Facebook network, taking pictures of each cup and asking her friends to vote on how she should answer each inquiry. Gini reported that she experienced sadness when she received a cup that mentioned that Dan was going to be leaving Starbucks in a month: "I made a point of stopping by to meet and say goodbye to Dan on his last day at Starbucks, as he was going to pursue his pastry career at the Trump Tower. I think Dan epitomizes the best of Starbucks, particularly in his sustained efforts to maintain our unique and special connection and to really care about my husband and me."

Dan notes, "I worked for Starbucks for six years, and they encouraged me to grow and develop. I gained interpersonal and management skills that will help me run a kitchen. They taught me what it means to be customer-focused. I am extremely pleased that Gini took the time to meet me. I really didn't think I was doing anything special; I was just playing my part in Starbucks culture by connecting personally—even if her person wasn't ever physically available."

Need I say more? Let me leave you with one question:

Bibliography

CHAPTER 1

"*Entrepreneur* magazine ranks the company among the ten 'most trusted' businesses": Paula Andruss, "Secrets of the 10 Most-Trusted Brands," *Entrepreneur*, March 20, 2012, http://www.entrepreneur.com/article/223125.

"*Fortune* magazine places it among the 'most admired' global brands": "World's Most Admired Companies," *Fortune*, March 21, 2011, http://money.cnn.com/magazines/fortune/mostadmired/2011/full_list/.

"U.S. president Barack Obama placed a call to the chief executive officer of Starbucks, Howard Schultz, because of Howard's leadership on job creation": David A. Kaplan, "Howard Schultz Brews Strong Coffee at Starbucks," *Fortune*, November 17, 2011, http://management.fortune.cnn.com/2011/11/17/starbucks-howard-schultz-business-person-year/.

"*Fortune* magazine has named Howard Schultz as businessperson of the year": Richard McGill Murphy, "2011 Businessperson of the Year," *Fortune*, November 17, 2011.

Joseph A. Michelli, *The Starbucks Experience: 5 Principles for Turning Ordinary into Extraordinary* (New York: McGraw-Hill, 2006).

"While our financial results are clearly being impacted by reduced frequency to our U.S. stores": Howard Schultz, "Financial Release: Starbucks Reports Second Quarter Fiscal 2008 Results and Announces Long-Term Financial Targets for 2009 to 2011," Starbucks Investor Relations, April 30, 2008, http://investor.starbucks.com/phoenix.zhtml?c=99518&p=irol-newsArticle&ID=1137657&highlight.

Howard Schultz and Joanne Gordon, *Onward: How Starbucks Fought for Its Life Without Losing Its Soul* (New York: Rodale, 2011).

"Adherence to these seven bold moves has resulted in desired financial outcomes, as evidenced by 13 consecutive quarters of global comparable store sales growth greater than 5%.": Information as of Q2FY13 furnished by Starbucks, Q2FY13 Earnings Transcript.

"The number of formal bankruptcy filings in the 12 months ending June 2010 . . . increased by 10% . . . and the year over year increase between 08 and 09 was 50%": Dun & Bradstreet, "D&B U.S. Business Trends Report," October 2010, http://www.dnb.com/content/dam/english/economic-and-industry-insight/us_business_trends_2010_10.pdf.

"Good management is largely a matter of love. Or if you're uncomfortable with that word, call it caring, because proper management involves caring for people, not manipulating them": James A. Autry, *Love and Profit: The Art of Caring Leadership* (New York: Avon Books, Inc., 1991).

"Great brands always make an emotional connection with the intended audience": Leonard L. Berry, *Discovering the Soul of Service: The Nine Drivers of Sustainable Business Success* (New York: Free Press, 1999).

"The City Council called for hearings and solutions": Petula Dvorak, "Encounter with a Homeless Man Touches a Virginia Starbucks Manager": *Washington Post*, June 18, 2012, http://articles.washingtonpost.com/2012-06-18/local/35460526_1_homeless-population-long-term-homelessness-dominic.

CHAPTER 2

"Steve Chou, the founder of Bumblebee Linens, reports that his online store went from zero earnings to more than $100,000 profit in a single year": Steve Chou, "Why You Don't Have to Love What You Sell when Starting an Online Store," mywifequitherjob.com, http://mywifequitherjob.com/why-you-dont-have-to-love-what-you-sell/.

"Not passionate about shoes at all": Joseph A. Michelli, *The Zappos Experience: 5 Principles to Inspire, Engage, and WOW* (New York: McGraw-Hill, 2012).

"Tony has reported he owns three pair": Justin Fenner, "You'll Never Guess How Many Shoes Zappos' CEO Owns," *Styleite.com* (blog), November 17, 2010, http://www.styleite.com/media/tony-hsieh-three-shoes/.

"Passionate about customer service and company culture": Valerie Khoo, "The Celebrity CEO: Zappos's Tony Hsieh," theage.com.au,

February 17, 2012, http://m.theage.com.au/small-business/managing/blogs/enterprise/the-celebrity-ceo-zapposs-tony-hsieh-20120216-1ta85.html.

"Passion is the indefinable something that creates and builds interest and excitement on the part of the customer": Troy Harrison, "Sales Without Passion Isâ€¦Well, It Isnâ€™t Sales," *salesforcesolutions.net* (blog), 2013, http://www.salesforcesolutions.net/blog/hotsheets/sales-without-passion-isâ€¦well-it-isnâ€™t-sales.

"As he described in his book *Onward*, he gained an enriched awareness of the 'magic' of coffee": Howard Schultz and Joanne Gordon, *Onward: How Starbucks Fought for Its Life Without Losing Its Soul* (New York: Rodale, 2011).

"To inspire and nurture the human spirit—one person, one cup and one neighborhood at a time": Our Starbucks Mission Statement, http://www.starbucks.com/about-us/company-information/mission-statement.

"Our Coffee. It has always been, and will always be, about quality": Our Starbucks Mission Statement, http://www.starbucks.com/about-us/company-information/mission-statement.

"Pouring espresso is an art, one that requires the barista to care about the quality of the beverage": Howard Schultz and Joanne Gordon, *Onward: How Starbucks Fought for Its Life Without Losing Its Soul* (New York: Rodale, 2011).

"As events which communicate and reinforce desired performance and values": S. Chris Edmonds, "Use Social Rituals to Reinforce Your Desired Culture," www.drivingresultsthroughculture.com, December 20, 2010, http://drivingresultsthroughculture.com/?p=871.

"When I was first learning about coffee three years ago at a Starbucks in Connecticut, I tasted Caffè Verona®": "Ratatouille Taught Me How to Taste Coffee," *www.coffeeandthecity.com* (blog), January 17, 2011, http://www.coffeeandthecity.com/2011/01/ratatouille-taught-me-how-to-taste.html.

"Rewards can perform a weird sort of behavioral alchemy: They can transform an interesting task into a drudge": Daniel H. Pink, *Drive: The Surprising Truth About What Motivates Us* (New York: Riverhead Books, 2009).

"Jim Collins . . . asserts that visionary companies are led by individuals": Jim Collins, "Aligning Action and Values," www.jimcollins.com, June 2000, http://www.jimcollins.com/article_topics/articles/aligning-action.html.

"Were a dangerous enemy in the battle to transform the company": Howard Schultz and Joanne Gordon, *Onward: How Starbucks Fought for Its Life Without Losing Its Soul* (New York: Rodale, 2011).
"I am in the process of becoming a Coffee Master": Paul Quinn, Starbucks community, http://community.starbucks.com/message/6853#6853.

CHAPTER 3

"Starbucks is at its best when we are creating enduring relationships and personal connections": Howard Schultz and Joanne Gordon, *Onward: How Starbucks Fought for Its Life Without Losing Its Soul* (New York: Rodale, 2011).
"Transformation Agenda includes . . . re-igniting our emotional attachment with our customers by restoring the connection our customers have with you, our coffee, our brand, and our stores": Howard Schultz, "Transformation Agenda Communication #1," starbucks.tekgroup.com, http://starbucks.tekgroup.com/article_print.cfm?article_id=76.
"Our Customers. When we are fully engaged": Our Starbucks Mission Statement, http://www.starbucks.com/about-us/company-information/mission-statement.
"Consumer data, consistently reflected in studies such as the American Express Global Customer Service Barometer, validate the perspective that customer service is chaotic, unpredictable, and in decline": "2012 Global Customer Service Barometer: Findings in the United States," a research report prepared for American Express, Echo, about.americanexpress.com, http://about.americanexpress.com/news/docs/2012x/AXP_2012GCSB_US.pdf.
"Memorable experiences": B. Joseph Pine II and James H. Gilmore, *The Experience Economy: Work Is Theater and Every Business a Stage* (Boston: Harvard Business School Press, 1999).
"McDonald's very business model seeks a highly cookie-cutter approach": John Shook, "A Lean 'Teachable Moment': Starbucks in the Wall Street Journal," Lean Enterprise Institute, August 7, 2009, http://www.lean.org/shook/displayobject.cfm?o=1085.
"The goal is to make as many things as possible routine so that the barista can spend just a few more": John Shook, "A Lean 'Teachable Moment': Starbucks in the Wall Street Journal," Lean Enterprise Institute, August 7, 2009, http://www.lean.org/shook/displayobject.cfm?o=1085.
"For companies looking to make an emotional connection with consumers": Nick Chiles, "Corporations Use Music to Make Emotional

Connection to Consumers," *Atlanta Black Star*, July 26, 2012, http://atlantablackstar.com/2012/07/26/corporations-use-music-to-make-emotional-connection-to-consumers/.

"As part of its commitment to evolve and enhance the Customer Experience with innovative": "Starbucks Acquires Evolution Fresh to Establish National Retail and Grocery Health and Wellness Brand," news.starbucks.com, November 10, 2011, http://news.starbucks.com/article_display.cfm?article_id=587.

"Our intent is to build a national health and wellness brand leveraging our scale, resources and premium product expertise": "Starbucks Acquires Evolution Fresh to Establish National Retail and Grocery Health and Wellness Brand," news.starbucks.com, November 10, 2011, http://news.starbucks.com/article_display.cfm?article_id=587.

"Evolution Fresh is Starbucks newest addition to health food": Emily K., yelp.com, July 30, 2012, http://www.yelp.com/filtered_reviews/666xh85KxFjcBVFqsTQy0w?fsid=r8JwQGC9dQ2YFYcbr0g3bg.

"Tazo, the Oregon company that once aspired to be the Starbucks of teas, has been bought out": "Company News: Starbucks Acquires Tazo, a Tea Retailer in Oregon," *New York Times*, January 13, 1999, http://www.nytimes.com/1999/01/13/business/company-news-starbucks-acquires-tazo-a-tea-retailer-in-oregon.html.

"Starbucks built Tazo from an $8.1 million purchase price in 1999": Lisa Baertlein, "Starbucks Plans to Open Tazo Tea Store This Year," Reuters.com, June 20, 2012, http://www.reuters.com/article/2012/06/20/us-starbucks-tea-idUSBRE85J17620120620.

"Into a brand with more than $1.4 billion in sales": Kelly Blessing, "Starbucks to Open Tazo Tea Store," Bloomberg.com, June 20, 2012, http://www.bloomberg.com/news/2012-06-20/starbucks-to-open-tazo-tea-store.html.

CHAPTER 4

"It is our belief that social justice begins at home": The Learning Network, "Jan. 5, 1914: Henry Ford Implements the $5-a-Day Wage," *New York Times*, January 5, 2012, http://learning.blogs.nytimes.com/2012/01/05/jan-5-1914-henry-ford-implements-5-a-day-wage/.

"This crisis of trust in our basic institutions is so troubling precisely because the lack of trust": Dov Seidman, "The Case for Ethical Leadership," *Academy of Management Executive* 18, no. 2, 2004, http://home.sandiego.edu/~pavett/docs/gsba532/ethical_leadership.pdf.

"The results were dismal. Over two-thirds (71%) of the Americans polled": Dov Seidman, "The Case for Ethical Leadership," *Academy of Management Executive* 18, no. 2, 2004, http://home.sandiego.edu/~pavett/docs/gsba532/ethical_leadership.pdf.

"Reflecting back on your high school or college coursework, you may recall that Maslow's 1943 paper 'A Theory of Human Motivation'": A. H. Maslow, "A Theory of Human Motivation," *Psychological Review* 50, 1943, 370–396.

"Are you competent?": Ed O'Boyle, "B2B Customers Have Feelings Too," *Gallup Business Journal*, May 14, 2009, http://businessjournal.gallup.com/content/118339/b2b-customers-feelings.aspx.

"A detailed exploration of the 11 questions that Gallup used in the CE-11 can be found in my book *The New Gold Standard*": Joseph A. Michelli, *The New Gold Standard: 5 Leadership Principles for Creating a Legendary Customer Experience Courtesy of The Ritz-Carlton Hotel Company* (New York: McGraw-Hill, 2008).

"Virtue has been, is, and always will be its own reward": Dov Seidman, "The Case for Ethical Leadership," *Academy of Management Executive* 18, no. 2, 2004, http://home.sandiego.edu/~pavett/docs/gsba532/ethical_leadership.pdf.

"Significant change was about to occur, and our people would want to know what it meant for them and their jobs": Howard Schultz and Joanne Gordon, *Onward: How Starbucks Fought for Its Life Without Losing Its Soul* (New York: Rodale, 2011).

"People are not a company's most important asset": Ira A. Jackson and Jane Nelson, "Values-Driven Performance: Seven Strategies for Delivering Profits with Principles," quoted from a speech by Adrian Levy, founder of RLG International, March 2001, *Ivey Business Journal*, November/December 2004, http://www.humanresourcesoncall.ca/coach/coach_quotes.htm.

"Watson Wyatt shows that total return to shareholders in high-trust organizations": Steven M. R. Covey, *The Speed of Trust: The One Thing That Changes Everything* (New York: Free Press, 2008).

"But would Starbucks really replace *anything*? To find out": John Hargrave, "The Starbucks Prank: Will Starbucks Really Return Anything?," Zug.com, August 24, 2009, http://www.zug.com/live/82273/The-Starbucks-Return-Prank-Will-Starbucks-Really-Return-ANYTHING.html.

"Psychologists Daniel Kahneman and Amos Tversky began a revolution in economics by focusing on the role of emotional factors in decision making": David Laibson and Richard Zeckhauser, "Amos Tversky and the Ascent of Behavioral Economics," *Journal of Risk and Uncertainty* 16, no. 1, April 1998, 7–47, http://link.springer.com/article/10.1023%2FA%3A1007717224343-page-1.

"A brand you recommend to friends wholeheartedly, even evangelically": Kate Newlin, *Passion Brands: Why Some Brands Are Just Gotta Have, Drive All Night For, and Tell All Your Friends About* (New York: Prometheus Books, 2009).

CHAPTER 5

"For the past two decades, Starbucks has been one of the only retailers with a stock program that includes part-time hourly partners": Howard Schultz, internal memo to partners, 2011. This memo was provided by Starbucks.

"In 2012, 28% of all firms that offer health benefits offer them to part-time workers": "2012 Employer Health Benefits Survey," Kaiser Family Foundation/Health Research & Educational Trust (HRET), 2012, www.kff.org/insurance/ehbs091112nr.cfm.

"I can also say in all seriousness that I owe Starbucks my life": Barista-Berry, *blogs.starbucks.com*, March 29, 2011, http://blogs.starbucks.com/blogs/customer/archive/2011/03/29/onward.aspx.

"Originally, this article was going to be 'Why I love Starbucks.' As a former barista": Caitlin Muir, "33 Companies That Can Save You from College Debt," *collegeplus.org* (blog), http://www.collegeplus.org/blog/33-companies-that-can-save-you-from-college-debt.

"In response to the question 'My organization recognizes excellence,' the organizations that scored in the lowest fourth overall": Adrian Gostick and Chester Elton, *The Carrot Principle: How the Best Managers Use Recognition to Engage Their People, Retain Talent, and Accelerate Performance* (New York: Free Press, 2009).

"Organizations with highly engaged employees achieve seven times greater 5-year TSR": "The Impact of Employee Engagement," Kenexa Research Institute, 2008, http://www.kenexa.com/getattachment/8c36e336-3935-4406-8b7b-777f1afaa57d/The-Impact-of-Employee-Engagement.aspx.

"By increasing employees' engagement levels, organizations can expect an increase in performance of up to 20 percentile points": "Driving Performance and Retention Through Employee Engagement," Corporate Executive Board, mckpeople.com.au, 2004, http://www.mckpeople.com.au/SiteMedia/w3svc161/Uploads/Documents/760af459-93b3-43c7-b52a-2a74e984c1a0.pdf.

"While other fast-food retailers lost staff at rates as high as 400% a year, Starbucks' turnover was a relatively low 65%": Andrew Lowery (quoting Richard Lofthouse, a writer for *CNBC Business*), "The Changing Landscape in the Restaurant Industry," *Restaurant Industry 1.0* (blog), November 19, 2012, http://restaurantindustryblog.wordpress.com/2012/11/19/the-changing-landscape-in-the-restaurant-industry/.

"Reached onto the counter and patted my hand, extending her sympathy and telling me the drinks were on them": "BetterBefore," *blogs.starbucks.com*, March 31, 2011, http://blogs.starbucks.com/blogs/customer/archive/2011/03/29/onward.aspx.

CHAPTER 6

"Some people might like being called by their first name, but I think many will be indifferent, and some might feel awkward": Vanessa Barford, "Will You Tell Starbucks Your Name?," *BBC News Magazine*, March 14, 2012, http://www.bbc.co.uk/news/magazine-17356957.

"We all want to be recognized for our loyal patronage. . . . Starbucks is a company that others look to as a model": Ron Lieber, "The Card-Carrying Starbucks Fan," *New York Times*, June 7, 2008, http://www.nytimes.com/2008/06/07/business/yourmoney/07money.html?pagewanted=all.

"In April 2012, nearly 60,000 Starbucks partners and customers, local organizations, and community members provided more than 700,000 individual community service acts that made a difference in more than 34 countries": "Community Service: Every Starbucks Store Is a Part of a Community, and We're Committed to Strengthening Neighborhoods Wherever We Do Business," starbucks.com, http://www.starbucks.com/responsibility/community/community-service.

"One additional example that had reach both within the United States and across international borders was an alliance forged between Starbucks leadership and the HandsOn Network": "Starbucks I'm In! Campaign," handsonnetwork.org, http://www.handsonnetwork.org/starbucks.

"The chic interior, comfortable lounge chairs, and upbeat music are not only differentiators that set Starbucks apart from the competition":

Helen H. Wang, "Five Things Starbucks Did to Get China Right," *Forbes*, August 10, 2012, http://www.forbes.com/sites/helenwang/2012/08/10/five-things-starbucks-did-to-get-china-right/1/.

"Today is the day! . . . We stopped by our favorite neighborhood Starbucks and there . . . low and behold . . . the Mother Ship . . . Red Cup Day": Chrissy, "Starbucks Red Cup Day Is the Happiest Day of the Year," *thymeinmygarden.com* (blog), November 2, 2010, http://www.thymeinmygarden.com/starbucks-red-cup-day-is-the-happiest-day-of-the-year/.

"During the past 10 days, sweaty queues of up to 50 people have formed outside an old colonial building in downtown Mumbai": Shymantha Asokan, "India's First Starbucks Branches Draw Long Queues," guardian.co.uk, October 29, 2012, http://www.guardian.co.uk/world/2012/oct/29/india-first-starbucks-long-queues.

"As in the US before Starbucks came along, there are few places in Latin America": Pan Kwan Yuk, "Starbucks in LatAm: Selling Ice to Eskimos?," *blogs.ft.com*, June 21, 2012, http://blogs.ft.com/beyond-brics/2012/06/21/starbucks-in-latam-selling-ice-to-eskimos/#axzz2Ab61xixC.

"With high-store margins and low-store penetration": Kim Peterson, "Starbucks' Next Growth Area: Asia," *MSN Money*, August 13, 2012, http://money.msn.com/investment-advice/article-2.aspx?post=53fc5012-8606-4deb-b1e6-adf22572a73d.

CHAPTER 7

"The root cause was baked into our early decision where we didn't build these products based on a deep study of the countries": Chris Beier and Daniel Wolfman, "Intuit's Scott Cook on Failed Global Expansion: 'We Should've Known Better,'" *Inc.com*, http://www.inc.com/chris-beier-and-daniel-wolfman/intuit-quicken-scott-cook-global-expansion-failed.html.

"In recent years, anthropological studies have built a strong empirical case. . . . [that] consumers often appropriate the meanings of global brands to their own ends": Craig J. Thompson and Zeynep Arsel, "The Starbucks Brandscape and Consumers' (Anticorporate) Experiences of Glocalization," *Journal of Consumer Research* 31, 2004, http://zeyneparsel.files.wordpress.com/2010/06/thompson-arsel-jcr.pdf.

"Hiring people locally who can go in and understand the customer cold and design what the solutions should be": Chris Beier and

Daniel Wolfman, "Intuit's Scott Cook on Failed Global Expansion: 'We Should've Known Better,'" *Inc.com*, http://www.inc.com/chris-beier-and-daniel-wolfman/intuit-quicken-scott-cook-global-expansion-failed.html.

"[India] is a very complex market to enter. At one point we thought we could come here alone and we overestimated the complexity": Sonali Krishna, "India's Coffee Market Competition Is Ferocious: Howard Schultz, Starbucks," *Economic Times*, October 25, 2012, http://articles.economictimes.indiatimes.com/2012-10-25/news/34729911_1_starbucks-howard-schultz-tatas.

"Are bringing an unparalleled experience to India customers": Mark J. Miller, "Starbucks Expands to India with Mumbai Flagship Opening," brandchannel.com, October 19, 2012, http://www.brandchannel.com/home/post/2012/10/19/Starbucks-Opens-India-Store-101912.aspx.

"Location of this Starbucks is somehow characteristic, as it stands on the main approach to the Dazaifu Tenmangu": Kengo Kuma and Associates, "Starbucks Coffee at Dazaifu Tenman-gū," *Dezeen.com*, February 23, 2012, http://www.dezeen.com/2012/02/23/starbucks-coffee-at-dazaifu-tenman-gu-by-kengo-kuma-and-associates/.

"Shortly thereafter, a headline in the London *Telegraph* read, 'Starbucks' UK sales boosted by extra shot of espresso'": Nathalie Thomas, "Starbucks' UK Sales Boosted by Extra Shot of Espresso" *Telegraph* (London), April 26, 2012, http://www.telegraph.co.uk/finance/newsbysector/retailandconsumer/9229791/Starbucks-UK-sales-boosted-by-extra-shot-of-espresso.html.

"Its origins are still a subject of debate, but the first printed reference to the phrase 'location, location, location' appears to be a real estate advertisement in the *Chicago Tribune* in 1926": William Safire, "Location, Location, Location," On Language, *New York Times*, June 26, 2009, http://www.nytimes.com/2009/06/28/magazine/28FOB-onlanguage-t.html?_r=0.

"Aiming at the young urban Chinese demographic, and store locations are comfortable and offer a social setting—a welcome break from cramped apartments": Moe Nawaz, "'Starbucks-China' Plans to Open 8,000 Branches," mastermindcoach.com, http://www.mastermindcoach.com/business-ideas/starbucks-china-plans-to-open-8000-branches/.

"Liz Muller, a Dutch-born designer and Starbucks concept design director, worked with 35 craftsmen and artists to make the underground store locally relevant and sustainable": Dave, "Starbucks 'the Bank' Concept Store in Amsterdam," *Contemporist*, March 6, 2012, http://www.contemporist.com/2012/03/06/starbucks-the-bank-concept-store-in-amsterdam/.

"All of the displays and materials and design are from the Netherlands. . . . The space is designed to encourage interaction": Qaalfa Dibeehi, "The Destination Starbucks—a Concept Customer Experience," *beyondphilosophy.com* (blog), September 5, 2012, http://www.beyondphilosophy.com/blog/destination-starbucks-concept-customer-experience.

"China is not one homogeneous market": Helen H. Wang, "Five Things Starbucks Did to Get China Right," *Forbes*, August 10, 2012, http://www.forbes.com/sites/helenwang/2012/08/10/five-things-starbucks-did-to-get-china-right/2/.

"The Starbucks offerings were my focus during my visit (three in one weekend, in fact)": Nicole Mancini, "Frappes, Lattes, & Liquid Gold: Starbucks Opens in Disney's California Adventure," DIS Unplugged, August 11, 2012, http://www.disunplugged.com/2012/08/11/frappes-lattes-liquid-gold-starbucks-opens-in-disneys-california-adventure/.

CHAPTER 8

"In a 2012 *Time* magazine survey, people were forced to choose one item to take to work: their wallet, their lunch, or their mobile device": *Time* Mobility Poll, in cooperation with QUALCOMM, "Poll Results," August 2012, http://www.qualcomm.com/media/documents/time-mobility-poll-cooperation-qualcomm.

Joseph A. Michelli, *The Starbucks Experience: 5 Principles for Turning Ordinary into Extraordinary* (New York: McGraw-Hill, 2006).

"Starbucks was selected by *Forbes* as one of the top 20 innovation companies in 2011": "The World's Most Innovative Companies," *Forbes*, http://www.forbes.com/special-features/innovative-companies-list.html.

"Recognized by General Sentiment's QSR MediaMatch report in 2012 as having the highest impact value": "Starbucks Named Top QSR in Media Impact Value," *QSR*, June 13, 2012, http://www.qsrmagazine.com/news/starbucks-named-top-qsr-media-impact-value.

"Because of its openness and seamless approach, Square at Starbucks is better positioned than any other technology to become": Marcus Wohlsen, "Square Launches at Starbucks—You Think You Won't Use It, but You Will," *WIRED.com*, November 8, 2012, http://www.wired.com/business/2012/11/square-launches-at-starbucks/all/.

"Using game-type mechanics in non-game businesses to increase efficiency, customer loyalty and engagement": Amish Shah, "The Art and Science of Gamification," *ipadbiz.ulitzer.com*, August 2, 2012, http://ipadbiz.ulitzer.com/node/2323173.

"Checking out Starbucks Twitter page, it's visible that most of the tweets are directed at": Kylie Jane Wakefield, "How Twitter Helps Starbucks Brew Up an Excellent Customer Experience," *contently.com* (blog), February 23, 2012, http://contently.com/blog/2012/02/23/starbucks-twitter-strategy/.

"Starbucks is constantly expanding its content channels and exploring new formats to connect with its customers": Matt Wesson, "How to Use Content to Raise the Bar for Branding," Content Marketing Institute, July 12, 2012, http://contentmarketinginstitute.com/2012/07/content-raises-the-bar-for-branding/.

"To achieve this successful social media engagement, Starbucks focused its Web page, Facebook page and television advertisements": "Starbucks Rates Number 1 in Study of Most Socially Engaged Companies by Research Firm PhaseOne," PhaseOne, March 28, 2012, http://www.phaseone.net/news/starbucks-rates-number-1-in-study-of-most-socially-engaged-companies-by-research-firm-phaseone/.

"Where traditional companies push out messages and products, these companies pull customers in. Instead of treating customers as passive targets": Mark Bonchek, "How Top Brands Pull Customers into Orbit," *Harvard Business Review Blog Network*, March 5, 2012, http://blogs.hbr.org/cs/2012/03/how_top_brands_pull_customers.html.

"For me, consumer-initiated ads are the future of advertising, not only on Facebook, but across other social networks too": Dave Williams, "How to Work Your Facebook Following," *blog.creamglobal.com*, February 23, 2012, http://blog.creamglobal.com/right_brain_left_brain/2012/02/how-to-work-your-facebook-following.html.

CHAPTER 9

"Due in large part to Howard Schultz's careful nurturing and development of the Starbucks Experience, the company has been able to leverage its increasingly strong brand": Ranjay Gulati, Sarah Huffman, and Gary Neilson, "The Barista Principle: Starbucks and the Rise of Relational Capital," *Strategy+Business*, no. 28, http://www.auburn.edu/outreach/ecdi/documents/wfd_barista_principal.pdf.

"I am not sure people today even know we are roasting coffee": "Starbucks Chairman Says Trouble May Be Brewing," Media and Marketing, *Wall Street Journal*, February 24, 2007, http://online.wsj.com/article/SB117225247561617457.html.

"Starbucks captures only a small portion of the $100 billion coffee, tea, and ready-to-drink beverage market globally": Robert Lillegard, "How to Win in Retail," *QSR*, July 2012, http://www.qsrmagazine.com/growth/how-win-retail.

"The key is choosing a partner. . . . Everybody thinks most licenses succeed—it's absolutely the opposite": As quoted in Robert Lillegard, "How to Win in Retail," *QSR*, July 2012, http://www.qsrmagazine.com/growth/how-win-retail.

"Even long-standing relationships can grow sour. Starbucks and Kraft had a very ugly public split in 2011 after the coffee giant claimed that the distributor wasn't doing enough": Robert Lillegard, "How to Win in Retail," *QSR*, July 2012, http://www.qsrmagazine.com/growth/how-win-retail.

"Starbucks is positioning VIA against its own fresh brewed coffee, challenging people to see if they can taste the difference": Steve Tobak, "Starbucks Via: How to Blow a Turnaround," *CBS Money Watch*, September 30, 2009, http://www.cbsnews.com/8301-505125_162-28242944/starbucks-via-how-to-blow-a-turnaround/.

"Through their collaboration, Starbucks is the exclusive licensed super-premium brand for GMCR's traditional Keurig and Vue brewers": "Starbucks Corporation and Green Mountain Coffee Roasters, Inc. Enter into Strategic Manufacturing, Marketing, Distribution and Sales Relationship," news.Starbucks.com, March 10, 2011, http://news.starbucks.com/article_display.cfm?article_id=504.

"A 2012 Reuters survey suggests that about 10 percent of the world's workforce works from home": Patricia Reaney, "About One in Five Workers Worldwide Telecommute: Poll," Reuters, January 24, 2012, http://www.reuters.com/article/2012/01/24/us-telecommuting-idUSTRE80N1IL20120124.

"We announced that Starbucks will introduce an instant coffee, providing our customers with great tasting Starbucks coffee, anywhere and anytime": Howard Schultz, "Staying Real in an Instant," *Huffington Post*, February 17, 2009, http://www.huffingtonpost.com/howard-schultz/staying-real-in-an-instan_b_167381.html.

"I know some will question our decision, and I understand this reaction. Expectations from brands like Starbucks are high": Howard Schultz, "Staying Real in an Instant," *Huffington Post*, February 17, 2009, http://www.huffingtonpost.com/howard-schultz/staying-real-in-an-instan_b_167381.html.

"Sampling is a time proven method for facilitating consumer trial. Starbucks having ultimate control in their own stores orchestrated sampling customers with free VIA coffee": Domenick Celentano, "Most Memorable New Product Launches Part 2," foodbeverage.about.com, February 2009, http://foodbeverage.about.com/od/Food_Entreprenur_Spotlight/a/Most-Memorable-N.

"You just can't get away from the fact that social media in food [promotion] is powerful and Starbucks being marketing geniuses know this": Domenick Celentano, "Most Memorable New Product Launches Part 2," foodbeverage.about.com, February 2009, http://foodbeverage.about.com/od/Food_Entreprenur_Spotlight/a/Most-Memorable-N.

"The fourth possible peril is this: A combination of brand fatigue (too much Starbucks distributed through too many market channels) and unbundling the beverage from the iconic ritual": Jane Genova, "Starbucks: Humbled in the Grocery Aisle?," *beta.fool.com* (blog), March 28, 2012, http://beta.fool.com/janegenova/2012/03/28/starbucks-humbled-grocery-aisle/3185.

CHAPTER 10

"Fundamental assumptions that did not allow top management to adjust to new market realities": Andrea Nagy Smith, "What Was Polaroid Thinking?," *Yale Insights*, November 2009, http://qn.som.yale.edu/content/what-was-polaroid-thinking.

"In 'the early stages of growth,' 'the second inning of a nine-inning game,'": Joseph A. Michelli, *The Starbucks Experience: 5 Principles for Turning Ordinary into Extraordinary* (New York: McGraw-Hill, 2006).

"Drippler.com, an electronic gadget news source, reported a substantial rise in site visitors in 2012": "iPod and Other MP3 Player Sales Fade as iPhones, Androids and Other Smartphones Take Over as the Digital Music Players of Choice," PR Web, February 29, 2012, http://www.prweb.com/releases/gadgets/iphone/prweb9236591.htm.

"Starbucks no longer seems to perceive its future as depending on an ability to clone its essential store concept ad infinitum": Jon Gertner, "For Infusing a Steady Stream of New Ideas to Revive its Business," *Fast Company*, 2012, http://www.fastcompany.com/most-innovative-companies/2012/starbucks.

"Design will allow Starbucks baristas to handcraft espresso beverages more efficiently and consistently": "Fact Sheet: New Milk Steaming Pitcher," news.starbucks.com, March 6, 2012, http://news.starbucks.com/article_display.cfm?article_id=627.

"Implementing mobile pay in the Drive Thru took a few more considerations than it did inside the store. For one, we needed something that would allow": Dana K., "The Starbucks App Is Now Drive Thru Friendly!," *starbucks.com/blog*, March 26, 2012, http://www.starbucks.com/blog/the-starbucks-app-is-now-drive-thru-friendly-/1172.

"We just did something in China that I think is one of the most innovative things we have ever done in our history": "Howard Schultz on Global Reach and Local Relevance at Starbucks: An Interview with the CEO," *BCG Perspectives*, October 17, 2012, https://www.bcgperspectives.com/content/videos/leadership_management_two_speed_economy_howard_schultz_global_reach_and_local_relevance/.

"Still the company's main instigator—has a kernel of an idea. . . . He then activates": Jon Gertner, "For Infusing a Steady Stream of New Ideas to Revive its Business," *Fast Company*, 2012, http://www.fastcompany.com/most-innovative-companies/2012/starbucks.

"It was absolutely delicious. Lots of people liked it.": Melody Overton, "Starbucks Sorbetto: The 2008 Delicious Test Product That Didn't Make It (A Piece of Starbucks History)," *starbucksmelody.com* (blog), October 20, 2010, http://www.starbucksmelody.com/2010/10/20/starbucks-sorbetto-the-2008-delicious-test-product-that-didnt-make-it-a-piece-of-starbucks-history/.

"Rate of change in the world today is going up. It's going up fast, and it's affecting organizations in a huge way": John Kotter, "Can You Handle an Exponential Rate of Change?," *Forbes*, July 19, 2011, http://www.forbes.com/sites/johnkotter/2011/07/19/can-you-handle-an-exponential-rate-of-change/.

"The Café Starbucks concept includes a wait staff, seating for up to 65, and a menu that covers all dayparts beginning with full breakfasts": Roseanne Harper, "Starbucks Percolates Its Third Full-Service Restaurant," *Supermarket News*, November 30, 1998, http://supermarketnews.com/archive/starbucks-percolates-its-third-full-service-restaurant.

"Surrounded by San Francisco's pricey new loft apartments, [Circadia] resurrects the feel of the 1960s coffee shops of Greenwich Village": Mark Gimein, "Behind Starbucks' New Venture: Beans, Beatniks, and Booze," *Fortune*, May 15, 2000, http://money.cnn.com/magazines/fortune/fortune_archive/2000/05/15/279773/index.htm.

"Starbucks pitched a new game plan . . . a healthier breakfast line-up with fewer calories and more protein": Erin Zimmer, "Starbucks Introduces a New Line of 'Healthier' Breakfast Foods," *Serious Eats*, September 4, 2008, http://www.seriouseats.com/2008/09/starbucks-new-healthy-breakfast-options.html.

"Starbucks Diet": "Woman Claims She Lost 75 Pounds on 'Starbucks Diet,'" *New York Daily News*, September 17, 2012, http://articles.nydailynews.com/2012-09-17/news/33907123_1_diet-starbucks-woman-claims.

"Sometimes you just want a glass of wine and a delicious bite to eat": "Starbucks Evenings," Starbucks.com, http://www.starbucks.com/coffeehouse/starbucks-stores/starbucks-evenings.

"Starbucks opened a store unlike any before it. There are no leather chairs or free power outlets": Mark Wilson, "An Experimental New Starbucks Store: Tiny, Portable, and Hyper Local," *Fast Company Design*, http://www.fastcodesign.com/1670889/an-experimental-new-starbucks-store-tiny-portable-and-hyper-local#1.

"In Seattle's Best Coffee's latest divergence from corporate parent Starbucks": Melissa Allison, "Seattle's Best Coffee Plans Thousands of Drive Thru-Only Cafés," *Seattle Times*, November 13, 2012, http://seattletimes.com/html/businesstechnology/2019676822_seattlesbestxml.html.

"Any company, small or large, consumer or otherwise, that is going to embrace the status quo": Howard Schultz, "Innovation," YouTube.com, May 16, 2011, http://www.youtube.com/watch?v=ll-64gNuT3E.

CHAPTER 11

James Kouzes and Barry Posner, *A Leader's Legacy* (Hoboken, NJ: John Wiley & Sons, 2006).

"Since Starbucks earliest days, I have believed in a strong link between our company's performance, our values, and the impact": Howard Schultz, "2012 Global Responsibility Report, Message from Howard Schultz," Starbucks.com, 2012, http://www.starbucks.com/responsibility/global-report/leadership-letter.

"Green building skeptics sometimes argue that it's difficult or even impossible to build green without paying a big cost premium": Natural Resources Defense Council, "Fact Sheets: How Much Does Green Building Really Cost?," http://www.nrdc.org/buildinggreen/factsheets/cost.asp.

Green Building Design Award: Bonnie Christian, "Global Green USA Honors Adrian Grenier, Starbucks with Sustainable Design Awards," *Huffington Post*, November 15, 2011, http://www.huffingtonpost.com/2011/11/15/global-green-usa-adrian-grenier_n_1095304.html.

2012 Good Design Is Good Business Award: Linda Lentz, "2012 Good Design Is Good Business Award Winners," *Architectural Record*, April 23, 2012, http://archrecord.construction.com/news/2012/04/2012-Good-Design-is-Good-Business-Award-Winners.asp.

Green Power Leadership Award winner: "Starbucks Listed on EPA's Top 50 Green Organizations," FastCasual.com, April 24, 2012, http://www.fastcasual.com/article/193480/Starbucks-listed-on-EPA-s-Top-50-green-organizations.

"Without compromising its thermal properties, the new sleeve uses 35 percent less paper and is made from 85 percent postconsumer recycled fiber: "New Starbucks EarthSleeve™ Blends Performance with Environmental Sensibility," news.starbucks.com, July 19, 2012, http://news.starbucks.com/article_display.cfm?article_id=681.

"Ensure 100% of our coffee is ethically sourced by 2015": "Starbucks Global Responsibility Report: Goals and Progress 2011," http://globalassets.starbucks.com/assets/c007fb25782442ac8283b154364c1016.pdf.

"Through our partnership with Starbucks, we were able to serve as an economic catalyst in urban cities through the creation of new jobs": "Starbucks Acquires Remaining Interest in Magic Johnson

Enterprises' Urban Coffee Opportunities (UCO)," news.starbucks.com, October 21, 2010, http://news.starbucks.com/article_display.cfm?article_id=452.

"Starbucks is partnering with two organizations doing heroic work": "Starbucks Announces Store Partnership Model with Community Organizations in Harlem and Los Angeles," news.starbucks.com, October 4, 2011, http://news.starbucks.com/article_display.cfm?article_id=574.

Howard Schultz and Dori Jones Yang, *Pour Your Heart into It: How Starbucks Built a Company One Cup at a Time* (New York: Hyperion, 1997).

"Ethos Water, which is now a Starbucks subsidiary, has made more than $7 million in grants in support of that mission": "2012 Global Responsibility Report: Year in Review," starbucks.com.

"There are more than 1.2 billion 15 to 24 year olds, the largest global cohort of young people in history": "Youth Leadership Grants," starbucks.com, http://www.starbucks.com/responsibility/community/youth-action/grant.

"Let's tell our government leaders to put partisanship aside and to speak truthfully about the challenges we face": Howard Schultz, "An Open Letter: How Can America Win This Election?," starbucks.com, June 29, 2012, http://www.starbucks.com/blog/an-open-letter-how-can-america-win-this-election/1207.

"Until the Congress and the president return to Washington and deliver a fiscally disciplined long-term debt and deficit plan to the American people": Cameron Joseph, "100 CEOs Promise No Campaign Contributions," *The Hill* (blog), August 25, 2011, http://thehill.com/blogs/ballot-box/presidential-races/178211-100-ceos-promise-no-campaign-contributions.

"It didn't take long for Starbucks to find the perfect financial partner": Joe Nocera, "We Can All Become Job Creators," *New York Times*, October 17, 2011, http://www.nytimes.com/2011/10/18/opinion/nocera-we-can-all-become-job-creators.html?_r=0.

"We're getting money in the hands of [CDFIs], (who then) lend it to small businesses, create jobs in start-ups and existing businesses": "Starbucks CEO Touts Program to Create U.S. Jobs," *CBSNews.com*, April 3, 2012, http://www.cbsnews.com/8301-505268_162-57408557/starbucks-ceo-touts-program-to-create-u.s-jobs/.

CHAPTER 12

"Any consumer brand today—whether Starbucks or a product like Tide—[must] create relevancy": John Gertner, "Starbucks CEO Howard Schultz on Connecting With Customers Everyday, All Day," *Fast Company*, November 26, 2012, http://www.fastcompany.com/3003147/starbucks-ceo-howard-schultz-connecting-customers-everyday-all-day.

"Material risks to Starbucks recent expansion efforts. While going global is a great idea, moving outside of one's niche": Reuben Gregg Brewer, "The Good and Bad of the Cool Caffeine Store's Expansion," *Motley Fool Blog Network*, November 20, 2012, http://beta.fool.com/reubengbrewer/2012/11/20/the-good-and-bad-of-the-cool-caffeine-stores-expan/16903/.

"I am going with Schultz—not against him—because it has been a horrendous bet to go against Schultz": Drew Sandholm, "Starbucks CEO Draws Comparison to Steve Jobs," Mad Money w/ Jim Cramer, *CNBC*, September 20, 2012, http://www.cnbc.com/id/49111861.

Much of the content of this book emerged from face-to-face meetings, telephone interviews, and other forms of support involving Starbucks partners. These partners include, but are not limited to:

Adam Brotman, Adam Novsam, Aimee Johnson, Al Griggs, Alex Wheeler, Alisa Martinez, Alison Edwards, Andrea Bader, Andrew Linneman, Anna Konopke, Annie Young-Scrivner, Anthony Perez, Arthur Rubinfeld, Barbara McMaster, Belinda Wong, Ben Packard, Blair Taylor, Brad Anderson, Brad Nelson, Brett Buchanan, Carlos Jimenez, Carol Wise, Carolina Morales, Catherine Chu, Cecilia Carter, Cecilia DeFranco, Cecile Hudon, Charles Cain, Charles Douglas III, Chris Bruzzo, Chris Carr, Christina McPherson, Christina Ryan Foster, Clarice Turner, Cliff Burrows, Corey duBrowa, Corey Lindberg, Craig Russell, Curt Garner, D. Major Cohen, Dan Berger, Dan Kassa, Diana Barnes, Diana Kelly, Dirk Nickolaus, Dub Hay, Elisha Trombley, Emma Evans, Ernst Florian, Feng Bao, Frank Wubben, Gabe Wiborg, Gina Woods, Heidi Durham, Heidi Peiper, Howard Schultz, Janeen Simmons, Jean-Marie Shields, Jenny Cui, Jim Hanna, Jim Olson, Joe Young, John Culver, Juan Rivers, Kalen Holmes, Katie McMahan, Kaycee Kiesz, Kelly Goodejohn, Kevin Petrisko, Kimberlee Sherman, Kris Engskov, Laura Baker, Linda Mills, Lionel Sussman, Lisa Passé, Lissa Law, Liz Muller, Maggie Jantzen,

Marthalee Galeota, Megan Adams, Meredith Bell, Michelle Bonam, Michelle Gass, Mick James, Mike Peck, Paula Boggs, Peter Gibbons, Rebecca Alexander, Rich Nelsen, Rob Naylor, Rob Porcarelli, Rob Sopkin, Rodney Hines, Ruth Anderson, Ryan Hudson, Samantha Yarwood, Sandra Bucher, Shao Wei, Stacy Speicher, Stephen Gillett, Tam Marpoe, Thom Breslin, Thomas Mayer, Tina Olsson Schulz, Tom Barr, Troy Alstead, Valerie O'Neil, Virgil Jones, Vivek Varma, and Wang Bin Wolf.

Index

About the Author

Dr. Joseph Michelli helps companies and organizations develop leaders, engage employees, elevate human experiences, master service skills, and innovate relevant solutions.

To achieve these measurable outcomes, Dr. Michelli provides:

Keynote speeches

Workshop presentations

Panel facilitation

Leadership retreats

Customer experience audits

Daylong and extended customer experience–
and leadership-focused consulting services

Dr. Michelli is the chief experience officer of the Michelli Experience, where he has dedicated his career to helping leaders achieve loyalty-building customer experiences and dynamic workplace cultures. In addition to writing the book you are holding, Dr. Michelli is a *New York Times*, *Wall Street Journal*, *USA Today*, and *BusinessWeek* bestselling author who has also written:

The Zappos Experience: 5 Principles to Inspire, Engage, and WOW

Prescription for Excellence: Leadership Lessons for Creating a World-Class Customer Experience from UCLA Health System

The New Gold Standard: 5 Leadership Principles for Creating a Legendary Customer Experience Courtesy of The Ritz-Carlton Hotel Company, and

The Starbucks Experience: 5 Principles for Turning Ordinary into Extraordinary

In addition, Dr. Michelli and John Yokoyama, the owner of the World Famous Pike Place Fish Market in Seattle, Washington, coauthored *When Fish Fly: Lessons for Creating a Vital and Energized Workplace.*

For more information on how Dr. Michelli can present at your event, provide training resources, or help you with your products, your people, or your customers' experience, please visit www.josephmichelli.com.

Dr. Michelli is eager to help you *lead the Starbucks way.* He can be reached through his website, by e-mail at josephm@josephmichelli.com, or by calling either (734) 697-5078 or (888) 711-4900 (toll free within the United States).

GRANDMA'S MARATHON STARTING LINE

1836
716

MARATHON
10
1
3
18

U R
AMAZING
DADDY
GO DADDY GO

F1222
4444

2926
F965

MDRA
1589
1731

USS

INISH LINE
F2300

adidas
IRONMAN
WELLS FARGO
Grandma's Marathon
half marathon
FINISHER
20
YEARS

4014
F9019

the family) and running the household, or a balance of the two. Both spouses need to agree and support the individual for the betterment and maximization of the whole (family). Otherwise, someone will feel cheated, unappreciated and unfulfilled. The results can be horrible.

I saw the positive side of this firsthand with my parents. Both my mom and dad had well-defined responsibilities and both took pride in their respective roles. Dad had a career and a desire to succeed. He had a passion and a direction for how he wanted his business to flourish. My mother was the CEO of the family and consummate supporter of the family business, whether it was entertaining, agreeing to move or making short-term sacrifices so the family business would succeed long-term. They both understood the power of building personal and professional relationships and they knew how to say thank you. They were a team. My dad succeeded because my mom succeeded in her role as mother and CEO of the house and in her unwavering commitment to supporting my dad.

Support at work

Whether you are a business owner, corporate executive or individual contributor, understand that the team is what is needed to win. And, as with all teams, not everyone will be an MVP (most valuable player). The real job is not to find fault—that's always the easy way out, as in, you're "out" as soon as you become known as one of the water cooler complainers, those who are soon quietly overlooked for promotion and, possibly, not so quietly, asked to find a new employer.

I recently heard James Owens, CEO of Cub Foods, a Minnesota grocery chain, give a talk at Augsburg College's

Strommen Executive Speaker Series. Mr. Owens noted that to succeed in corporate life you need a champion in the "promotion committee room." It's that group who all know who the team supporters are and those who look to place blame. Those complainers and non–team players are known all too well.

Mr. Owens went on to say that it is equally important to find that mentor within the organization, someone who is not threatened by your career path and drives, someone you trust and can learn from. They will have a good feel for the culture and personality of the organization and the skills needed to flourish. That type of support is more valuable than an MBA, says Owen. In addition, he said, it is critical to look for the fun and the positives in your life and in your work environment. The rewards will come when you least expect them and from people that you did not think even knew who you were. When he was asked by a student in the audience what single thing he did that contributed to his success, Owens replied, "I sought out and learned from everyone around me."

Support in your life and relationships

If you really study those around you, those you know, you will find something remarkably obvious: People surround themselves with others who share common beliefs and attitudes. As Lisa T. stepped up her running, she joined a running club and found that her fellow runners had similar personality characteristics. "They were motivated, educated and had tons of life experiences," she says. "The moms, like me, had professional backgrounds. We had a lot in common. Runners are fascinating, positive and focused people."

Think about your own interests and what's important to you. Do you have a network you can contribute to and receive from? Those who are socially minded often have friends that are part of socially minded organizations. Those who enjoy the arts and culture get involved in related activities. Some place a high value on their spiritual lives and work to place their faith and the church as the foundation of their family life.

Being connected to something informs our sense of identity and can support a positive outlook on life. When working toward a goal, look for the strengths versus the weaknesses in others. It is not surprising that those who are the loudest complainers often look for fault in others first and surround themselves with like-minded people. They have no compassion, grace or capacity to forgive or to accept that we are all human and entitled to making mistakes. Do you want someone like that on your team?

All of this reinforces that we are not designed to be solitary creatures. We need support, help and encouragement from others to define and achieve our purpose. At the base of our psyches is the basic human need to belong.

Raise the Bar for Yourself:

How might you go about connecting with others who share your values and can support your goals? Think about what's important to you and what you enjoy. What organizations and activities encompass similar attributes? How might you engage with them? Also, look within your company and seek out a mentor for professional coaching. Or create your own personal board of directors!

CHAPTER 6

WHAT'S LUCK GOT TO DO WITH IT?

Shallow men believe in luck or in circumstance. Strong men believe in cause and effect.

—Ralph Waldo Emerson

I am not a big believer in luck. Now, it could be argued that there are situations where "luck," however you term it, could contribute to the outcome. Yet as a general rule, plain old luck usually doesn't come into play. Winning the lottery may be one of those situations where I could be persuaded differently, but most all other outcomes can be contributed to factors other than luck.

I hear people say:

"He was lucky to make the team!" But this person isn't aware that the athlete worked at their sport daily during the off season, refined their skills, developed their physical strengths by going to the gym, sought out competition and challenges and made sacrifices. Was making the team "lucky"?

"How lucky was he? He got that new sale . . . or expanded an existing client . . . it was a big deal!" However, if you followed that individual you would see nearly two years of relationship building, a great sales record, honing professional skills, asking questions and taking the time to discover what's important to the client. Was the sale "lucky"? No, it was the result of patience and clearly putting the client first.

"She got lucky in qualifying for the Boston Marathon!" Again, I doubt luck was the factor. This gal trained daily, put her trust in a coach, changed her diet and, likely, had to forgo some nights out with friends. She put in her miles. She prepared mentally for the challenge and sought advice from elite runners. She surrounded herself with a great support team during the training and the race. She *earned* the right to go to Boston; she didn't rely on luck.

It's All about Preparation

I prefer to say that I was *fortunate* to have had the experience, to be part of the team, to have a great client, to participate in a marathon that I had to qualify for. I was *fortunate* to have the experience. I'm so glad I earned this right and feel fully satisfied with the accomplishment.

In Chapter 2 of this book, I refer to an article, "Mind over

Miles," by Jerry Lynch, PhD, that appeared in the May 1996 *Runner's World* magazine. This article not only discusses some of the principles and beliefs I have found helpful in pursuing my goals, including "stay relaxed" and "strive for your best," but also helps us better understand how to "get lucky" in running.

There's more to it than just putting in the training miles, no matter what kind of marathon you're preparing for. Let me summarize Dr. Lynch's list of ten key mental attributes, skills and commitments that are critical to success in achieving goals of all kinds:

1. **Motivation** – "To stay motivated you must love what you do!" What a compelling statement that deals with more than just running.

2. **Goal Setting** – Goals are essential. Without them you do not know how you are doing, yet goals based solely on achievement can create tension and anxiety.

3. **Visualization** – If you cannot visualize the desired outcome, you likely won't achieve it. Every time I run (jog) a marathon, I find that I must visualize how I will feel when I see the next support person along the route. I visualize crossing the finish line. Visualization supports and reinforces my motivation.

4. **Yielding to Fatigue** – Fatigue is a normal byproduct of striving for success. What Dr. Lynch contends is that rather than fight fatigue, accept it and take it along as part of the experience. I tried his suggestion on a recent training run and "talked to the fatigue." Sounded corny, but it has merit. "Welcome fatigue,"

I said to myself. "So you finally arrived. Join me and if needed, hop on my back and I will carry you for a while and, if necessary, to the finish line." It was interesting how effective that simple idea was. I accepted the fatigue and moved beyond it.

5. **Focus** – This is a matter of perspective. When I participate in a marathon, I do not focus on the 26.2-mile journey in front of me. I focus on the next water stop—typically every two miles. I focus on a series of thirteen two-mile runs. I've adopted Craig T.'s ritual of dedicating each of the last six miles to one of the important people in my life. It gives me an extra boost. I focus on what is important.

6. **Relaxation** – Easier said than done. Who doesn't get uptight running 26.2 miles? One of the keys to completing a successful run or goal of any kind is to remain relaxed and in control.

7. **Self-Talk** – We have a choice between positive or negative self-talk. Each has an impact on results. I have experienced this in my training. Negative self-talk drains my energy, motivation and fortitude, and it destroys my results. Being kind to yourself will buoy up your brain and your body.

8. **Excellence** – Dr. Lynch says, "Strive for excellence, not perfection." I don't know about you, but striving for perfection drives me crazy. I am a passionate golfer but no matter how good a day I have on the golf course, it's never perfect. I've discovered that doing my

best and preparing for the challenge will provide me an excellent experience, one I can feel good about.

9. **Determination** – Remember the children's story *The Little Engine That Could*? This is a classic lesson about the importance of determination, positive self-talk, focus and having a well-defined purpose. I encourage you to read the story again.

10. **Dance** – I like how Dr. Lynch sums it up: "Excellence in running is a dance of body, mind and spirit." It is all a frame of mind. I'd expand it to say, Excellence in life is a dance of body, mind and spirit!

Success doesn't happen by accident and shouldn't depend upon luck. To achieve success is to be filled with *intentionality* and supported by *preparation*.

Dr. Lynch's ten principles of "Mind over Miles" is clearly a concept that can translate to life, career and business, even relationships. The elements necessary to achieving success or a fulfilling life don't happen by accident. We can't count on luck to get us where we want to go. We must prepare for our purpose.

> *I'm a great believer in luck, and I find the harder I work the more I have of it.*
> —Thomas Jefferson

Put in the Miles

Katie R. shares moving testimony about the importance of "putting in the miles," laying the groundwork necessary for achieving a goal. Katie ran Grandma's Marathon—her first one—two weeks before her fortieth birthday.

"I grew up with the notion that I could not run and that I was not an athlete," Katie says. "Negative comments from coaches and my own dad haunted me as a child and into adulthood. I lacked confidence and it showed. I believed I could never run a mile, let alone a marathon. In 2010, I was challenged to a 5K. I never intended to run a marathon; I never thought I was capable of doing it. I just didn't think I could . . . it goes back to being a kid. I was never an athlete. I ran track when I was ten years old. I was in this race and ended up coming in last. After that, I was really self-conscious. I grew up with a reputation for not being athletic."

Approaching forty and a University of Minnesota–Duluth graduate, Katie made Grandma's Marathon in Duluth her ultimate goal. "Completing the marathon has been the most rewarding and important accomplishment of my life," she says. "The positive energy of the racing environment and feeling of accomplishment is addictive."

When asked if she ever questioned finishing, Katie responded, "Oh yes. I was crying when the race started. I was so nervous. This lady next to me hugged me and said, 'It's going to be okay.' When I was running the first few miles, I thought 'What did I get myself into?'"

Katie says twenty-six weeks of training is the marathon. "Marathon day is the prize."

Crossing the finish line was an emotional experience for Katie. "Several of my friends were there. I was so happy. I've never felt that sense of accomplishment in my life. I spent so many years battling that self-esteem thing and I did it."

When asked about her inspiration, Katie had one person in mind: "My dad. He's battled alcoholism. In the year I was training, he was getting sober for the second time. He was in treatment. I have to run for four hours, he has to work hard every minute of every day. I only had a hill to climb, but he had this mountain. What I faced in running was only a drop in the bucket."

Katie's example of putting her mind over the miles has led to healing, a greater self-awareness of her strengths and a new chapter of purpose and fulfillment.

Raise the Bar for Yourself:

Taking Katie's experience, think about how you might reframe a negative or hurtful experience in your life and use it to learn from and grow. How might you challenge yourself to turn this into an opportunity?

CHAPTER 7

DEALING WITH FAILURE

Failure is only the opportunity to begin again more intelligently.

—Henry Ford

I was unlucky today; I did not finish the Napa Marathon. This was the ninth time I had walked through the same morning routine: I had gotten up early, had some breakfast, took a long shower and thought about the journey ahead as I paced around the room. I then headed to the starting line a quarter-mile away.

As I walked this cool, dark morning with other runners, I was filled with a mix of excitement and anxiety. I could visualize the course and various points along the way. I knew support was there, just waiting for me. However, I wasn't in my best shape . . . not bad shape in any sense of the word . . . I felt I was ready enough. I could visualize and look ahead to feel the elation, the satisfaction and relief that would come as I crossed the finish line. I was brought back into the moment as "The Star Spangled Banner" was being sung. Then the starter's pistol went off and I was off.

As I got underway I knew I wasn't feeling like I should so early in the run. The first hill, I thought, was more of a drain than it should be. I reminded myself to relax. It takes some time to get in the groove, in the zone, as they say. All will be fine, you are tough, Bob, I told myself. Yet with some stomach issues, leg cramps and the inner voice that says today is not the day . . . I dropped out.

As I write this I am reminded of the deep emotions that accompany the sense of failure. In this case I had not accomplished my three goals for the marathon: enjoy the experience, finish and make sure there were others behind me! Although I did enjoy the experience, I did not finish, and as such, there was no one behind me.

Was I mentally weak that day? What did I learn from this experience of personal failure in accomplishing my objective?

What I've Learned

What I know is that if you fall off the bike—fail—in the sense of not accomplishing a goal, you are at a "Y" in the road. Now you have a choice as to how you are going to react. You can either quit or get back in there and attempt the event, job or task again. I hope you choose to get back on the bike, readjust and try again.

If you stumble, use it as a learning and growth experience, not an experience of failure.

Personally, I chose to see the Napa experience as a learning and growth opportunity—not an experience of failure—and have already started to prepare differently for my next marathon, Grandma's Marathon, this summer. I have taken a few days to reflect and have come to some conclusions as to what went wrong.

Assess the Process

I need to assess my process, my checklist in preparation for this marathon, to see where I went wrong. This requires brutal honesty with oneself. What could I change? Where could I improve? How could I make adjustments to minimize the chances of this happening again?

- Was my purpose for running Napa true and well grounded? – Yes
- Was I mentally prepared and could I visualize the journey and outcome? – Yes
- Was my race-day preparation, food, sleep and clothing appropriate for race-day conditions? – Yes
- Were there places along the race route where I'd find emotional and personal support? – Yes
- Did I put in the training as I had in the past? – Not sure!
- Did I utilize the foundation of training found in most marathon books? –Nope

- Was I in good shape for a sixty-year-old male? – Yes, but a bit overweight for a 26.2-mile jog.

Bingo. As I studied and reflected on two key areas, it was not that I was unlucky, it was that I didn't do all that I should have to be as ready as I could.

I also realize that despite all the perfect plans and preparation, the goal still may not be achieved. The body may have a different plan on race day. However, in assessing and preparing, I am stacking the cards in my favor to increase the probability of success.

My post-race assessment is the same process that needs to occur wherever you feel you have not been as successful as planned. Stop, assess, review, adjust and get back on the bike. Reinforce what was good and improve on what missed the mark. In the case of the Napa Marathon, it wasn't a lack of mental and mechanical preparation. It wasn't a lack of focus on my purpose, goal and process. It was the lack of physical preparation. I didn't put in the miles, the training required to help me accomplish my goal.

Dealing with the Unexpected

Things do go wrong in sports, business and life. In an article "When Things Go Wrong," written by John Blue for *Freeplay Endurance Sports* magazine, an elite runner shares revelations she gained when she encounters the unanticipated while preparing for a race. Here's a snippet from the article:

"In our training, charts, pace calculators and race plans, everything operates in a world of math and perfect performance.

Meanwhile, each race is like life. The actual races occur in the real world, tossed with chaos and conflict. Weather happens, spectators get in the way, dogs run on the course, lead bikes go off the course, shoes become untied, you trip, the person in front of you trips and you may even trip over them. It's also possible that you might stop to help someone who's fallen down."

So what do you do when confronted with the unexpected? Keep things in perspective: Realize that you've prepared for it and just deal with it!

Doesn't that sound like a great mindset for life, business and your career? Does it not sound like the right mindset for relationships? We do not live in a perfect world that will be free of speed bumps.

However, the *Freeplay* magazine article also goes on to say that no matter how much pre-race planning you do, you can't always avoid difficulties or missteps. "You can double knot your shoelaces and put on some anti-chafing ointment—but you can't possibly plan for every contingency."

Redirecting after a Letdown

What do you do when something goes wrong?

We learn to suck it up and deal with it. Odds are your preparation will position you to be up to the challenge.

So can failure breed success? Are there lessons learned from failure? The answer to both is YES! This is not rocket science if your attitude is right. The right "success-driven attitude" enables you to take responsibility and look for ways to correct the problem. If the purpose is well grounded, then the attitude needs to be closely aligned.

While I clearly prefer success—it's more fun, feels better and breeds confidence—I also have learned to value what comes from failure. If looked at from the right perspective, failure can set the stage for more learning and more growth.

Failure often results due to a lack of mastery of a skill or behavior. If mastery has not been achieved, then stopping to assess the failure (like I chose to do after the Napa Marathon) offers an opportunity to change direction, attitude and behavior with better results following.

Learning from Failure

If you Google "Lessons Learned from Failure," you'll find dozens and dozens of pages of references. I stopped looking after forty pages. However, the "Top Ten Lessons to Learn from Failure" list on the SuccessStories website, by Mousumi Kumar Saha, really resonates with me. I've adapted this to incorporate some lessons I've learned from running and in business.

Patience

Achieving success, whether in life, relationships or running a marathon, takes time, dedication to stay with the plan and a commitment to not lose focus of your goal. Even a well-defined, visualized and internalized goal may not be achieved the first time out. You need to constantly assess, readjust and try again. I believe patience is a virtue, but don't let it be a curse.

Humility

You don't need to aim to be the absolute best. Remember, it's not about achieving perfection. You'll only drive yourself nuts. In life, we fail at relationships, career moves, parenting, golf and so on. There will always be someone who has more or done better.

I am of the belief that the happy and content person has a personal purpose and conviction for their life's journey. They strive to do their best and when they reach the finish line they feel happy, fulfilled and successful. The manner in which they handle this success is critical. Learning humility along the way makes the success all the sweeter.

We all love to win, yet no one wins 100 percent of the time. The ability to handle failure or disappointment is a developed strength. When I was coaching, I told my team, "We need to learn to win with class and lose with class." That's where a healthy sense of humility comes in. It attracts others to you. It makes others more inclined to help you. Remember, we do not succeed alone. The antithesis of humility is arrogance. It is harder to help an arrogant soul than a humble one.

Learning humility along the way makes success all the sweeter.

Pursue Your Passion

Simply put, find your passion and then pursue it. It will be that passion that will formulate your purpose, define your goals, instill motivation and result in personal success. Consistent failure may be a hint that you are not as focused or committed to your passion as you should be. Or perhaps you need to create a new strategy. Greatness lies in pursuing your own dreams, understanding your own plan and walking your own path.

Proper Planning

Success as a general rule is not an accident; it is a byproduct of a plan. The saying goes: Without a plan, any road will get you there, but will the destination be what you are looking for? You may encounter turning points that alter the journey and lead you in another direction. The result may pleasantly surprise you.

Goals can only be attained with a plan we fervently believe in and vigorously act upon. Since time is so critical and one of our most precious commodities, we must beg the question after a failure, was my planning appropriate and did I work the plan well?

Faith

If you do not believe, if you do not have faith that the goal is yours and is attainable, it will most likely not be achieved. Cement in your mind, heart and soul, not only your commitment, but the belief that you can win.

Retain Your Success

Learn to own each success and store it in your heart. No one can take success away from you. Success breeds further success and provides resilience when there is a challenge and you are faced with your own Lemon Drop Hill.

Warning: Taking success for granted can be a quick eye-opener when you get set back on your heels and lose. You are reminded that success is not automatic and there must be a constant intentional act of progress and effort to stay on task and committed to improving. It happened to me at the Napa Marathon: I took my training for granted and probably lost some focus. After all, I had succeeded eight times in a row. Why would this race be any different? I lost perspective and it came back to bite me.

Be Creative

Easy to say, hard to do. We shouldn't fear failure but rather learn from it as we try and try again. There is no crazy idea, just an idea that did not work well in a given situation. So find another idea. Failure can open the door to creativity if you are open to change. Nothing of significance occurs without some challenge. Nothing accomplished of significance is as rewarding as success after hard work, failure and challenge. Experiment with alternatives to what was done in the past to see if something works better, not just works. The foundation for creativity is acceptance that failure does occur. Fear of failure or discounting a "crazy idea" is a wet blanket to creativity!

Be Strong

Strongly hold onto your passion, your personal conviction, your personal worth and your focus, and maintain a solid commitment to those around you. No one succeeds alone; embrace your relationships and find a reason to say "thank you." It takes effort to fail gracefully but retain your commitment to your goal. There is a saying, which clearly applies to marathons of all kinds: "If it was easy, everyone would do it!" Be strong and anticipate and prepare for the need for strength.

Bring Value

Start with making sure that your beliefs have value. Do not compromise what you believe. Bring value to those around you, not necessarily in a tangible way, but at an emotional and personal level of appreciation and care. Living in Minnesota all my life I can't tell you how many times I've heard the complaint, "I hate cold snowy weather." However, without the bitter cold and dreary days we wouldn't appreciate our beautiful summer and fall weather as we do. This too applies to failure. Failure helps hone a worthwhile purpose, cause and life. Failure helps us to appreciate the successes all that much more. Failure helps us make good choices in life. Failure places the spotlight on value.

Failure places the spotlight on value.

Conquer Yourself

Conquer your fears, conquer your personal doubt. Focus on what is important to you; don't compare yourself to others, but to who you are, who you want to be and the value you provide. Conquer yourself with the help of others. Those around you who can support you are as important as anything else you do to reach the finish line. Others, too, face this same challenge. You are a part of that mechanism for them. This support creates bonds that will last a lifetime.

Stepping Stones

Failure does beg the very personal question that we must ask ourselves: "Is this important? Am I tough enough to conquer this?" More important, don't just ask the question, but act to conquer the little red devil that sits on your shoulder following a missed goal. He's whispering in your ear to accept defeat and sit on the sideline. He's the source of your negative self-chatter. However, listening to that voice will leave you unfulfilled and lacking in true self-satisfied purpose. View your failures as stepping stones that will help you redefine your purpose, renew your motivation and energy and continue pursuing your goals.

In 1963, Mary Kay Ash left her job in traditional sales after yet another man she'd trained was promoted ahead of her. She went on to build her own business, Mary Kay Cosmetics. Today the enterprise boasts annual sales exceeding two billion dollars. Here are sage words from her experience: "When you reach an obstacle, turn it into an opportunity. You have the choice. You can overcome and be a winner, or you can allow it to overcome you and be a loser. The choice is yours and yours alone. Refuse to throw in the towel. Go the extra mile that failures refuse to travel. It is far better to be exhausted from success than to be rested from failure."

Making a Comeback

In the fall of 2011, Adrian Peterson, one of the great running backs in the NFL, incurred a devastating injury when he took a helmet to the knee, tearing his ACL and MCL. It was characterized as one of the most severe injuries of the season. Compared to Peyton Manning and Eric Dickerson, Peterson was in the prime of his career and a critical player for the Minnesota Vikings. Everyone speculated about his future. Would he be back for the 2012 season and, if so, would he return to his previous greatness?

Well, the history books have been written on that one. Peterson not only returned for the first regular season game, but he also nearly broke the single-season yardage record, falling just nine yards short. He was named the NFL's Offensive Player of the Year (2012) and received the NFL's MVP award.

Adrian Peterson returned, not to his past level, but surpassing it. This didn't happen by accident. He prepared for greatness and accepted nothing less for himself. Earlier in his career, he told a reporter his goal was "to be the best player to ever play this game." That mindset explains his unprecedented return from major knee surgery. Peterson didn't simply want to resume his career—he wanted to do it more quickly, and better, than anyone else in the history of the sport. Less than ten months after an injury that very well could have ended his career, he returned to lead the NFL in both yardage and yards per game.

Adrian Peterson worked with his trainers and medical team to control the pace of his return in order to guarantee the greatest chance at success. As he worked through healing from a major injury (or setback), he prepared and trained to react naturally but at a slower rate and rebuilt his agility, balance and range of motion. This type of focus, patience and preparation, in addition to commitment and intentionality, is what ultimately led to the next chapter in a successful athletic career.

Getting Back Up

We all have failures and setbacks that can get in the way of accomplishing our goal. What's important is how we learn from them and whether we choose to get back up and continue on. How much fight do you have? How easily do you give up once you get knocked down? Adrian Peterson could have chosen to retire from the sport, but he wasn't done living his dream and pursuing his goal. Instead he worked with his team, leaning on their encouragement and expertise, blending that with his own will to get back up with renewed vigor and drive.

I have seen this time after time in athletics. I have seen the high school athlete who was not recruited or selected to participate on a Division I team walk away and live their dream. The movie *Rudy,* based on a true story, is an iconic example of a young man overcoming incredible adversity and setbacks to accomplish a personal goal of making the Notre Dame football team, a journey that most of us would never have endured.

Can you see yourself with that level of fortitude and resilience? Stop and rethink your purpose in life, what's important to you and what you want to achieve. Once that is well grounded, fortitude and resilience become a natural part of the mix.

Raise the Bar for Yourself:

How do you deal with failure? Is there teeth gnashing and rending of garments involved? Or can you keep failure in perspective, see it as a temporary setback and resolve to try again?

Think about a recent failure at work, in a relationship or regarding a personal goal such as losing weight or achieving a perfect downward dog in yoga class. Go back and assess your process and preparation. Where did things go wrong? Now think about what you might change and where you might improve. What adjustments can you make to minimize the chance of it happening again? Now get back on the bike and try it again!

CHAPTER 8

HAPPINESS AND SUCCESS

Success is not the key to happiness.
Happiness is the key to success. If you love
what you are doing, you will be successful.

—Albert Schweitzer

At the start of this book I wrote that I hoped you would find a personal nugget of value from the stories shared herein. The purpose of this book is to share the stories of runners who have taken lessons learned from running and used their experiences to enhance the quality and significance of their life and relationships to inspire you to find your own purpose and set goals for your life.

We often feel we will be happy once we are successful while the truth is that happiness is found in the journey. Happiness lies in putting our heart, mind and soul into what we love doing. Success is discovering what we love to do and excelling at it.

Success has abundant and varied definitions. For some, it is a very personal and subjective thing, often related to attaining contentment and happiness in life. It may be finding that quality relationship that will never require you to sacrifice your friends, your dreams or your dignity. Others may define success solely as the attainment of financial wealth or status. Some may believe success is a combination of both.

Why is it important to define success and find a meaningful purpose for yourself?

Success will be elusive to you when another person's definition of success preys upon your own vision and resolution. While others' experiences might guide you toward something positive in your own life, don't compromise your unique experience by following another's path. *You need your own definition and a clear vision of success, something that is consistent with your values, character and abilities.*

For many, success symbolizes the sense of accomplishment and fulfillment that comes from creating something; one's commitment to work or avocation; or a sense of using one's resources to make a positive impact in an area important to the individual.

What Really Matters

Don't cheat yourself or others of the full experience of navigating the bumps along the journey to the finish lines in life. The real value of the journey is the struggle, the sweat, the work that goes into earnestly achieving something for ourselves. A successful life isn't something we can give someone else.

A few years back, I collaborated on a book, *Beating the Midas Curse,* designed to advise families on how they can meaningfully and effectively transfer wealth not only from one generation to another but in a purposeful and conscientious manner to reflect their values and "what really matters." Too often, families can become misguided by the best of intentions: they want to use money as a tool to cushion or protect their loved ones from pain and struggle. However, the underlying premise in *Beating the Midas Curse* is that facing struggle and adversity is invaluable in building strength of character, and helps us learn to recognize and hold onto what really matters.

In my business as a financial planning consultant, all too often the discussion of transferring wealth focuses only on money, when in reality the wealth of a family is far more than that. The term "affluenza" means having a dysfunctional relationship with money. Money does not bring happiness in itself, yet viewing money as a responsibility and privilege is the key to the meaningful transfer of wealth and all that comes with it.

As we wrote the book, we were convinced by the example of countless families where the transfer of wealth without well-thought-out intention and meaning, beyond money, can result in a tragic outcome. Let me give an example, found within the book, that speaks to the importance of recognizing the role struggle and adversity play in creating character and making success all the sweeter. The lesson here is that trying to subvert or avoid challenges or bumps in the road of life, for ourselves or those we care about, comes at a heavy cost.

When Good Intentions Backfire

William came from a middle-class family. His father was a pipe fitter and his mother took in sewing and laundry. William excelled in high school but his family couldn't afford college. A scholarship only paid part of the tuition. William worked his way through school. During the year, he worked as a waiter, a short-order cook and a plumber's assistant. Each summer he worked as a deckhand on an Alaskan fishing boat.

William's work ethic, enthusiasm and drive were amazing. No one was surprised when he graduated at the top of his class. He went to work for a machine parts manufacturer and took on every job they had from maintenance to machine operations, outside sales to personnel management. William learned the business inside and out. Just eight years later, he started his own manufacturing business in a small rented warehouse. At the age of fifty-nine his net worth was in excess of ten million dollars.

Like many people who become successful through hard work and great personal sacrifice, William vowed his kids would never have to work as hard as he did. They wouldn't have to give up parties or football games or buy their clothes at thrift stores—they would have everything he didn't and more. William's children spent their summers at expensive camps and had credit cards by age fourteen. At sixteen they were given keys to their own cars. When it came time for college, William made sure they would be able to concentrate on studies and social activities and not worry about holding down part-time jobs.

William made sure his kids grew up without a single one of the challenging experiences that had shaped his own life. How have his children done?

William's three children, ranging in age from twenty-three

to thirty, have two failed marriages, one bankrupt start-up business and several drug and rehab stays between them. Two graduated from college but only one currently holds a full-time job. William tried to bring them into his business but they just weren't interested. He is so distressed by their lack of ambition and motivation that he has decided to sell his business rather than leave any part of it to them.

The Value of Adversity

As we learned from earlier examples, there is value in dealing with adversity. Struggles build strength of character and generate greater knowledge of self. In addition, struggle does affect our perspective and how we view the world around us. Experiencing struggle and challenge influences our value system and enables us to develop a sense of perseverance, focus and a deeper appreciation and understanding of purpose in life.

A Life of Value and Purpose

In reality, the definition of success rests on each of us, yet a fundamental aspect of a successful life is happiness and being content that life has been lived with value and purpose.

Spiritual leader, physician and well-known author Deepak Chopra has engaged various celebrities in Twitter conversations around social consciousness, connectedness and the pursuit of happiness. In one such conversation, with hip-hop mogul Russell Simmons, the two men talked about the value of incorporating a sense of spirituality and connectedness into our work and avocation.

Chopra and Simmons touched on many of the principles that resonate with *The Finish Line.* Here are some of the key points of their discussion:

- Happiness vs. Pleasure: Too often these two terms are used interchangeably, or in the same context. However, there is a difference between them. Having a glass of wine, going out for a game of golf with your friends, having sex or going shopping do not make us happy as they are short-lasting "feel good" experiences that wear off rather quickly. These things bring you pleasure. Pleasure is important and part of happiness, yet these things do not equate to lifelong happiness.

- Long-term success: In business, if you want to achieve long-term success, you must bring the same level of happiness to those around you—to your employees and customers—that you want for yourself. Think about your career, business or job. Are you committed to bringing happiness to your customers? How many industries, services or products can you name that strive for this level of service? A product or service that can offer a sense of pleasure as well as long-term happiness will engender loyalty and an unusually strong relationship with customers.

- The fastest way to be happy is to make somebody else happy; not just pleased, but happy in a meaningful way.

- And, finally, Delta's *SKY* magazine printed an interview with Deepak Chopra about finding fulfillment at

> work. Chopra referenced research which found that if a boss (I'll expand to include supervisor or co-worker) ignores you, the likelihood of your disengagement goes up 45 percent and your productivity goes down. However, employee disengagement goes down only 20 percent if the boss highlights a deficiency daily. This is an interesting outcome: at least the boss cares enough to be noticing and will take the time and energy to comment. It's far better than ignoring you!

But here is the real message: If you actually notice and acknowledge the strength of someone around you and you provide genuine positive feedback or some form of recognition, the disengagement factor falls to less than 1 percent.

Success is not a final destination that takes you somewhere based on the accomplishment alone, nor is it a status that can be attained by accumulation of material wealth, favor or position. Success is about harnessing a fire inside you to triumph over challenge. Success is not static—it's dynamic and provides the fuel to take on new ventures. I believe that one of the keys to success is staying a worthy course of continual action, moving toward something, without losing your devotion, enthusiasm and perseverance. Success means laying a firm foundation for persistent growth and progress while walking through disappointments and overcoming stumbles along the path.

Finding Inspiration

My goal with *The Finish Line* is for you to find inspiration to pursue your purpose and passion in life with boldness and fervor. However, who can't use a little motivation to get the wheels turning? I've been fortunate to have some great mentors and advisors in my life whose own experiences have taught me so much. In researching this book I came across dozens of examples of others whose journeys were filled with bumps and unexpected turns and others who faced circumstances of great adversity and failure. The common thread: They never gave up. They persevered, overcame the challenges, found their purpose, sometimes refining and retooling it, and ultimately crossed incredible finish lines along the way that can inspire us today.

Facing Adversity

I have personally experienced failure and disappointment. I have felt deep loss due to mistakes I've made. Despite those negative and painful experiences, I have grown from each and learned a great deal about myself in the process. I have discovered the power of compassionate people to help me through adversity and continue to learn and find happiness, purpose and success in life. I choose to grow and improve rather than risk, as my friend Karen puts it, "starting the slippery slope downward."

You may be surprised to know that Walt Disney, whose enduring legacy includes the creation of the iconic Mickey Mouse and dozens of other timeless characters, more than eighty feature films and the birth of Disneyland and Disney World, failed repeatedly throughout his career. He faced bankruptcy in his twenties, a mental breakdown, the loss of control over one of his character creations and a strike, to name a few. Early in his career he was fired as an artist for a Kansas City newspaper because of his "lack of creativity." He once said, "You may not realize it when it happens, but a kick in the teeth may be the best thing in the world for you." Disney learned how to pick himself up and persevere through serious setbacks.

Attitude

Miseries or happiness, obstacles or opportunities, failure or success in life: All are a matter of perception. For those of us who run marathons, we clearly have experienced this: Many of our friends don't understand why someone would choose to run 26.2 miles. You can find happiness in miseries, opportunities among obstacles and success in failure. This also works in the opposite: miseries in happiness, obstacles in opportunities or failure in success. It's attitude that can polish out the gems from rock.

The self-made steel magnate and philanthropist Andrew Carnegie survived acute childhood poverty and spent days and nights without food. As a boy, he immigrated to the United States from Scotland and got a job at a cotton mill where he worked twelve-hour days, six days a week. Later, a friend got him a job with the Pennsylvania Railroad. The Civil War sparked the growth of the iron industry along with Carnegie's entrepreneurial spirit. By 1900 Carnegie Steel was a world leader in steel production. Despite the sorrows and miseries of his early life, Carnegie developed an unbending commitment to the principles of hard work, determination and honesty to positively transform his life. A great believer in the power of education, he spent much of his collected fortune on establishing more than 2,500 public libraries as well as supporting institutions of higher learning. At the time of his death, Carnegie had given away 350 million dollars.

Accept Change

Making a big life change is pretty scary. But know what's even scarier? REGRET.

No matter the size or nature, change is scary to most of us. Change is a norm without which perfect composure in any respect is impossible. The cold, harsh winter prepares the ground for the bursting forth of new life in spring. The freshness of spring prepares us for the vivid and dazzling summer. The shorter days and cooler temperatures of fall prepare nature for a restorative rest, and the cycle continues. Change brings us surprises and opportunities to evolve and flourish.

> *Courage is being scared to death—and saddling up anyway.*
> —John Wayne

Rethink the Impossible

Oftentimes, FEAR can prevent us from taking action toward achieving our desired goal. We are afraid of stumbling over obstacles. Confidence and perseverance won't make fear go away but will help you move beyond, over, around and through it.

Are you faced with a seemingly impossible situation? Perhaps you have a new idea but you can't get anyone to believe in you. Maybe you have a dream and a goal but the road ahead seems impossible. Reframe your perspective and see what happens. Turn the impossible into the possible. You'll be in good company!

- Jessica Cox became the world's first armless licensed pilot. Born without arms, she uses her feet as most people use their hands. She is able, among other things, to drive a car, play the piano, type on a computer and pump her own gas. She's also earned two black belts in tae kwon do. At the age of thirty she travels the world as a motivational speaker and serves as an advocate for disability rights. She uses her own life as an example of what can be achieved if one wants it badly enough.

- British novelist J.K. Rowling was a newly divorced, unemployed single mom living on government aid when she wrote the first Harry Potter book. In 2008, she addressed the Harvard alumni association where she talked about "The Fringe Benefits of Failure, and the Importance of Imagination." About her life she said, "Failure meant a stripping away of the inessential. I stopped pretending I was anything other than what I was, and began to direct all my energy to finishing the only work that mattered to me. Had I really succeeded at anything else, I might never have found the determination to succeed in the one area where I truly belonged. I was set free, because my greatest fear had been realized, and I was still alive, and I still had a daughter whom I adored, and I had an old typewriter, and a big idea. And so rock bottom became a solid foundation on which I rebuilt my life."

- At the age of six, Aduei Riak was separated from her family during a civil war in Ethiopia. Alone, she joined the thousands of orphans from similarly torn-apart families who walked over a thousand miles to find refuge. She eventually found the Kakuma

> Refugee Camp in Kenya, where she remained for several years. In 2000 Aduei arrived in the United States as one of eighty-nine girls in a group of more than four thousand orphans in a Lost Boys and Girls resettlement program. She joined a foster family in Massachusetts, and began attending high school despite the fact that she spoke little English. She devoted herself to her studies and mastered the language by spending hours watching *Sesame Street.* Aduei quickly became a top student, and in 2003 she was accepted at Brandeis University, one of the most prestigious schools in the country. Upon graduation Aduei was recognized for integrating social activism and academic study. Since graduating, Aduei has campaigned against genocide in Darfur, was a keynote speaker at the International Women's Leadership Conference and is starting a foundation to help girls in Sudan receive an education.

Determination, resilience and a relentless pursuit of one's purpose in life: There are countless people who have hurdled seemingly impossible odds to create a new chapter in their lives. People overcome bankruptcy, divorce, serious injury or illness, a lack of formal education, discrimination and more to achieve what they strive for in life.

Let's Do It!

As we approach the finish line of *The Finish Line*, I thought I would leave you with a visual collage that represents my visualization board. It's a great reminder that continually helps me focus on what I'm striving for in life, my purpose and what really matters. If you haven't done so already, get out a pair of scissors, some old magazines and a piece of tag board and create your own. I think you'll be pleasantly surprised by what this simple exercise will do to get the juices flowing as you think about what you want to achieve in your life.

And, finally, I hope this book and the stories shared herein provided a nugget or two to inspire you as you strive toward the finish lines in your own life. Here's to making the most of the journey!

MEET THE RUNNERS

Jim Hanson

"As every marathoner knows, nobody gets through it without hurting....it's a perfect metaphor for life: You have to have perseverance and a willingness to fight through the pain. It's how you deal with the adversity and pain that is important. Very few people get to know themselves without adversity in their lives."

CAMERA SHY

Adam S.

"Training is the hard part, the marathon itself is the victory lap!"

Allison McVay-Steer

"Runners are committed people. If you are a runner in Minnesota, Grandma's Marathon is the marathon to do. It encompasses what it means to be from Minnesota."

Amanda Akason

"I was competing against myself and my goals. After finishing, I thought, what am I going to do next?"

Amy Cherko

"I was at a crossroads in life when I found running. Now it's one of the things I've checked off my 'to do' list. Love the Grandma's Marathon and town, THEY JUST GET IT!"

Ann Jones

"Running has given me a piece of the puzzle I never had when I was younger: it introduced me to my inner athlete. Now running with my husband is a way to quietly inspire our children. We have a tradition of going to Hell's Kitchen the morning after the marathon for an amazing breakfast I know I couldn't eat in good conscience if I didn't finish the run. That and seeing my husband at the finish line are two of my ongoing motivations to finish!"

Bill Cayley

"Why Grandma's? I've always enjoyed the North Shore and it's really a fun and pretty race."

Bob Kovell

"The real purpose of running is not to win a race, it's to test the limits of the human heart."

Brice Andree

"I run for myself and my mind. I run because I was told not to! I run because I need to challenge myself and I know that it's as much a mental challenge as a physical one."

Dan Lindberg (son Davis)

"There is no way I could have trained for a marathon without a great support system at home. I always stop and say hello to my wife and son during a race. No time would be worth just running by my family."

Dan Rassier

"Bottom line..IT JUST FEELS GOOD TO FINISH. At fifty-seven and having run over two hundred races, I continue to strive to do my best. Focus is required when you have everything stacked against you. However, the age and injuries just fuel the excitement of finishing the race."

Dan Staberg

"I am grateful for what running has given me. Earlier in life I did things I shouldn't. Once I started running, it changed my life. I became a better brother, husband and son. For me, crossing the finish line is very emotional and a huge accomplishment."

Debbie Allen

"The feeling of crossing the finish line is a rush like no other. I feel like Superwoman. I am addicted to that feeling of accomplishment!"

Gina Phearman

"I'm slow, but I run marathons! The first time I crossed the finish line was quite an experience. I was so incredibly high; it's incredibly emotional."

Greg Merth

"At sixty-three, I got a late start in running marathons. Running is 50 percent training, 25 percent heart and 25 percent total and absolute insanity."

Jen MacKay

"Coming down Superior Street between miles twenty-four and twenty-six is the best. My family is always on the last turn. It gets me every time. The atmosphere of Grandma's is unmatched because there are people everywhere creating a warm atmosphere for every runner."

CAMERA SHY

Jimmy M.

"I never questioned whether I would finish; my biggest concern was where the next water was!"

Katie Radeke

"My inspiration? MY DAD! When I crossed the finish line, I said to myself 'I DID IT!' It was so emotional."

Margaret Hvatum

"My running has turned into an effort to raise money for leukemia and related causes."

CAMERA SHY

Kristi K.

"Grandma's Marathon is one of my absolute favorites. There's never a dull moment. It's full of wonderful people and an over-exuberant amount of energy. I've learned to set goals just a smidgen beyond achievable. You surprise yourself and reach them!"

CAMERA SHY

Jordan H.

"When I did my first run seven years ago, I was eighty-five pounds heavier and on high blood pressure medication. I had recently quit smoking. I had two little kids and a beautiful wife. I wanted to make sure I was there for my family. When I started running, I was pretty depressed. Running changed my whole life. I feel better about myself and I'm more happy and healthy for it."

Crystal Deschinney

"Running connected me to life following a cancer diagnosis. It did more for me than anything. I was so overwhelmed with the support at Grandma's. I felt like they were all cheering just for me!"

Lisa Terrell

Lisa (left) finds that runners have similar personality characteristics. "They are intelligent, dedicated and focused people." She recommends Grandma's Marathon, for its no hassle, fun atmosphere for families and runners alike.

Jim Guettler

"My marathon journey began in a hospital bed in 1985, two months before my twentieth birthday. Six years later, in 1991, I nervously stood on the starting line of Grandma's. I was feeling that cocktail of nerves. After Lemon Drop Hill, I realized I had five miles to go. Could I make it? I was feeling rough, but once I saw my family I knew I would make it."

CAMERA SHY

Adam B.

"The great thing about the marathon isn't about winning. The end, the goal, is the finish line!"

Alissa Mrozinski

"While my father wasn't a huge motivator in my younger years, he became one when I started running. He was always saying, 'Let's run to the next pole,' or... 'the next sign!' My dad motivated me big time!"

Amanda Williams

"My grandfather ran Grandma's on the day I was born, June 18, 1987. I received a pink Grandma's baby shirt from him. My motivation is my grandma. We are very close. My mom and aunt were my accountability partners in my training."

CAMERA SHY

Brandon S.

"After donating a kidney, I felt lost. I needed something to drive me. Running helped me rediscover my identity, it gave me a reason to get going each morning."

Cassie Flynn

"Duluth has turned me into a runner! The entire city supports the race. And the UMD students? Their enthusiasm keeps us going!"

Craig Toerpe

"If you want to be treated like a rock star, run Grandma's Marathon. When I run a marathon, I dedicate each of the last six miles to a different member of my family. It motivates me to keep going for them!"

Emily Hanson

"My grandma was very important to me. I grew up with her and spent much time at her house. I ALWAYS want to be with her. The marathon is my tribute to her. When I run by 21st and London (in Duluth), I get very emotional."

CAMERA SHY

Joshua K.

"I'm a recovering alcoholic and running has become my outlet. Instead of hitting the bottle, I hit the pavement!"

Katy Kiger

"I run for God's purpose. God not only drives me to run, but makes me focus on my task, whether it be running to raise money to support a cause or praying during my runs."

Ken Palmer

"When I started running I was going through a divorce. Running helped me deal with the pain of a failed marriage with each mile."

Phil Gustamante

"I've gained a personal sense of inner power from running. If you're a marathon runner you can commit to a lot of things you did not think you could do."

ABOUT GRANDMA'S MARATHON

"I am most proud of the fact that Grandma's Marathon is ingrained in the community and without family, friends and the entire community's ongoing support, this event would not have the success it has had."

– Scott Keenan, Founder and Executive Director, Grandma's Marathon

Grandma's Marathon has been a fixture in Duluth for well over thirty years and serves as an unparalleled platform for connecting with people who have lived the power of running (or race with a reason). Why Grandma's? Here's a sampling of what runners say . . .

"If you want to be treated like a rock star, run Grandma's Marathon! The community opens its doors and embraces the running community. The entire city wants you there."

—Craig T.

"Grandma's Marathon is one my absolute favorites. There's never a dull moment, it's full of wonderful people and an abundance of energy. And, it's just so beautiful to run alongside Lake Superior."

—Kristie K.

"I was overwhelmed with all of the spectator support. It felt like they were cheering for me! Grandma's will always be the race that connected me to running."

—Crystal D.

"The crowd at Grandma's is outstanding. It motivates you to push to the end. I know they will be there and it's like a celebration when you finish."

—Adam B.

In 1977, as president of the North Shore Striders, a Duluth running club, Scott Keenan developed Grandma's Marathon as an annual event with the *purpose of putting on an official marathon and hopefully having some fun along the way.* Over the years, that fundamental purpose has expanded. Yes, fun remains part of what attracts more than eight thousand runners each year. However, community, collaboration and service form the bedrock of its foundation.

"There were three principles that have not strayed over the years," says Scott. "One: Do the basics well. Two: Get the elite runners involved. And three: Embrace in every way possible the spirit of community."

This notion of giving back is symbolic of Scott's philosophy and that of Grandma's Marathon, as well as its runners. Grandma's Marathon has a purpose beyond the race!

"As I reflect back on the first race in 1977 and the journey that Grandma's Marathon has taken over the past thirty-six years, I am overwhelmed with a great sense of pride in knowing that Grandma's has touched the lives of tens of thousands of people. We have developed many lifelong partnerships. Our volunteers are the best in the world, our sponsors are always extremely generous, and our runners are the most loyal group of individuals you could ever imagine. However, if there is one theme that has remained constant at our event since the beginning, it's 'Let's have some fun!'"

—Scott Keenan

YOUNG ATHLETES FOUNDATION

In 1990, the Young Athletes Foundation (YAF) was established as a way for Grandma's Marathon to give back locally and regionally. The YAF assists in the promotion, development and growth of youth athletics. Since its inception, the YAF has contributed more than $600,000 to nonprofit youth athletic organizations and programs in Carlton, Cook, Lake, St. Louis (Minnesota) and Douglas (Wisconsin) counties.

I'm a huge fan of the Young Athletes Foundation. I've seen the impact fitness and athletics has on kids of all ages, regardless of their ability. The big, proud smile and positive sense of self a boy or girl experiences while challenging him or herself physically, builds character, inner strength and confidence. I'm pleased to provide the YAF with $1 for every copy of *The Finish Line* that rolls off the press.

If you'd like to learn more about the Young Athletes Foundation and what they're doing for kids, go to: **www.youngathletesfoundation.com** or **www.grandmasmarathon.com**

Young Athletes Foundation
C/O Grandma's Marathon
P.O. Box 16234
Duluth, MN 55816
218-727-0947
grandmas@grandmasmarathon.com

ACKNOWLEDGEMENTS

First and foremost, I wish to thank and acknowledge Scott Keenan, founder and executive director of Grandma's Marathon in Duluth, for your trust and confidence in collaborating with me on this book. Your vision of a great marathon organization that has community and youth in the forefront is a tribute to you, your staff and board.

Thank you to the magnificent staff I've worked with at Grandma's, including Dani, Zack and Bob, who supported the research and outreach to current and past runners in getting the stories for this book.

I thank all those runners who responded to our survey to be interviewed and allowed us permission to use your stories throughout this book. Each of you lives your life with purpose and I'm honored to have had this experience to get to know you a bit.

Thank you to my editor, Jennifer L. Hipple, who made me look a better writer than I am.

And to Beaver's Pond Press in Minneapolis for your guidance, input and publishing expertise.

BIBLIOGRAPHY

Jobs, Steve. 2005 commencement address at Stanford. http://news.stanford.edu/news/2005/june15/jobs-061505.html

Horan, Jim. *The One Page Business Plan.* PAP/COM edition, 2004.

Donald, Brooke. "Stanford psychologist: Achievement goals can be shaped by environment." *Stanford University News.* May 2012. http://news.stanford.edu/news/2012/may/shape-achievemement-goals-051012.html. A 2012 study by Stanford psychologist Paul O'Keefe, Adar Ben-Eliyahu of the University of Pittsburgh and Lisa Linnenbrink-Garcia of Duke University.

Lynch, Jerry. "Mind over Miles." *Runner's World*, May 1996.

Pink, Daniel H. *Drive: The Surprising Truth About What Motivates Us.* Riverhead Books, 2011.

Huxley Running Company, "Getting the Scoop From . . . Neely Spence, 1st Non-African World XC." http://huxleyrunningco.org/2013/03/26/getting-the-scoop-from-neely-spence-1st-non-african-world-xc/

Mackay, Harvey. "What's Your Next Marathon?" *Minneapolis StarTribune*. Feb 13, 2013. http://www.startribune.com/business/189419971.html?refer=y. Feb 13, 2013

Working Moms Only.com. http://www.workingmomsonly.com/mary-ellen-tribby/

Karp, Jason R. *Running Marathons for Dummies*. New York. John Wiley and Sons, 2012.

Blue, John. "When Things Go Wrong." *Freeplay, Endurance Sports Magazine for Women,* January–February 2013.

Saha, Mousumi Kumar. "Top 10 Lessons to Learn from Failure." http://www.successstories.co.in/top-10-lessons-to-learn-from-failure/

Cochell, Perry L. and Zeeb, Rodney C. *Beating the Midas Curse.* Heritage Institute Press, 2005.

Rowling, J.K. "The Fringe Benefits of Failure and the Importance of Imagination." http://news.harvard.edu/gazette/story/2008/06/text-of-j-k-rowling-speech/

ABOUT THE AUTHOR

The descendant of a long and proud—but somewhat reserved—Norwegian heritage, Bob Strommen has lived a full and rich personal and professional life that is reflected in *The Finish Line* as well as in the creation of **purpose+3**, the platform for his writing and speaking career. Incorporating the personal stories of dozens of Grandma's Marathon runners, *The Finish Line* touches the heart and will resonate with anyone who wants to grow in life, their relationships and their career.

Graduating from Augsburg College with BAs in education and psychology, Bob enjoyed a career in teaching and coaching high school soccer. In the fall of 1978, ready for a new challenge, Bob joined the family's financial services business, Strommen and Associates, and became co-owner in 1980 when his father was recruited to lead Lutheran Brotherhood (now known as Thrivent for Lutherans) as president and CEO.

In 1988, Bob left the family business to venture out on his own in the financial services business under the Strommen and Associates name. In 1989 the business expanded and acquired a third-party retirement plan design and administrative firm, Corporate Benefits Administrator, Inc. CBA grew from 100 to more than 450 retirement plans when Bob sold CBA to two key employees in 2007. Expanding on his financial services practice, Bob collaborated with fourteen professionals from across the country on a values-based estate-planning book, *Beating the Midas Curse.*

In addition to his writing and speaking, Bob currently enjoys a successful career in the financial services industry with Strommen and Associates, LLC. He is also a managing member of CheckPoints Consulting, LLC, focusing on corporate retirement plan consulting and fiduciary responsibilities.

A lifelong resident of Minneapolis–St. Paul, Bob is an ardent supporter of his alma mater, Augsburg College, a dedicated runner and golfer and an avid traveler.

www.purposeplus3.com
Facebook: purpose+3
www.checkpointsconsulting.com
www.strommen.com